LIQUID MEXICO

FESTIVE SPIRITS, TEQUILA CULTURE, AND THE INFAMOUS WORM

Bilingual Press/Editorial Bilingüe

Address:
Bilingual Press
Hispanic Research Center
Arizona State University
PO Box 875303
Tempe, Arizona 85287-5303
(480) 965-3867

Liquid Mexico

Festive Spirits, Tequila Culture, and the Infamous Worm

Becky Youman & Bryan Estep

Bilingual Press/Editorial Bilingüe
TEMPE, ARIZONA

ISBN 1-931010-26-9

Library of Congress Cataloging-in-Publication Data

Youman, Becky.
Liquid Mexico : festive spirits, tequila culture, and the infamous worm / Becky Youman and Bryan Estep.
p. cm.
ISBN 1-931010-26-9
1. Tequila. I. Estep, Bryan. II. Title.

TP607.T46Y68 2004
641.2'5—dc22

2004040994

PRINTED IN THE UNITED STATES OF AMERICA

Front cover art: A Large Margarita *(2003) by Frank Ybarra*

Cover and interior design by John Wincek, Aerocraft Charter Art Service

In some cases, names have been changed to protect people's privacy.

ACKNOWLEDGMENTS

First, we would like to thank all the people mentioned in the book who shared their expertise, knowledge, and time with us.

Our readers, Ace and Alice Forsythe and Ginger Geyer, helped us make the book tighter, clearer, and more interesting than it would have been otherwise. Sandy and Dudley Youman and John Leonard generously made guest bedrooms available for long stretches of time during our research and writing. Muchísimas gracias.

Finally, we want to thank Gary Keller and all the dedicated editors, readers, designers, and marketers at Bilingual Review Press.

¡Salud!

CONTENTS

PROLOGUE

RAMÓN'S WEDDING

Becky and I peer through our reflections in the tinted back window of our Ford Explorer, concerned that the wedding gift will not be safe. We've draped an old blanket over it, a pathetic disguise intended to outwit the thieves that rule Mexico City these days. Though the country is nearly recuperated from an economic crisis, metropolitan crime is the last complication to abate, hanging on like a raspy cough. We are leaving the gift in the car because we're not exactly sure of the proper way to unload it. Becky's hunch is that a table will be set up at the ceremony, while I favor taking it to the reception. I finally convince her not to take it to the church, but now worry about the gift's allure and vulnerability. I glance away, and then try to observe the inflated blanket for the first time, as a thief would. I see a Lilliputian circus tent, a dormant ghost, or a Bedouin's doghouse and I suppose it will be OK.

To get here we spent the past two days driving from Becky's parents' house in Austin. Returning to Mexico is a homecoming of the vagabond sort for both of us. Though I grew up in the Seattle area, our youthful ambitions paralleled as we both sought stints in Mexico early in our careers. We first arrived in this imposing megalopolis without acquaintances or job offers, just the desire to live and work in a foreign country. We had little notion of the challenges we would encounter, nor of the lasting impact that the country would have on our lives.

The two people with whom I worked most closely during my expatriate days were a pair of Ramóns, father and son. Ramón *hijo* is to be married today. Ramón *papá* is to blow puffs of cigar smoke between tried and tested wedding quips such as "A man is incomplete until he is married—then he is really finished."

As we walk to the church, I take comfort in the fact that our car is among the least notable in this affluent Lomas neighborhood located in the western hills of the city. We observe that no one carries gifts, so it appears my instincts are right on this issue.

We slide into a pew of the airy church. It would be indistinguishable from a modern Catholic sanctuary anywhere else in the world, except for the stained-glass portrayal of the indigenous peasant Juan Diego encountering the Virgin of Guadalupe on a hill spiked with agave plants.

The agave, like the holy encounter, is an integral part of Mexican identity. Two hundred species of this cousin of aloe, often mistaken for cacti, burst from the Mexican countryside. Known as *maguey* in Spanish and nicknamed the "century plant" in English, agave provides the raw material for three famous Mexican spirits—pulque, mezcal, and tequila. Different species and processes are used to concoct each of the libations, yet to most, even those who consider themselves aficionados, the distinctions are nebulous. As we wait for the bride to appear, I admire the sunlight tumbling through the triangular leaves into emerald green shafts.

We haven't met Ramón's fiancée yet so we can't help but conjecture what she will be like. The wedding march blasts from the organ, prompting all to rise. Ramón's intended glides down the aisle tall, slender, brunette, as captivating as any bride could hope to be.

To our relief, the car windows remain unshattered. On our way to the reception, we discuss the prospect of lasting through the marathon affair. When we started working in Mexico, part of our cultural adaptation was learning to endure inebriant business lunches that averaged four hours and occasionally continued past midnight. Now, however, we are out of practice, unsure of our commitment to such prolonged indulgence. A Mexican wedding celebration is highlighted by dinner, but lasts until breakfast is served.

Though I should be less apprehensive, I sweat cultural formalities. I feel the pressure of doing things right, hoping not to look quite so foreign. Ramón's wedding gift triggers such angst. The how-about-a-blender method remains the custom for wedding gift selection as opposed to choosing from a preplanned, itemized gift list. We crossed the border empty-handed, so a shopping foray was necessary this morning. In a glitzy department store, we hemmed and hawed, then chose a crystal decanter for the newlyweds.

The thing about life abroad is that simple tasks like wrapping a wedding present turn to intrigue. The employee in the gift wrap department placed the decanter on an immense velvet-covered cardboard platform, adhered a card bearing our names, then hung an enormous cloak of cellophane over it. She took aim with a hair dryer and spent five minutes blasting the wrap until it shrunk to a tight, clear epidermis. A bow was added to the gift, which now appears to be an architectural creation that might debut at a world's fair.

The reception is staged in the garden of the Hacienda de los Morales, a restaurant situated on a sixteenth-century Polanco ranch, now surrounded by skyscrapers. We cross the manicured lawn with our conspicuous gift in hand, exchanging urgent whispers as a thousand eyes survey us. There is nowhere to set presents, we are told, because the tradition is to send them directly to the bride's house. A gift table must be set up specifically for the gringos. There always seems to be more to learn.

Two Mexican friends have saved seats for us at a large table. Three chairs are occupied by elegant grandmothers, old friends of the bride's mother. Primness battles vogue in silk dresses, strands of pearls, hefty rings, coquettish lipstick, and hair-spray helmets. One of the women is in her nineties, so it surprises us when she orders straight tequila, as do her companions. The rest of us at the table follow suit. Our tequila arrives as double shots in brandy snifters. We toast—*salud!*—sip the smooth, oaky libation, then douse the embers with a quaff of a spicy tomato-citrus chaser called *sangrita.*

The fact that these gracious tequila-tippling seniors do not share Pancho Villa's guise or bar manners is an indication that Mexico's drinking traditions are as rich and intriguing as the rest of its culture. We had hoped to encounter such nuances when we started this trip.

The idea for *Liquid Mexico* was conceived in a Mexican restaurant in a colonial Ecuadorian town. We were finishing work on an Ecuador travel guide, so the meal was part duty and part craving. While sipping tequila and Corona, nostalgia kicked in full force, inspiring us to discuss the possibility of returning to our favorite country for our next project. We asked ourselves, What is an intriguing and folkloric aspect of Mexico, a narrative that begs telling? The answer was in our hands and on our lips.

We decided to investigate the history, customs, music, festivals, and locales associated with Mexican hooch. Our interest is definitely more cultural than technical or commercial, though knowledge of the latter areas was necessary. To create an itinerary we identified places aligned, either by origin or custom, with typical Mexican beverages. We then spent several months in the University of Texas at Austin's Nettie Lee Benson Latin America Library doing research.

Alcohol has played a role in religion, medicine, cuisine, celebrations, and business and social gatherings in most civilizations. It also contributes to crime, accidents, and disease. We view alcohol neither as a demon nor a guiding light. It is, however, an undeniable part of Mexico's culture as well as our own.

The library provided a bounty of leads. Portable files are stuffed thick with notes while classic books on Mexico tear at the seams of our duffel bag. We are eager to confront the enigmatic spirits that our preliminary research has conjured up, but first we must survive our reinitiation.

The bride and groom arrive an hour and a half—and several rounds—after our first tequila. The guests, of mostly European descent, applaud. We are all ravenous. Cheese soup with grapes, veal Marsala, and chocolate pastries for 500 are served and devoured.

The band plays everything from old world *paso dobles* to tropical salsa to the farcical "YMCA." Becky goes wild on the dance floor most of the night while I mingle with old business associates, though it is understood that the relationships go beyond commerce. Business is personal here and I appreciate that. It is great to exchange *abrazos* and bullshit with these earnest, savvy men who in truth are friends.

The gringos are fading. We've been at the reception for seven hours already, but when we tell Ramón *papá* goodbye, he insists we stay until breakfast is served. Another hour later the mariachi musicians burst into the garden. A buffet line is set up with *chilaquiles*—tortillas and chicken baked in red and green hot sauce topped with sour cream. *Churros*, somewhat like donut sticks, and rich Mexican hot chocolate are offered. The *churros*, dipped into the frothy chocolate, are so savory that they revive us for several more songs, just when we thought we could exult no more.

TEQUILA

TEQUILA, JALISCO

We are handed a four-page tequila menu, which we open with eager delight. Our anticipation turns to disbelief when we see the prices. They are double if not triple what we paid for tequila when we lived in Mexico City three years ago.

The manager is quick to defend his establishment. He lowers his voice and looks nervously around the room. "It's not just here. You might not be aware of this, but there is a shortage of blue agave, the plant that tequila comes from. Tequila prices are going through the roof."

Bryan and I are both a little suspicious. It sounds like a story to justify absurd bar profits. In terms of selection, however, we have come to the right place to kick off our investigation of the drinks of Mexico. Guadalajara, the capital of the Mexican state of Jalisco, is a city ringed by tequila producers. The Destilería Restaurant, located in an upscale suburb of town, offers a wide sampling of the region's famous libation. After a quick count Bryan tallies thirty-two *blancos*, white tequilas; fifty *reposados*, slightly aged tequilas; and twenty-six *añejos*, well-aged varieties.

The restaurant is decorated with tools and symbols of the industry. A large mural features spiky agave, known in Spanish as *maguey*, the plant from which tequila is made. A creaky wooden cart, once used to haul agave, fills the corner next to us. Across from the bar a giant stone wheel, utilized to crush agave hearts, sits ready for action. Looking over this menu I imagine rustic factories—workshops really—where our favorite Mexican elixir is created.

The years we lived and worked in Mexico City did more than stoke our tequila fancy. Tequila, for us, has become inexorably associated with this country. When we take a sip of tequila, we are imbued with strong emotions for this culture that has captured our hearts. Our understanding and appreciation for Mexico, as central to who we are as agave is to tequila, is symbolized for us in this special drink.

We're looking forward to the chance to taste some of the high-quality local product that never makes it out of Jalisco. We ask our waiter for a recommendation.

"Umm. How about this one?"

He points to a brand commonly found not only on the supermarket shelves around Mexico, but also in liquor stores in the United States. We were hoping to sample a treasure from a small local company. He points to another tequila made by a large manufacturer. Realizing that employee training hasn't included much information about tequila, we make our own choice. We recognize a brand we've heard good things about and order one of their *añejos,* aged tequilas.

Looking around the restaurant, we spot a few tables of gringos. No surprise, considering tequila's popularity in the United States. The fastest-growing spirit in the country, tequila has shed its border-brawl image to make its way into the inventories and liquor cabinets of many American restaurants and homes. Americans drink 82 percent of the tequila exported from Mexico. No longer a drink to slam and regret, premium brands of tequila are now being sipped and savored like a fine scotch.

When it's time for the next round we bypass our waiter. We explain to the manager our quest to sample a quality brand we haven't tried before. He recommends two tequilas from a relatively new high-end exporter, El Conquistador. We order one that has been slightly aged, *reposado*, and another one that has been aged longer, *añejo*.

Recent magazine articles about tequila have waxed lyrical over the subtle flavors that supposedly complement the agave. Some of them sound like complete baloney. Tequila, after all, is 40 percent alcohol. How much subtlety can you get with 80 proof? We want to test whether we can come up with some lines like ones we read recently in a *Fortune Magazine* article about certain high-end tequilas.

> Overtones of flowers, herbs and pine . . . hints of lavender, dill, fresh flowers and brine . . . look for a floral nose and a palate with hints of white pepper, fresh cut wood and herb . . .

Our second round of tequilas is set down in front of us. They arrive at the table in two different types of glasses. The slightly aged *reposado* stands tall in the long, slender Mexican shot glass known as a *caballito*. The *añejo,* however, is presented in a brandy snifter, to concentrate its pleasurable bouquet. We try to taste the difference between the two. While we can discern that the aged one, *añejo*, is creamier and has a richer oak flavor than the *reposado*, that's about the best we can do. No matter, even if we can't taste herbs and flowers, both are excellent. This success with a new brand of tequila bodes well for the rest of the trip.

Although our investigation into the culture and traditions of Mexican drinks started with Ramón's wedding, this is really the first leg of our journey. We left our car parked in front of a friend's house in Mexico City this morning, crossed our fingers that it would still be there when we got back, and hopped on a plane to Guadalajara. We will cover this part of the country in taxi, rental car, and even train.

The Guadalajara station, clean and cavernous, serves only one passenger train a week, the Tequila Express. A young Mexican woman wearing a white polo shirt and starched jeans greets us at the door. About fifteen of her similarly dressed co-workers dash around helping patrons in both English and Spanish. The Tequila Express, billed as "the best train tour ever," transports people from Guadalajara to the nearby town of Tequila. We're looking forward to learning a lot more about the tequila-making process, trying some new brands, and exploring the town.

Our fellow passengers are a mixed group of Mexicans and foreigners. There are gringo businessmen trying unsuccessfully to look casual, a few groups of American retirees, and numerous Mexican families.

The number of little kids and pregnant women on what is essentially a drinking tour surprises us, but it shouldn't. We've learned that Mexican clans stick together. That's one of the things we've always found enjoyable about parties hosted by our Mexican friends—all generations congregate together. Instead of segregating by age, Mexicans invite the whole gang. From infants to geriatrics, everybody joins in the fun until the wee hours of the morning. Celebrations involve an inclusiveness that seems healthy to us.

Suddenly the lonely wail of a trumpet introduces a full mariachi band. Singing and pounding their instruments, the band belts out traditional Mexican music. The crowd gathers around, clapping and whistling. After a few songs the conductor steps in front of the mariachis, cups his hands to his mouth and yells, "Allll Aboooaaarrrrrd!" The words roll, bounce, and echo off the high ceiling of the station.

The men and women are separated into two lines. Bryan and I are confused until we realize that armed train robbery is always a possibility. The men are forced to walk through a metal detector while we women have the contents of our bags inspected.

The mariachis continue to belt out tunes from the platform while the employees help people find their seats. Waiters with bow ties and green vests walk through the cabin offering trays of cold beer.

The train moves slowly through town. The mariachi tunes have been replaced by soft Mexican vocals piped through the stereo system. Gradually the city gives way to parched fields perforated with dried corn stubble. The husks, pushed into heaping piles, catch the light like Monet's haystacks. I decline the beer because I'm waiting to sample good tequilas side by side, like a wine tasting.

Amanda, one of the employees assigned to our car, turns on a microphone and begins to speak a few sentences in Spanish, followed by a few in English. Those of us who speak both languages are stuck in a bilingual echo chamber.

"Welcome to the Tequila Express. You're going to have a great day. Are you all excited to be here?"

A few tentative yeses and sís sally forth.

"That's pathetic. Come on, people. Are you excited to be here?"

The group of retirees in the back gives a hearty yell.

"That's better. You need to get ready to party. As you know, we are on our way to the town of Tequila, seventy kilometers northwest of Guadalajara. Tequila, the drink, was first made in Tequila, the town. That's how the drink got its name. The town was named after the Teqwila Indians who lived there when the Spanish arrived. We'll give you more information later, but now it's time to boogie."

With that the music switches over to the macarena. The organizers run through the car forcing people to stand up and prance in the isles. A silver-haired woman, wearing pink Keds and a matching shorts set, sashays to the front of the train. Her companions in back love it.

"Ya gotta swing it faster, Wilma!"

"Marge is the drinker so you're the dancer!"

The dance brigade goes on for at least an hour. The organizers finish the set with the macarena again—not once, not twice, but three times. I can't take it any longer. I run to the front of the car and plead for a new song.

As the train glides through the dry countryside, Amanda returns to the microphone.

"Agave, the plant that tequila is made from, grows best in semi-arid climates. The particular species of agave used to make tequila, called Blue Weber, thrives in the sandy, iron-rich soil found around Tequila."

I expected to see acre upon acre of Blue Weber on the ride. Instead, we only see a few rows of tapered azure agave leaves cupping the clear morning sunshine. Maybe there really is some sort of shortage.

"If you look out the window now you'll see a field of young agave. It takes eight to ten years for the Blue Weber plant to mature. A long time, no? When it matures, the plant is harvested and then crushed to get the agave juice to make tequila."

It's easy to see where the Blue Weber got its name. The spiky starbursts exploding out of the scarlet soil are almost turquoise.

Amanda enthusiastically regales us with more tequila trivia.

"The Mexican government oversees the entire tequila industry. The regulations define tequila as a double distilled spirit made from at least 51 percent Blue Weber agave. The agave is only allowed to come from five Mexican states. The states are Jalisco, where we are now, as well as Nayarit, Michoacán, Guanajuato, and Tamaulipas. If the agave is not from one of these states, the product cannot legally be called tequila."

We pull into the Tequila train station. The trip lasted almost two hours but we were never offered any sipping tequila. I guess the logistics of sampling are too complicated for the train. We'll do it here in Tequila, I'm sure.

The air smells sweet, like fermentation. We are immediately loaded onto buses where a police escort with sirens blaring leads us all of a quarter of a mile to the town's main plaza. The sirens seem to wail, "The tourists are coming, the tourists are coming." Already the Tequila Express is wearing thin.

The square is filled with locals who come by for the free show every week. The grandstand is decorated with bunting, a stage stands in front of it, and a large tent shading rows of plastic chairs is set up beyond that. The Champs' one-word song "Tequila" blares out of loud speakers. This is why I always travel with earplugs. I clog my ears and the din is reduced to a tolerable roar. More cold beer is passed through the crowd while ambulatory vendors do a brisk business in potato chips and fried pork rinds.

Blue agave, pictured here, is the principal ingredient in tequila. The finest tequilas are made from 100% blue agave, also called Blue Weber, which takes eight to ten years to mature.

A Blue Weber agave as big as a washing machine is hauled onto the stage in front of us. The music is still blaring. A *jimador*, an agave harvester, walks over to the plant, which looks like a giant thin-leafed artichoke, and begins to shear it. It takes him about thirty seconds to cut all the leaves around the base of the plant, leaving what looks like an oversized pineapple. This agave heart, really the central mass of the plant, weighs about one hundred pounds on average. I think Bryan and I are the only ones watching the demonstration. Most of the crowd is more concerned about the beer and snacks.

A loud inner voice is telling me that the Tequila Express was a mistake, but I try to ignore it, still harboring hopes for the tequila-making tour. We are loaded back onto the buses and transferred to the Sauza family estate. Sauza is one of the largest selling brands of tequila both in Mexico and abroad. It was the first company to export tequila to the United States, sending six barrels and six earthenware jars of their family product to El Paso, Texas, in 1873.

The "factory" is not even a working plant, but rather a mock-up of one. There is no tequila tasting. After a ten-minute tour we are led around to the back of the hacienda where a bland buffet lunch awaits. We're starving. Admittedly, the lettuce, wilted and soaking in water, gives us pause, but we dig in.

As we walk to a table, two guitarists and a woman in a cowgirl outfit take the stage in front of the dining area. It's another show, this one with singing and dancing. We still haven't done any tequila tasting. Bryan and I sit in numbed realization that a tour is a tour is a tour. Even if the subject matter is our favorite alcohol, we are just not tour group types.

I sweet-talk a bottle of tequila from the bartender, who says we can keep it. Finally, a regional brand we can't find in the United States. The tequila, Mayor, is made from 100 percent agave. It is a *reposado*, slightly aged, so it has a bit of oak flavor. Removing ourselves to the shade of a stately elm in the back, we sip the amber nectar for the first time today.

A dance contest has started. We can't take it another minute. We start to scheme. We were going to come back to Tequila, anyway. What if we simply run away from the tour and stay here overnight? Our hotel room in Guadalajara is so cheap that we can just leave our stuff there. We don't have a problem wearing the same clothes for a few days.

We toast to our idea and inform Amanda that we're leaving the group.

"But how will you get back to Guadalajara? You'll miss the rest of the fun. We still have some dance shows and singers and then there's the ride back. . . ."

The sound of her voice fades as we stride toward the front gate and freedom.

Crowing roosters substitute for a 6 AM wake-up call. We get a completely different perspective on Tequila today. It is a mellow, pleasant place when the Tequila Express is not in town. We buy tortillas, fresh out of the rumbling machine of the *tortillería*, and huge orange juices, squeezed while we wait. To-go cups are an expensive luxury here, as in much of Mexico. Our juices are served in the standard plastic sandwich bag with a straw.

Neither one of us has much of an appetite this morning. Our stomachs are distended and we both feel a little queasy—the revenge of the Tequila Express buffet.

At the main plaza, the stage and tents from yesterday's show have been broken down. Mango and orange trees, heavily laden with fruit, bend over benches decorated with metal agaves. A memorial dedicated to the town's early defenders is sprinkled with names like Sauza and Cuervo.

The word tequila comes from a Nahuatl phrase that means "place of work." It's also the name of an extinct volcano that sits like a fat toad at one end of town. Sunrise brands vermilion patterns on houses and cornfields as we head up a narrow cobblestone road that winds eighteen kilometers to the top of the volcano.

Bouncing along in the taxi, bump by bump by bump, our stomachs start to feel even worse. To distract ourselves we ask our driver about his tequila preferences. An international treaty has been signed stating that tequila must originate in Mexico, in the same way that cognac must come from France or bourbon the United States. Over 50 percent of the tequila produced in Mexico is made in Tequila, so who better to ask than a Tequila native?

"I usually drink Sauza or Cuervo. I like them both and have been drinking them for years. My father drinks them too. We both drink *un cuarto* of tequila every night. No more, no less. Every night. For our health."

Sauza and Cuervo are the best selling brands in Mexico, each with almost 20 percent of the market. It's interesting to us that even in a place like Tequila, the small producers and premium brands are only for real aficionados. Most people still prefer the traditional, less expensive favorites.

Over the course of our climb the fields give way to oaks and then to pines. As we near the top, almost 8,500 feet, the foliage opens to reveal panoramas of the rumpled Amatitán and Atemajac valleys. I'm surprised when I look more closely to see that there aren't many fields of blue agave.

Our driver laments, "This used to be called 'the land of two skies' because the hectares and hectares of blue agave were like a second sky. It was really impressive. Now it's different. There's a disease in the valley that effects the agave when it's four years old. It just shrivels up and dies. Most of the farmers have switched to other crops with shorter growing cycles and more sure outcomes. It's mainly the tequila companies that are planting agave now and they're not doing it around here because of the disease."

It's clear from our vantage point that the situation is extreme, especially in and around Tequila. Our driver can't resist throwing us a little morsel of gossip.

"I heard that they are bringing agave in from states that aren't included in the official Mexican tequila regulations. I also heard that some of it isn't even blue agave. *¿Quién sabe?* It wouldn't surprise me, you know. There's a lot of money to be made in tequila—maybe too much to follow all the rules when there's an agave shortage."

Ismael Gama has worked as a *jimador*, agave harvester, for twenty-eight years. He is now the chief harvester for José Cuervo. We arranged, through the Cuervo headquarters, to visit the agave fields with him. He picks us up near the town plaza and we cram ourselves into the cab of his dusty pick-up truck. Ismael started harvesting agave when he was eleven years old. Handsome and tan, with a dark handlebar mustache that seems to hurdle his teeth when he smiles, he is Tequila's version of the Marlboro Man. A straw cowboy hat perches on his head and a leather knife sheath hangs like a holster off his right hip. His white shirt is undone to the waist and the bottoms of his pressed jeans cover a pair of *huarache* sandals.

We stuff ourselves into the truck and start for the agave fields. We're heading to the countryside because of the scarcity of mature agave close to town. When we finally arrive at a field owned by Cuervo, we find row after row of blue agave bursting upward toward a similarly brilliant sky.

Ismael talks about the plant. "Lots of people think that agave is a kind of cactus, but it's not. It's actually closely related to the lily. There are over 300 species of agave in Mexico, but as you know, tequila is made from the Blue Weber variety.

"Unlike grapevines for wine, an agave plant is uprooted when it is harvested to make tequila. That's eight or nine years of growing for a single use. And you have to care for it the entire time. The blue agave should be cut exactly when it reaches maturity. If you harvest it too soon, it won't be ripe, but if you do it too late, it will be dried out."

Every *jimador* is paid according to the weight of the agave he harvests. The hearts, or *piñas*, weigh roughly 100 pounds each. A skilled *jimador* like Ismael can reap up to three or four tons of *piñas* per day.

A *jimador* like Ismael is entrusted with a huge responsibility. It's up to him to determine which plants should be harvested each day. If he's wrong, eight years of investment go down the drain. Unlike many other crops, there is no "harvest season" for agave. It is reaped every day, all year, to feed the ravenous demand for tequila production.

We ask Ismael about the difference between tequila and mezcal. He looks at us aghast.

"Tequila is a very special type of mezcal. Mezcal can be made with the juice of any type of agave. Tequila has to come from Blue Weber agave, the most refined, flavorful agave there is.

"Tequila is simply far more distinguished than mezcal. I mean, some mezcals even have a worm in the bottom of the bottle. Tequila never, ever has a worm."

After straightening us out on that obviously touchy subject, Ismael walks over to a mature agave. He begins by removing and saving the plantlings that are growing around the base of the parent plant. He then whacks off the prickly ends of the leaves so the mature agave, about five feet tall, will be easier to handle. Using a specialized handmade tool called a *coa* he uproots the plant and heaves it over on its side with his sandal-covered foot. The *coa* looks somewhat like a shovel with a sharp, rounded blade.

Ismael uses the *coa* to deftly slice off all the leaves around the base of the plant, creating the pineapple-looking agave heart. This *piña* is about the size of an ottoman. His demonstration is over in less than a minute.

We ask him how he knows that particular plant was ready to be harvested.

"Well, you just look at it, that's all. *Mira*, this one is mature and that one isn't. See how the mature one is a little yellowish on the inside near the base?"

We study the two plants he has indicated. They look identical in every way. That's why he's the expert.

He uproots another agave and turns toward me with the *coa*.

"Your turn."

He had put his foot on the plant to stabilize it while he worked. I raise my shoe to place it on the agave and he quickly jumps in.

"Don't put your foot up there! You might misjudge with the *coa* and cut it off. I'd get in trouble then."

I know the *coa* would easily cut through my shoe, but at least I'm not wearing sandals. Some *jimadores* must walk around on fewer than ten toes.

My first thrust doesn't make it all the way through the leaf. I try again, a little harder, and the blade of the *coa* slices cleanly through. Another thrust and another leaf is sitting on the ground beside the agave. I start to get the hang of it after a few leaves, but am much less fluid than Ismael. It takes me about five minutes because I have to go back over my work and trim it up.

"You'd be in trouble if you had to make a living this way," laughs Ismael.

Every *jimador* is paid according to the weight of the agave he harvests. The *piñas* average about 100 pounds each and many *jimadores* can reap up to three or four tons a day. I doubt, however, that their pay is increasing in relation to the rising price of agave.

Ismael cuts into part of the *piña* and hands us each a slice. It's much drier than I expected it to be. We both take nibbles. It tastes like jicama, but not nearly as moist.

Unlike grapevines for wine, an agave plant is uprooted when it is harvested to make tequila. Eight or nine years of growth go into a single use. There is no specific harvesting season for agave. It is reaped every day, all year, to feed the growing demand for tequila.

Bryan and I each harvest a few plants, but it is obvious we should stick to our day jobs. Ismael loads our agave hearts into the bed of the pickup to deliver them to the Cuervo factory. On the way back to town, we pass a large truck full of agave *piñas*. Ismael shakes his head and clucks his tongue.

"Look at that! Look how young those plants are! Some companies are picking their agave too early, way before the sugars are concentrated. It's all because of the shortage."

The José Cuervo factory, one block off the main plaza on Cuervo Street, is a yellow-walled hacienda-style building. A large iron cage at the entrance houses a monstrous black crow with a long, curved beak. His creepy presence is explained when I recall that *cuervo* means "crow" in Spanish.

Lulu Morales, a compact whirl of energy with a megawatt smile, greets us in the garden. Perfectly groomed, with long manicured fingernails and flawless make-up, Lulu's official title at Cuervo is "Social Superintendent."

José Cuervo, the eleventh largest food and beverage company in the world, has a long history as a tequila producer. In 1795, Spain's King Ferdinand IV granted a license, the first of its kind, to a man named José Cuervo in Tequila. This license was the inaugural permission for commercial production of agave liquor. Today the company is still in the hands of José's descendents.

The company's initial years at the beginning of the nineteenth century were a turbulent time in Mexican history. The struggle for independence from Spain was followed by decades of unrest. Establishment of the Porfirio Díaz dictatorship in 1876 finally brought the political stability that manufacturers needed for economic growth. At the same time, trial and error led distillers in the state of Jalisco to the one species of agave that produced the best tasting liquor. This blue agave (scientifically classified as *Agave tequilana var. Azul*) was classified and named in 1902.

The Cuervo plant is a huge operation. It processes roughly 182,000 gallons of tequila a day. We follow Lulu in her pink hardhat. At the back of the plant we come to the large adobe ovens where the agave hearts are cooked. Thousands of *piñas*, cut into quarters and stacked in piles taller than Bryan, wait their turn to be steamed. Blasts of vapor hiss from the edges of the ovens' doors.

Lulu explains. "When the agave hearts are steamed the starches in the plant are turned to sugars. It's these sugars that are released in the juice when the cooked *piñas* are crushed."

I have read about the crushing process. A large stone wheel like the one we saw at the Destilería Restaurant, a *tahona*, is rolled around a central axis. The wheel is pulled by mules or oxen. I ask Lulu about the Cuervo *tahona* and she laughs.

"No, no, no. *Tahonas* were used in the old days. Nobody uses them any more—they're inefficient. We have modern milling machinery that crushes the agave and washes the fibers to get every last drop of agave juice."

We follow her inside a large building where clanging metal and whooshing water create a production line cacophony. She plucks part of a steamed *piña* off a conveyor belt and pulls back the fibrous brown outer skin to reveal a fleshy pulp.

"Here, taste this."

The steamed *piña* tastes similar to sweet potato, but even more sugary. Almost like candy. It's delicious.

"That's the flavor of the juice. We call it *aguamiel*, honey water."

After milling, the "honey water" is transferred to gargantuan stainless steel vats for fermenting. We stand in front of tank number 9, which has a capacity of over 12,000 gallons.

"This is where the commercial yeast and catalyzers are added. We also add sugars in syrup form if the tequila is going to be a blend."

The majority of the tequilas that Cuervo makes are blends, aimed at the mass market. I think about the wicked tequila hangovers I had in college and wish that I had known that it is the added sugar in cheap tequila that produces much of the headache. Cuervo Gold, the best selling tequila in the United States, is 49 percent sugar. The gold color comes from added caramel, not aging in oak barrels. Like many blends, Cuervo Gold is shipped to the United States in tankers and bottled in American plants.

The grog from the gargantuan fermentation vats in front of us is transferred to copper tanks where it is distilled. During distillation the liquid is heated to a boil. The resulting steam is cooled so that it condenses into a pure, clear liquid. This liquid is boiled and cooled again to concentrate the alcohol even further. The end product of the second distillation is tequila.

Lulu continues her discourse. "There are four different types of tequila. Silver tequila, also called white, is not aged. It's the clear tequila you see in stores. Gold tequila, the second category, is mainly preferred outside of Mexico."

Bryan and I look at each other and roll our eyes. It's "preferred" outside of Mexico because many foreigners don't know any better than to drink blended tequila with artificial color and flavoring. Gold in this case does not imply excellence.

We walk into another building.

"These barrels hold the third kind of tequila, *reposado*. *Reposado* must be aged for a minimum of two months. The fourth kind of tequila is called *añejo*. It must be aged for a minimum of one year, but many times is matured even longer, up to four years. Aging a tequila smoothes it and gives it some of the flavors of the wood. It also makes the liquid a nice amber color."

She shows us stacks of oak barrels that house Cuervo's *añejos*. In one corner a stack of these casks is stamped with the words *Gran Reserva Tequila Añejo—Edición del Nuevo Milenio.*

"That's a special tequila, aged for three years. Its release was timed with the new century. We only made 312 barrels. It costs $18,000 per barrel and is not sold by the bottle. Sotheby's is auctioning some of it."

We ask Lulu how Cuervo is dealing with the agave shortage.

"We're fortunate in that 90 percent of the agave we use comes from our own fields. We have even set up a satellite system to monitor our 20,000 hectares of planted crops.

"To tell you the truth, though, the scarcity is only going to get worse before it gets better. Our studies have shown that the supply won't meet the demand again for at least five years. The next couple of years will be the most difficult ones for tequila producers who don't have their own supplies of agave. Very, very difficult."

fter another night in Tequila we venture into the countryside to visit some of the smaller tequila producers. Although Cuervo doesn't use old techniques like the stone crushing wheel, I'm hopeful that some of these operations still do.

Hacienda San José del Refugio is located in Amatitán, a small town between Tequila and Guadalajara, and the name means "place of the fig trees." A giant fig shades the courtyard of this family-owned estate. It is here that the Herradura brand of tequila is made. Sergio, an enthusiastic college student, has volunteered to show us around. Herradura is known for producing only 100 percent agave, high-quality tequila.

A few years ago Bryan and I went to our favorite restaurant in Austin, a high-end establishment specializing in food from Mexico's interior. Even though we primarily eat Mexican-influenced dishes at home, Fonda San Miguel serves some of the labor-intensive dishes that we don't have the patience to create in our own kitchen. My mother had called ahead and ordered us a bottle of wine as a gift. We decided fine tequila would be more appropriate. The bartender strongly recommended the newly released Herradura Selección Suprema. The name was so cheesy that we were wary about the product, but the man was adamant. Our shots arrived at the table in brandy snifters.

We took deep breaths and inhaled pure heaven. The scent that filled our lungs was rich and deep. There were no harsh alcohol fumes. One sip confirmed that this was the smoothest tequila we had ever tried. Oak and agave mingled together to create buttery perfection. We had always enjoyed Herradura's *reposado*, but the Selección Suprema, aged three to four years, made us Herradura fans for life.

Now we're actually at the Herradura plant. Sergio shares some information Herradura's owners would probably prefer be kept quiet.

"We used to be self-sufficient in our agave. It was one of our points of pride that only estate-grown agave from our own fields was used in Herradura products. We made a big deal about the fact that it helped us control the quality of every plant used. Now, with the shortage, we just don't have enough agave to do that."

That explains the huge sign at the hacienda's entrance. It reads, "Agave-growing friends, Tequila Herradura is buying your agave." After years of turning away independent growers, Herradura is now courting them.

Although a much smaller producer than Cuervo, Herradura is totally modern and mechanized. No stone crushing wheels here. We climb narrow metal ladders to the tops of huge bubbling fermentation vats. Unlike Cuervo, Herradura uses only naturally occurring yeast and does not add catalyzers to speed along the fermentation process. We stick our heads over the edges and are surprised by the heat coming off the frothy, churning brown liquid, called must, *mosto*. Each vat has been fermenting for a different amount of time. Sergio encourages us to stick our hands in and lick the liquid *mosto* off our fingers. The *mosto* that has been fermenting for just a few hours is as sweet as the steamed agave leaves. The four-day old product, strong and dark, puckers our mouths.

We make our way to the distillation tanks. Sergio dips a skinny pail into a tank and withdraws a long, narrow cylinder of the clear liquid. The tester inside is only a quarter full, so I have to tilt the cylinder far back. When I do, a flood of tequila pours into my mouth, down the front of my chin, and all over my shirt. The tequila is smooth, but I am not. Not only have I been wearing the same clothes for two days, now I also smell like a distillery.

Sergio shows us one of Herradura's new bottles. It's made of smoky glass with a single clear section through which you can see an etching of the Hacienda. He scoffs.

"Pretty bottles are a trend in high-end tequilas. Our regular bottle is basic and utilitarian, so we came out with this new design. These so-called bottle collectors don't know much about drinking tequila—there's not always a direct relationship between the price of a tequila and the quality of the product. This fancy bottle is filled with plain white tequila but costs as much as Herradura *reposado*."

Although only 10 percent of the company's product is exported, Bryan and I appreciate the fact that Herradura has become easier to find on menus and in liquor stores in the United States. We mention this to Sergio, who warns us that things could change.

"We used to make 2,600 gallons of tequila a day [about 1 percent of what Cuervo makes], but now we are down to half of that."

e stop by two even smaller producers on our way back to Guadalajara. Tinier tanks, smaller machinery, but clean, modern equipment is used by everybody. No stone crushing wheels to be found.

As we enter the city I am struck by the profusion of tequila billboards. Tequila consumption is up not only in the United States but also in its country of origin. Mexicans today drink three and a half times as much tequila as they did five years ago. I recall that I never saw the spirit advertised when I lived in Guadalajara for a few months in the early 1990s.

While in graduate school I attended a university in Guadalajara for the summer session. I had been working for a consulting company for a few years when I determined that I wouldn't be happy professionally unless I was involved with Mexico. I saw a master's in international management as my ticket to the type of job I sought. Spending a semester studying in Mexico was an added bonus.

I gained a lot of insight that summer, but even here in the heart of blue agave country I learned little about tequila. I drank plenty of margaritas, but was not very aware of the different types and quality levels of tequila that could be mixed in a cocktail. I thought José Cuervo was the gold standard. On those occasional crazy nights that I drank straight tequila, I slammed it in shots and always regretted it.

It wasn't until I moved to Mexico City after graduation that I started to learn about tequila. I was surprised that my Mexican friends would order a tequila to accompany quiet dinners. I had always associated the drink with wild partying, not quiet conversation.

I also observed that they were very specific and demanding about the type of tequila they drank. One of my friends, Ernesto, worked for a liquor distributor. He is a well-versed tequila aficionado, and I call him to find out his current favorite brands.

"You know, there are some okay tequilas coming out of the tiniest unknown factories, but in general I prefer the mid-sized, high-end exporters. They have excellent quality control. A lot of them have beautiful hand-blown bottles too, but what's most important is on the inside. If I'm buying tequila for a gift, I often buy Porfidio. I know I'm paying a lot for the packaging, but the tequila is first rate as well.

"When it comes down to buying for myself I focus entirely on what's inside the bottle. I usually spend my tequila allowance on names I can trust like Herradura, El Tesoro de Don Felipe and Don Julio. Their *reposados*, for instance, are aged for eight months instead of the legally required minimum of two. That just makes them a lot smoother and more complex than their counterparts.

"It's really important to buy from reputable companies. Recently an unscrupulous producer was penalized for bringing in non-blue agave from the state of Oaxaca. They make a lot of mezcal in Oaxaca, but you know it's from a different kind of agave plant. Because of the shortage, many manufacturers are being tempted to use the cheaper, more abundant Oaxaca agave. Officially, if a producer uses any agave other than Blue Weber, the end product can't even be called tequila. Some of the less stringent companies may not always abide by the rules, however. I even heard yesterday about a company caught making tequila with as little as 20 percent agave juice."

Another thing I learned from my Mexican friends was that they sipped, not slammed.

That wasn't always the case. Before tequila was regularly smoothed out by aging in oak barrels, Mexicans used to slam it too. In fact, old Mexican movies featuring shot-slamming mariachis helped popularize tequila and make it the country's undisputed national drink.

All the Best in Mexico, a travel guide from 1949, describes in detail the acceptable fashion for drinking tequila.

> First you shake on the back of your left hand (assuming the right to be your drinking hand) a dash of salt. Toss off the fiery drink at one gulp,

as if it were Swedish aquavit. Then suck a bit of lime and hurl the salt slug nonchalantly from the back of your hand onto your tongue.

That's exactly how I'd been taught to drink it. After all, that's how they drank it in the movies and that was how Shelly West sang about drinking it in her song "José Cuervo, You Are a Friend of Mine." They just happened to be about twenty years behind the times.

Bryan and I pass a billboard advertising a new brand of tequila called Perrísimo. I do a double take. *Perrísimo* is a Mexican word that has two different meanings based on tone. The original meaning of the term, based on the Spanish word for dog, is "wretched." If something is *perrísimo*, it is just awful. Young people, however, use the word entirely differently. In slang, *perrísimo* means "excellent." It's much like the English word "bad." It generally means "unfavorable," but used as slang it can mean "great." We have to check this stuff out.

Luis Alberto Martínez, age 24, is one of the three senior directors for Tequila Perrísimo. Young, hip, and engaging, he enthuses about his new brand of tequila.

"We wanted a tequila for young people, you know. Tequila is always associated with old fossils like mariachis, tradition, and hacienda owners named Don So-and-So. That's fine, and we respect that, but it's kind of irrelevant for our generation. We're about breaking existing paradigms."

I study the bottle. It too is a break with tradition. A finely crafted blue container shaped like a wine bottle, it is decorated with a silver top and silver highlights. Very Mexican, but very sleek and modern at the same time.

Luis Alberto continues, "Just because somebody is young doesn't mean he or she doesn't have good taste in tequila. Tequila Perrísimo is a very high-quality 100 percent agave *reposado*. We happen to be marketing it for people in their twenties and early thirties, that's all."

I ask him about the name. He sighs.

"Oh, that's a long, long story. We were looking for a name that would really capture the attention of people our age, but that older people might not understand. Kind of like an inside joke, you know? We first launched Tequila Perrísimo as Tequila Cabrón. That was a mess that I'm not supposed to talk about."

Tequila Cabrón? I'd say that would be a mess. The term *cabrón*, whose meaning is similar to "asshole," is a forceful slur in Mexico.

Like *perrísimo,* however, it has a different slang meaning. Between close friends, if somebody is labeled a *cabrón* in the positive sense, it means that he is a real stud. I can imagine that Luis Alberto's original brand name, Cabrón, had quite an impact.

"You know, the funny thing was that the public loved the name—especially our target market. Nobody complained. It was the government and some people in the industry that were mad about it. They called it *falta de moral.* We had to recall the bottles and change the name. That's when we came up with Perrísimo."

He turns the subject back to their company philosophy.

"There are lots of new tequilas out on the market right now, but they are all following in the footsteps of brands that are already out there. We're different. It makes sense, you know. I mean, tequila is made in the most modern and up-to-date plants around. They have great machinery, ISO9000 qualification. Why act like it's all old timey? Look at beer—it's 3,000 years old, but it's not marketed like some old-fashioned product. Tequila doesn't have to be, either. Especially to young people."

He's right. If there's one thing we've seen over the past few days it's that this is a modern industry. What was I thinking? Was I expecting to see mule-powered stone crushing wheels? This is an activity that sells millions of dollars of product a year and employs almost 40,000 people in the state. It's big business.

While most tequila comes from the Tequila area, there is another pocket of production east of Guadalajara in the highlands around Arandas. It's here that El Tesoro de Don Felipe, one of the brands my friend Ernesto recommended, is made. We pull up to La Alteña, the Tesoro distillery, expecting to see more of what we saw at the other plants we had visited.

Our host is a middle-aged man named Guillermo. I almost fall over when we are led into the production area. There it is—a stone crushing wheel. It's being pulled in circles by a tiny green-and-yellow tractor instead of a mule, but it is being used for tequila production.

Guillermo explains. "We believe in making tequila the old-fashioned way. We're the only ones who still do. We crush all of our agave for El Tesoro using this 2,000-pound *tahona.*"

A man in shorts and rubber boots stands ankle-deep in agave. As soon as the *tahona* passes by he fluffs the steamed agave fibers with a pitchfork so that they will get crushed evenly. I can't believe we've found the wheel. I take pictures and grin like a goon.

Slowly it dawns on me. El Tesoro and Perrísimo are not as far apart as it might appear at first glance. It all comes down to marketing. El Tesoro's unique marketing concept is that it is the only commercial tequila manufacturer that still uses traditional methods in crafting its liquor. It's this company's way of differentiating itself in this competitive business.

The end result, however, is some of the highest quality tequila in Mexico. Guillermo explains the importance of the wood barrels while we sample El Tesoro's *reposado* and *añejo*.

"When *reposados* are aged, it's for less than a year. The wood changes the chemical structure of the alcohol, making it softer, but it doesn't really have time to change the agave flavor. You get hints of oak and vanilla, but the central taste should be agave.

"The main impact of aging tequila for over a year is to transfer some of the characteristics of the wood to the alcohol. That's why the barrel is so important for the flavor. A new barrel gives off more tannins, creating body, but an old barrel will soften the drink more. Different barrels can give off smoky, butterscotch, or even mocha undertones. Our product is handcrafted to carefully blend tequila from old and new barrels to create the perfect flavor."

These are the finest tequilas we have sampled on this trip. We mention to Guillermo our concerns that the shortage will negatively impact the quality of tequila across the board. He calmly shakes his head.

"No, there are some manufacturers, like us, for whom quality is the single most important thing. We won't sacrifice it to cut costs. That may mean that we become a lot more expensive, but we will never, ever compromise our quality."

Bryan and I consider this statement while we linger over our last sips. We realize that while the shortage may inflate prices for the next couple of years, we'll happily pay whatever it takes for this pleasure. Tequila is more than just a drink for us; it's a touchstone of all our time in Mexico. No matter where we are in the world, the taste of tequila returns us to this land of sun and agave.

Resources

Álvarez, José Rogelio, ed. *Enciclopedia de México*. México, DF: Compañía Editora de Enciclopedias de México, 1987.

Barrios, Virginia B. de. *A Guide to Tequila, Mezcal, and Pulque*. México, DF: Editorial Minutiae Mexicana SA de CV, 1971.

Bender, Andrew. "A Field Guide to Fine Tequila." *Fortune*, October 30, 2000, 328.

Clark, Sydney. *All the Best in Mexico*. New York: Dodd, Mead & Co., 1949.

De Mente, Boyé Lafayette. *NTC's Dictionary of Mexican Cultural Code Words*. Lincolnwood, IL: NTC Publishing Group, 1996.

Estadísticas diciembre 1999. Guadalajara: Cámara Nacional de la Industria Tequilera, 2000.

Muriá, José María. *El tequila. Boceto histórico de una industria*. Cuadernos de Difusión Científica, Número 18. Guadalajara: Universidad de Guadalajara, 1990.

———. *Una bebida llamada tequila*. Guadalajara: Editorial Agata, 1996.

Sharpe, Patricia. "Viva Tequila." *Texas Monthly*, August 1995, 74-79.

SANGRITA

GUADALAJARA AND SOUTHERN JALISCO

A cab transports Becky and me from the village of Arandas back into Guadalajara. The capital of Jalisco swells outward in binges of factories, humble block dwellings, and commercial structures. In its heart, however, lies a beautiful historical center graced with neoclassical buildings and a pair of unforgettable blue-and-yellow-tiled cathedral spires. Glistening with fountain spray, several plazas link to form a jacaranda-embroidered cross, sentried by a bevy of national heroes in bronze. The grandeur can be misleading in a sense, because the *tapatíos*, as the residents of Guadalajara are known, readily adopted the musical and culinary ways brought by country folk. Many of these regional characteristics ultimately developed into the most typical of Mexican traditions.

When you order tequila here, two long, slender shot glasses promptly salute you. One is gilded with tequila, and the other is stoked red with the fiery chaser *sangrita*. *Reposado* tequila is sipped alternately with sangrita, without haste, so that luster, then incandescence, can be savored. Ideally mariachi musicians encircle your table, strumming, plucking, and thumping guitars, and blasting on horns. You and your friends sing along or perhaps someone in your group will be talented or simply daring enough to stand and perform solo. Sip, sip, sing.

All over Mexico people now drink tequila with a side of sangrita (not to be confused with the wine-based *sangría* from Spain) but that doesn't mean it's the only way to imbibe. In any establishment that serves upscale tequila, a variety of approaches are used. One person uses beer laced with lime juice as a chaser. Another person drips lime directly into his tequila. Another splashes sangrita into hers. It is still quite common to be served salt and lime with a shot of tequila, but the norm of yesteryear—lick the salt, shoot the tequila, suck the lime—is passé because tequila quality has improved dramatically. You would be considered a rube to squander fine tequila by shooting it. A good strategy is to line up the full arsenal in front of you—tequila, lime, salt, beer, and sangrita—then grab whatever tempts your palate at the moment. Your method develops spontaneously.

I love to smother and stoke tequila's smooth burn with a blazing quaff of chilled sangrita. The name, given to the drink for its color and consistency, means "a little blood" in Spanish. By making "blood" diminutive, the speaker sounds bolder, dauntless when confronted by what makes most squeamish. When those who have a love affair with their tequila ritual say it, it seems more like cooing.

Sangrita is concocted by blending until smooth two pounds of peeled tomatoes, the juice of three oranges, the juice of three limes, one chopped onion, and chili to taste. Recipes vary. Some add grenadine syrup, Worcestershire, or Salsa Maggi, a brand of sauce found primarily in Latin America, and a few omit the tomatoes. The chili is preferably fresh *puya*, *guajillo*, or *chile de árbol*, but hot sauce like red pepper (such as Tabasco brand) or habanero can be substituted. There are a few brands of sangrita bottled commercially, the most ubiquitous of which is La Viuda de Sánchez, but it is awful stuff, a Tang-flavored forgery.

I prefer sangrita to be homemade, viscous with tomato pulp and onion bits, sweet with freshly-squeezed orange juice, torrid with *guajillo* chiles, and served with a tequila *reposado*. Tequila's other ideal companion, mariachi music, must also be present. Sip, sip . . .

I suddenly realize, to my great dismay, that I don't know the complete words to a mariachi song.

The revelation strikes me as Becky and I walk down Plaza Tapatía. I've hummed a hundred mariachi songs, yet I can't evoke the entire lyrics to any one of them. Oh, sure I can jump in on the chorus lines like everyone else, but if the necessity arose, I couldn't perform a mariachi song on my own. This newfound deficiency gnaws at me to the point of distraction, and then devours me as only a true obsession can.

Here's the thing. When you go to a cantina where mariachi music is the central attraction, it is a chaotic affair. Tequila and sangrita flow, several bands play different songs simultaneously in the same confined area, and everyone is yelling across tables to converse. There is always one patron who appears more self-satisfied than everyone else. The audacious and somewhat cheesy character brandishes a wad of cash that induces mariachi groups to dote on him all evening as he belts out song after song with great bravado. When seated, the macho's legs are spread and sturdy, his elbows rest in the most commodious spots, and he grins with the pride of the creator of song. When he stands, all eyes are on him; the musicians and even the bandleader are waiting for his cue to play. He is the focus and the power and the glory. With a blinding surge of aspiration, I yearn to match his boldness and aplomb. I want to dictate what song is played next. I want . . .

"We're here," Becky says.

"Huh?"

I look around. "Here" is the Cabañas Cultural Institute. We've come to this former orphanage built in the early 1800s to check out the murals painted by José Clemente Orozco. He painted these from 1936 to 1939, toward the end of the muralist movement when this was one of the last bare—thus greatly coveted—public spaces. Born in provincial Jalisco, Orozco spent five of his boyhood years in Guadalajara before his family moved to Mexico City. Adorning his home state's most revered edifice was a fitting climax for an extraordinary artist.

Orozco painted these murals in the colors of ash, earth, blood, and fire and he did so with one hand. As a teenager he was trying to make fireworks out of gunpowder and blew off several fingers. Ensuing infection and surgery reduced his left hand to a stump. The accident inspired him to paint hands in Herculean proportions, like those created by El Greco and Rodin.

This mural is entitled "Man of Fire" and it runs the length of a forty-meter vaulted ceiling. The best way to view the masterpiece is to lie on one of the wooden benches set up for the purpose. We gaze at the interior of the central dome. In this focal point four natural elements are represented by male nudes. Three of them, Man of Earth, Man of Sea, and Man of Air, form a ring around the circumference of the dome with their torsos, arms, and legs. At the apex, the Man of Fire, foreshortened and enveloped in flames, ascends toward heaven.

Inspiration comes in strange forms, but even Orozco was moved by agave, which he depicted as a central subject in his lithograph "Nopales and Maguey." As I gaze up at the dome I imagine the celestial burning man as me sipping a torrid sangrita while singing "Cielito Lindo."

Resolving to transform myself into that archetypical crooning maverick that rules the cantina, I tell Becky that I will debut here in Jalisco, the very birthplace of mariachi music. I discount the fact that I'm often the person botching the words to the latest pop song, and frequently go silent amid verse that should be ingrained into my memory such as camp songs, carols, and nursery rhymes. I ponder how anxiety might ambush me, freezing my grandiose gestures and pinching my vocal chords shut. I need time, that's all—a few days to memorize the lyrics and muster the nerve. We map out a loop around the south of Jalisco, an inspirational odyssey intended to graft us with the historical roots of mariachi.

They say that this town, Cocula, is the birthplace of mariachi music. Citizens of Cocula don't just say it; they postulate, testify, document, and agonize over it. In the short publication "De Cocula es el Mariachi" by Germán A. Méndez Rodríguez, which outlines the history of the genre, a native son builds his case in the most erudite and convincing manner, drawing on evidence that goes back as far as the original indigenous inhabitants. After calmly building an irrefutable argument over seven pages, the author suddenly breaks out in screaming caps, "COCULA IS THE BIRTHPLACE OF MARIACHI."

No one seems to listen. They listen to the music, all right. Often the most famous group in the history of the genre, Mariachi Vargas de Tecalitlán, plays it. That is exactly why the folks in Cocula have to shout; they are trying to make themselves heard over the cumulative volume of eight decades of Mariachi Vargas popularity. If only Mariachi Vargas hadn't included "de Tecalitlán" (from Tecalitlán) in its name, then that town across the *sierra* wouldn't be mentioned so frequently as the birthplace of mariachi music, and Cocula would bask in undisputed glory.

Franciscan monks brought European music to Jalisco. They taught litanies and hymns to the indigenous Coca people in the area that now is Cocula. With the instruments and skills intended for religious music, the native players picked up Spanish genres such as Jarabe and Son. During the last half of the nineteenth century their tunes evolved into folk music. The quartets were composed of two violins, a small guitar called a *vihuela*, and a harp. The *guitarrón*, "guitar" in the augmentative, transforming it to mean "huge guitar," really is a gargantuan guitar. Many of the musicians can barely fit their arms around it. The hollow-sounding *guitarrón* was invented in Cocula and added to the arrangement at the end of the century, just when the music was becoming popularly known as "mariachi." Trumpets were adopted later, after the Mexican Revolution, when Mexico City's Garibaldi Plaza turned into the country's musical hub.

A cornerstone of the Cocula's mariachi birthplace theory is that this is where the first *guitarrón* was created. We've driven seventy kilometers south from Guadalajara to this town of 25,000 to meet a *guitarrón* maker. The central plaza is exceedingly pleasant with park benches that curve like big pink parentheses amid fountains, statues, and trees heavy with oranges and red gramophone flowers. A visit to the cathedral reveals that the varying shades of pink brick are simply painted on the façade. The faux mortar is thin gray lines that ripple when confronted with protuberant square columns. Nestled in the cracks of the real stones of the steps are bits of bright confetti from a recent wedding.

It is often reported that the word "mariachi" came from the French word for marriage—*mariage*. The basis of this theory is that during the French occupation of Mexico, 1863-1867, musicians in Guadalajara played for French weddings. While simple and sweet, the mariachi expert Méndez asserts that the theory is unlikely to be true because the word "mariachi" as applied to a modern musical group didn't come into popular use until three decades after the French were tossed out. Moreover, "mariachi" was used for centuries in the regional dialect of Nahuatl to describe a tree, a small dance platform made from its wood, and to a lesser extent the dance and musical group associated with the platform. It is a distinct probability that Nahuatl provided the true etymological root of the word.

We stop at a metal shack for a couple of OJs. The owner pulls down on the lever of her manual juicer with admirable might. We consult her about finding a *guitarrón* maker in town. She informs us that there is only one, the grandson of Camila Flores. We can find his house by asking around on Juárez Street a few blocks away.

An octopus arm of the outdoor market snatches us just behind the juice stand. We pass a stall selling belts with big, fancily stitched leather buckles. On another table crowd a hundred plastic bags of spices, the tops rolled down like bobby socks to unveil diverse colors, textures, and aromas. The next stand exhibits bulk breakfast cereals, brandless Cheerios, Fruit Loops, and Cocoa Puffs, in huge clear plastic bags.

We stop in front of two speakers booming out *ranchera* music to survey an impressive selection of bootleg cassette tapes. This is an upscale operation in that each cassette includes a color photocopy cover of the original tape sleeve. I find what I'm looking for, a Mariachi Vargas tape with "Cielito Lindo" on it so I can practice the words while we drive. The price is under a dollar, so we look to see if there is anything else that catches our fancy. Becky picks up a copy of *15 Auténticos Éxitos de Santana.*

The young vendor, dressed in a polo shirt, gold-rimmed Yves Saint Laurent shades, and purple-and-gold Miami Dolphins hat, certainly as genuine as his wares, speaks to us in international slacker's English, "He's from here, man. Carlos Santana borned here."

"Santana is from this town?" I ask, surprised.

"From this state—Jalisco, man. His town is Autlán de Navarro, south from here. Everybody thinks that he borned in Tijuana, but no, he is *jalisciense*."

After buying the tapes, we ask our way along Juárez Street until we arrive at the home of Camila Flores's grandson. We inquire of the cheery gray-haired woman who answers the door about the possibility of meeting the craftsman. We expect to enter a compact dwelling, but the *señora* leads us through a long, narrow corridor along which open a living room and bedrooms. Two teenage girls smile and giggle when we pass the ample kitchen. The wall above the sink is decorated with miniature ceramic mugs in a large spiral, with the cups increasing ever so slightly in size along the spiral arm.

Since there are few doors in the house, we pass directly from the kitchen into the back courtyard, an extension of the corridor minus the roof. Lining one side are birdcages with parrots, canaries, and cardinals segregated by squawk and song. The *señora* stops us suddenly with a thrust of her arm. A teenager drops a flaring match into a two-foot-high black cylinder, which is partially filled with gasoline. The flame's peaks leap from the cylinder like a blue cat trying to claw its way out of a metal pen. The young man bends a strip of wood around the hot cylinder, endowing it with the voluptuous curves of a guitar torso. The *señora* finally interrupts his work by shouting, "Javier!"

The last crafter of *guitarrones* in Cocula is seventeen years old. He wears a baseball hat with a Billabong logo pulled backward on his head and a faded Maui & Sons T-shirt, both brands of surfwear companies. Guadalajara is within weekend driving distance of the beach, so surfing is a popular sport, and the brands and clothing spawned from it even more so. Javier doesn't surf, though. You would assume that his favorite sport is soccer, but it isn't. He prefers to play American football, which has become increasingly popular during the past decade. You can guess from his above-average height and formidable shoulders and neck that he is probably dominant on the field. His peach fuzz moustache, however, is more indicative of his personality than is his athletic build.

Javier holds up a finished *guitarrón* for us to admire. When asked for details about its construction, he murmurs, "The acoustic box is made of cedar and mahogany that I buy in Guadalajara. The cover is made from *tacota* wood found only in Jalisco."

Silence ensues. Becky encourages him. "Go on . . . "

"The neck of the guitar starts like that," he says as he points to a solid block of wood. "Then I carve it with a machete. I make two *guitarrones* at a time and it takes me about ten days to finish them."

Flat guitar patterns hang on the brick walls, as does a calendar featuring a photo of an open-armed Pope John Paul. Javier's workbench is cluttered with metal files, brushes, and cans of lacquer and glue. In addition to *guitarrones*, he makes the small Spanish guitars, *vihuelas*.

Becky asks if she can hold the *guitarrón* so we can inspect it more closely. The blonde *tacota* wood is engraved around the mouth with black looping spirals and pointed waves. The same designs border the body. Where the body meets the neck, Javier has burned in a simple line a drawing of a woman's face.

When I refer to his trade as a valuable legacy, Javier fidgets. "My grandfather taught me how to do this. Most of his clients still come to me. My father didn't want to learn. He found other work. I know there are good jobs with more money." He pauses. "I want to go to the university too."

Becky hugs the *guitarrón,* looking much like the beatific girl engraved on it. A mere glance in her direction provokes adamant justifications. "If you can learn the words to mariachi songs, then I can learn to play this!" She continues searching for the most convincing reason. "Someone has to buy these so he keeps making them to keep the tradition alive. What if he becomes a middle manager at Proctor y Gamble de México or something?" And finally, "This is an authentic piece of mariachi history."

We locate Autlán de Navarro, Santana's hometown, on the map. Our next planned stop is Tecalitlán, but it looks as if we can include Autlán by driving our rental car seventy miles south, then cutting east over the Sierra Tapalpa mountains. We are about to pop the bootleg Santana tape into the car's cassette player when we notice that the song titles are written on the tape in Spanish.

It makes us wonder if we're going to listen to a Mexican lounge singer playing an electronic keyboard. No, it's the sorcerer himself making those guitar chords uncoil and sway like a cobra. The tinny reproduction quality enhances our nostalgia as we listen to *Evil Ways*, *Black Magic Woman*, and *Oye Como Va* in succession.

Before his first wild peak of success with these songs in the early '70s, before dropping LSD with fellow hippies in Haight Ashbury, before seeking spirituality through Eastern mysticism, before learning to speak with angels, and before his *Supernatural* resurrection on the worldwide musical stage, Carlos Santana was a boy here. It represents a time of innocence, because afterward his family migrated to a Tijuana hovel where everyone had to work to make ends meet. Santana sold *chicles* and shined shoes. As a teen he earned money with his musical talent by playing guitar in strip joints that ranged from seedy to depraved.

His memories of his hometown are of "*mazapán* and *pitayas*—sweet things," he told a local radio station during his visit this year, the only time he has returned since childhood.

In Autlán's municipal building I am introduced to the catalyst of that visit. "The mayor," an assistant announces with solemn formality, and hands me a cordless phone, as if insinuating that the apparatus itself is the mayor.

"I convinced Carlos to come back after forty-five years. We are dedicating a park to him and I am pushing the council to name a street Calle de Santana. My public relations man, Edgardo, will show you around."

The assistant snatches the mayor away from me. Instantly my hand is grasped by Edgardo, a budding politician with a chiseled and polished ear-to-ear grin. He is barely thirty, with a dark, blockish face and a neatly clipped cushion of steel-wool hair. A starched white Nehru collar shirt and light linen pants adorn his husky frame.

"We can take the city van," Edgardo proclaims as he hands us each a folding chair. Neither Becky or I can figure out why we are carrying chairs until we see that the van has no seats, not even one for the driver. Edgardo explains this layout makes it easier to haul bulky stage set-ups.

Autlán serves as a commercial center for the surrounding farmers who raise sugarcane, tomatoes, squash, and corn. The drive around town is hot and soporific. We stop by the Carlos Santana Civic Plaza, which has been constructed piece by piece over ten years whenever Autlán can secure matching funds from the state. Some of the main components are in place now, including a pink-columned bandstand, a basketball court, and playground equipment, but there are also several projects still in the works. Someday the park will have a statue of the guitarist, and at his own suggestion, busts of other local musicians.

Wherever we drive, Edgardo honks, makes eye contact, and doles out unerring waves. Sometimes he stops for a salutation and a mini-summit. His popularity isn't only political; it's also literary. He writes a newspaper column about the colorful people of Autlán. One article was about a humble man whose unruly gang of street dogs pulled his shopping cart around town like an Alaskan sled. He used the clamorous vehicle to deliver tanks of gas and other cargo. One day a *norteño* came into town and gave the man a wad of money. (When *norteños*, people from the north of Mexico, visit Autlán, they are very loud and popular as long as their money lasts. After the money is spent, they are just loud). The day after receiving his endowment, the shopping cart man was found dead by the railroad tracks, his dogs still tethered and barking.

Edgardo explains that a lot of people he writes about are eccentric, which is why everybody knows them. "They are our community figures. They are part of us. I treat them with dignity because it is a form of self-respect."

Dark volcanic mountains surround Autlán. Edgardo points to one. "My wife is from there. She is a mountain woman, but has lighter skin than you. She is beautiful, maybe French, from a clan that dug in up there a century ago. I just taught her to dance. Can you imagine? She'd never heard salsa music growing up. That is how remote of a life she lived before I met her.

"I used to be too ambitious. My first marriage was for the wrong reasons, to advance my position mainly, and it turned out to be a bad situation. I was miserable. As penitence for my divorce, I pledged to the priest that I would walk barefoot forty kilometers to the Virgen de Cacoma in that village's church. I arrived there so remorseful, tired, and suffering. My feet were swollen and bloody from the walk. A stranger took pity on me and invited me into the shade of his home for a drink of water. Now that man is the grandfather of my son."

We stop in front of the house where Santana was born. It is a simple dwelling painted two-tone, the bottom half pink and the upper half lavender. During his visit Santana said that he remembered the mango trees planted here by his Uncle Juan and spending time with his other relatives, including his Aunt Teresa.

Aunt Teresa says she was surprised by her nephew's impromptu visit. She had a cold that day and wasn't made up. Today as we sit on the sheet-covered furniture in her living room she seems quite healthy and at ease. The octogenarian wears a gray sweater and a long, dark housedress over green slacks. She speaks with her back erect and her hands clasped to her knees. Aunt Teresa is happily retired now, but for decades she ran a popular local restaurant, and by her own account, was queen of that kitchen. The house specialties were *birria* tacos and *pipián*. On the wall behind her is a poster of the '70s Santana in silhouette, with afro-like hair, aviator sunglasses, and a bushy moustache. He is grooving on a guitar in front of a blue background airbrushed with a full moon and palm trees reflecting on the ocean.

"Carlos was a good boy," she says. "He loved his father."

In a *Rolling Stone* interview Santana recalls riding on the back of his father's bicycle to church and to his father's performances. "My father was a musician and my first memory of him was watching him play music and watching what it did to people—he was the darling of our town."

Aunt Teresa continues, "His father, my brother José, played in cantinas mostly. He also did serenades. They'd load a piano and the band into the back of pick-up and drive right up to the girl's house."

She points to some framed black-and-white photos. "That's José on the wall next to Carlos."

We get up from our seats for a better look. In one of the silvery shots, eight members of a mariachi group pose in huge sombreros and dapper *charro* suits. The band's leader, José Santana, is surrounded by the other members on a stage. The curtain draped down behind them is decorated with paper cutouts of palm trees and a crescent moon, a crude version of the mod background on the poster of Carlos. The coincidence is moving.

Aunt Teresa closes her eyes. "Carlos makes the guitar sing just like his father made the violin sing when he was a mariachi."

On a country highway a coyote raises its head momentarily, then hunches its shoulders, trotting into a cornfield. We crest a ridge and marvel over a brilliant blue lake that covers the entire valley floor. As we descend, we realize that the lake is an illusion. This oval valley is sewn with blue agave; one of the experimental plots that the producers from Tequila planted here a few years ago. Most of the afternoon drive is spent peering over swaying green stalks of sugarcane at the smoke plume spiraling from the tan cone of the Colima Volcano. Religious pilgrims in straw cowboy hats walk along the roadside under shady pines where the highway crosses the mountain pass.

Tecalitlán is a quaint village, though not as charming as Cocula. A yellow church and two beautiful pine trees grace its square. We take a photo with the statue of Silvestre Vargas, sharing the shade of his ample sombrero. We hope to find mariachis here so I can make my much-anticipated debut, but when we ask around, we are informed that mariachis rarely play in Tecalitlán. The town continues to seed Mariachi Vargas with talent, but professional musicians must play in places like Mexico City, Guadalajara, and Tlaquepaque, where people have money. Here the people can only afford to give them *gritos*, enthusiastic hollers, which is just enough to bring the famous band home a few times per year. We are told that a mariachi museum opened a few months ago. I breathe a sigh of relief over averting my debut. At this point I prefer inspiration to performance.

We grab a bite in a typical country eatery with cheery cloth-covered tables and bare stucco walls. The place is exceptionally clean and the food is spicy and delicious. As we dine, the locals who enter the restaurant greet us with "*buen provecho,*" which roughly translates to "enjoy your meal." In big cities it is polite to say this to the people with whom you're dining before starting to eat. In small towns, additionally, you say *buen provecho* to each occupied table that you pass on the way into and out of the restaurant. You can really tell that you are in the country when this politeness is in practice.

The museum is a gorgeous little exhibition space with brightly painted walls highlighting mariachi memorabilia and outlining the history of the Mariachi Vargas de Tecalitlán. Musically talented but illiterate, Gaspar Vargas started a quartet with three other locals in 1898. They played mostly *son*. Three years later Gaspar's son Silvestre was born. Gaspar attempted to dissuade Silvestre from becoming a musician because it was a hard life, especially during the years of the revolution. One of the band members found the teenage Silvestre secretly playing a "violin" against his father's wishes. The instrument was constructed of a piece of dry sugarcane with strings attached to it. The band member convinced Gaspar to split the cost of a real violin with Silvestre who went on to lead the band to fame and fortune.

Mariachi music's popularity grew in the '20s and '30s. In 1934 the band finally made the big move to Mexico City, where musicians from around the country had descended on Garibaldi Plaza. The band added a trumpet player and landed a weekly radio show. While warming up to record an album, a few of the band members unleashed hoots and hollers, imitating the rowdy crowds in Tecalitlán. The producer loved it, recorded it onto the album, and such *gritos* have not only become a trademark of the group, but are also commonly heard whenever mariachi music is played.

Mariachi Vargas played in over a hundred films during Mexico's golden age of cinema with prominent stars such as Pedro Infante, Jorge Negrete, and Lola Beltrán. These films were exported all over Latin America. When a middle-aged Chilean, Peruvian, or Ecuadoran meets a Mexican, invariably the talk will turn to fond childhood memories of Mexican films and music. The impact that Mariachi Vargas had on the far reaches of Latin America is truly awe inspiring when you consider the group's origin in this humble and remote *pueblito,* Tecalitlán.

As I contemplate Silvestre's sorry little cane violin, I surmise that my rehearsals are now at least equal in quality to this simple instrument. I am ready to sing.

The stage will be Tlaquepaque's El Parián, an open-air cafe under arches built two centuries ago when the community was still a *pueblito*. Now the village has been consumed into greater Guadalajara. Visitors come to Tlaquepaque for pleasant strolls among myriad *artesanía* shops selling everything from the town's specialty, pottery, to wooden horses and religious sculptures. People also come to enjoy mariachi music and cool beverages in the toasty afternoon sunshine.

I grow more nervous by the moment as we try to decide which part of the huge restaurant will be the best spot for my debut. Bow-tied waiters induce people to their sections with promises of *cervezas bien heladas*, but we are drawn by the aroma of fresh, thick tortillas baking on a wide, flat grill. A wrinkled old woman with Clark Kent glasses wallops the tortilla dough into balls, then shapes them with her nimble fingers before tossing them onto the crackling grill. The dense corn flour tortillas serve as the base layer of *gorditas*, which are piled with toppings like bean puree, spicy chorizo sausage, lettuce, and salsa.

Before sitting down, I anxiously ask about the musicians. They are nowhere to be seen. The waiter advises us that the mariachis will arrive at any moment. My heart leaps to my throat. We order shots of Herradura *reposado* with sangrita on the side.

The day is filled with perfect heat and flowing purple bougainvillea. Some of my most memorable afternoon buzzes were caught in Tlaquepaque while I lived in Guadalajara during my initial foray into Mexico.

As a budding Latinophile, I decided to I wanted to somehow work in or with Latin America after college. I joined some friends who had moved from Seattle to San Diego to find work. The established pattern was that you saved up job-hunting funds, moved in with a buddy, attempted to look for a job, but instead spent all of your time learning how to surf. When the money ran out, you borrowed from your loved ones, really got into surfing now that you knew how to do it, then finally, as the borrowed funds dwindled, frantically searched for a job. I knocked on every export company's door in San Diego hoping for a sales job targeting Latin America. I found one selling agricultural products to Iraq.

Saddam Hussein was an ally then, bogged down in a long war with our common enemy Iran, so the United States was aiding his regime with billions of dollars of agricultural credit. About two weeks after I landed the job, my manager quit and I found myself taking regular trips to Baghdad. I returned from meetings with tacit Iraqi officials to my pad in Pacific Beach, where I'd immediately ditch the business suit for surf shorts, then skateboard to the beach with a surfboard under my arm. Iraq invaded Kuwait on the night of a close friend's bachelor party and although I got the news before I went to bed, it had to be repeated to me a few hours after I woke up. The death of my commissions was not a remedy for my hangover.

Though I had my heart set on working in South America, particularly Argentina, the potential of the unsigned North American Free Trade Agreement changed my mind. Mexico became my destination. Because of its proximity, I did not consider our southern neighbor a particularly exotic country at the time, but now marvel at how, when comparing it to dozens of countries I've traveled to, Mexico still consistently intrigues and surprises me like no other.

From San Diego I entered into an association with two American businessmen and two Mexico City businessmen, all about twenty-five years my senior, to form an agricultural trading company. My contribution would be opening an office in Guadalajara. I loaded my pick-up truck with a twenty-pound laptop, a fax machine, and my surfboard. I had never in my life experienced jitters like those that rattled me when I crossed the border to drive here alone.

I am bouncing my leg against the leather tabletop nervously when the waiter brings our order. He sets the shot glasses with tequila and sangrita down. The sangrita is radioactive orange in color and too watery to be handmade. The waiter informs us that it is *La Viuda de Sánchez*, the bottled brand.

"*Pinche Viuda*!" I curse the widow out loud.

"Excuse me?" the waiter says.

The waiter promises a homemade batch, but like the mariachis, it never arrives. I stare sullenly at my empty shot glass as its shadow lengthens, lamenting the practice I've done in vain.

After dinner that evening I consider the options. Our flight to Monterrey leaves tomorrow morning. Becky worked hard to arrange an interview at the Cuauhtémoc Brewery, so changing the schedule is not a possibility. I tell Becky that I've given up on the prospect of singing here.

"We can go to Mariachi Plaza right now," Becky encourages me, "You can do the song there."

"Mariachi Plaza? Isn't that supposed to be the most dangerous spot in Guadalajara?"

We select the browniest driver from the queue of cabs outside of our hotel. We tell him we just want to drive by Mariachi Plaza to see how dicey it looks.

"Oh, you have to be careful, all right," Raúl, our driver, confirms. "People get aggressive there."

A drive by the plaza confirms that it is no fancy ballroom. Mariachis, hoping to land an outside gig, wave to drivers-by. Cracked and peeling buildings encase the triangular plaza. A group of derelicts loiters on a dry fountain littered with shards of glass. The grungy men smoke, suck on bottles of cheap booze, and fulfill their role of appearing criminal. Raúl stops the cab so we can discuss the situation. In Mexico City's Garibaldi Plaza most of the problems occur when upon catching a cab home the driver turns out to be in cahoots with armed robbers. We study Raúl.

He prompts, "If it makes you more comfortable, I will go with you. It will be safer with a bigger group."

We picked him out of a queue. He didn't pick us. His offer seems genuine so we put our trust in our instincts and make our way to the plaza. At the entrance, there is a cluster of dozens of music cases in the shapes of violins, trumpets, *vihuelas*, guitars, and *guitarrones*. The charro-dressed men that go with the instruments mill around under the arches of the plaza, waiting for their leaders to give them instructions to play here or to pile into station wagons for serenades elsewhere.

The plaza is cordoned into several sections with tables that pertain to indoor bars directly behind them. We take a seat in the middle. A waiter, sleazy despite his bow tie and white shirt, gruffly demands our order. We are startled by his bark. I ask for a shot of Don Julio *reposado* and sangrita, then find myself mimicking a tough desperado in an old cowboy movie, saying, "*No quiero ver la pinche viuda.*"

He eyes me warily. I don't think he has ever heard a gringo swear in Spanish, at least not when referring to a widow. He replies, "Our sangrita is made on the premises."

Raúl, now informed of my objective, offers to call over a mariachi group. I prefer to take my time, loosen the vocal cords with some tequila and sangrita, and then make my move.

A stream of vendors flows by. One is selling a tiny plastic monkey that pees water on our table when he squeezes its belly. Another belts out "Electric Shock! Forty pesos! *El relax*!" This man is carrying a car battery with lines that flow into a gauge box, then out to two metal wands. The fun begins when two people in a group grab the wands as all hold hands to complete the circuit. The voltage increases until someone breaks the chain by dropping hands or simply crying, "stop!" It's an electronic version of "*¿Quién es más macho?*"

Raúl summons the leader of a mariachi group, a violinist in his sixties with Coke-bottle glasses and gold-capped Billy Bob teeth. The rate per song is a stiff seven dollars. It is no wonder I've never done this before. I request three songs, informing the leader that I'll sing the second one.

The mariachi group that arrives is so ragtag it seems the musicians were selected on the basis of grooming defects. The *guitarronista* wears a shrunken squirrel hair toupee. The shirt of one of the trumpet players billows through an open fly. All of the men are well past middle-age, so when I request one of my favorites, "Niño Perdido," Becky is amused that the oldest of them, perhaps seventy-five, acts out the role of the lost child. He hides on the other side of the plaza pushing air through his melancholy, searching trumpet while the rest of the band echoes in response around our table.

The group is slovenly to be sure, but these are my men now. I request "Cielito Lindo." The leader invites me to stand. I think of a boy who learns to a make a *guitarrón* from his grandfather, a mariachi's son who sweeps the Grammys, a boy who plays the violin on a piece of sugarcane. I imagine Santana's voice rising above the plaza's clamor: "We are multidimensional spirits with enormous potential." The music bursts out around me, all eight musicians play with vigor, and sweat floods my back as the leader nods at me.

"De la Sierra Morena, cielito lindo, viene bajando, un par de ojitos negros, cielito lindo, de contrabando."

I remember the words to the first verse completely—a *señorita* with perilous black eyes comes down from the mountains. I stumble on the timing, my voice isn't in perfect tune but, oh, here comes the chorus, which translates to "Sing, don't cry, because singing brightens heavy hearts."

"Ay, ay, ay, ay, canta y no llores, porque cantando se alegran, cielito lindo, los corazones."

When I was a high school exchange student in Brazil I went on an organized tour to the Iguazu Waterfall, a gloriously brutish semicircle of thunder and spray. A motorboat pilot offered to transport passengers to a rock in the mouth of the falls. Our guide forbade that anyone take such a risk, so an Israeli schoolteacher in the group and I snuck back later. I stood on that rock awed by the universe of water that churned past, leapt downward, and pummeled itself into mist. In a melodic sense I now feel something similar as the trumpets blast, the *guitarrón* twangs, the violins squeal, and I stand overwhelmed in the mouth of this cascade of music.

After I finish the song, I sit down. Becky caresses my arm. My knees are shaking, but my aspiration has been fulfilled.

I request the last song. My men react, the distinctive sounds of their instruments blending like the ingredients of sangrita into a zesty mélange.

"Guadalajara, Guadalajara, Guadalajara, Guadalajara . . ."

Sip, sip, sing.

Resources

Dutton, June. *Cocina Mexicana.* San Francisco: Determined Productions, 1969.

Heath, Chris. "The Epic Life of Carlos Santana." *Rolling Stone*, March 16, 2000, 38-48, 86-89.

Méndez Rodríguez, Germán. *De Cocula es el Mariachi*. Cocula, Jalisco: n.p., 1998.

Verti, Sebastián. *Tradiciones mexicanas*. México, DF: Editorial Diana, 1993.

MONTERREY

It's 9:30 at night when Bryan and I enter El Rey de Cabrito, a famous Monterrey eatery, to meet a friend for dinner. We scan the restaurant, seeing no sign of Paco. Ordering two beers to kill our thirst and take the edge off our appetites, we drop into our chairs. The beer arrives, still capped. Our middle-aged waiter whips an opener out of his pocket and frees the lids, allowing the cold beverages to emit a frosty sigh. We don't need to see a date on the amber lagers, a Mexican brand called Bohemia, to vouch for their freshness. They were made right up the street at the second largest brewery in the country.

El Rey de Cabrito is a lively restaurant with enough bizarre adornment to take our minds off our hunger for a while. Three stuffed goats cavort together in one corner, while in the back of the room two fearsome lions rear up on hind legs, forever locked in mortal combat. A large window display near the kitchen exhibits the specialty of the house, roasted goat. About twenty of them stretch out on individual spits behind the glass. Every time I look up I get the unappetizing mental image of big housecats, skinned and cooked. My hunger is no longer urgent.

Red and blue neon lights trim one wall, counterfeited in mirrors throughout the restaurant. An elevator to the second floor is decorated on each side with a painting of a buck. The call button is incorporated into the artwork as a bulging glass deer eyeball. Large photos cover almost every inch of hanging space in the room. Most of them feature El Rey de Cabrito, The King of Roasted Kid, accompanied by a lineup of friends and celebrities.

One of the pictures comes to life and starts walking our way. No, it's not a photo. It's a sighting. Here comes The King.

He stops and chats with the patrons at each table, working the room like a Hollywood star. When he gets to our table we invite him to take a seat. Bryan is starving and sees this as a way of getting served something to eat pronto.

Before Bryan can get a chance to ask for The King's recommendation, El Rey de Cabrito launches into a soliloquy about Monterrey's terrain, its most famous dish, its people, and its history.

"The land around here isn't good for much, but it's great for raising goats. Monterrey is goat country and *cabrito* is the signature dish of our region. You can see that we roast our goats whole, on iron spits.

One of the keys to good *cabrito* is using mesquite coals. You get a great woody flavor in the meat. The secret, though, is in the marinade. Our recipe, with over twenty herbs and spices, just can't be imitated."

Bryan holds up his finger to interrupt, but The King zooms ahead.

"Did you know that Monterrey has almost one hundred restaurants that specialize in roasted goat kid? What a city! I love it. I've traveled all over the country, but for me, there's nowhere I'd rather call home. I just don't feel comfortable in the rest of Mexico. There's not another place like Monterrey."

The King may be a big talker, but he's right. Monterrey is unique. Much of its peculiarity can be traced to its history, distinct from that of the rest of the country. Instead of being conquered, Northern Mexico, where Monterrey is located, was colonized. That made all the difference. The King is well aware of his city's history.

"When the conquistadors arrived in this region there were no large Indian civilizations here—the land was just too harsh. That meant that the Spanish who settled here couldn't count on slave labor to make a go of it. They had to depend solely on themselves. This attracted a different type of settler, hard-working men willing to claw away at their surroundings. The people who came here had to be resourceful to survive. There was no room for the pleasantries and pomp of easy city living. As a result *regiomontanos*—that's what we call ourselves—as a result, we're the straight shooters of the country."

We hear this same story from almost every person we meet in Monterrey. The propaganda campaign must start in the first grade. Bryan, now weak with hunger, is starting to slump over in his chair. In his desperation he digs a jalapeño out of the *escabeche* sauce on our table and eats that. It momentarily allows him to focus back on The King.

"I don't know if you've noticed, but people from here don't just act different; they look different as well. Because the indigenous population was so small, there was not much intermarrying between it and the Spanish colonizers. Even today, after hundreds of years of being in Mexico, people from here are taller than they are in other parts of Mexico."

Throw in their boots, and they tower over the rest of the country. I've always felt at home in Monterrey because the spirit of the city reminds me of Texas, where I grew up. The people here are the equivalent to the cowboys and oilmen of my home state. Monterrey is in fact just a few hours from the Texas border, another factor that has shaped the city. Its citizens have long taken advantage of their proximity to the American marketplace. Many regions of Mexico have an attitude that can be characterized as hostile to new ideas or suggestions. Not the North. Monterrey has been able to take advantage of technologies from the nearby United States without feeling insecure about it. *Regiomontanos* believe that they are the vanguard of the country and that they represent modern Mexico.

The King, as we might guess, is also well versed on the economic might of this city of almost three million.

"Do you know that we have only 4 percent of the country's population but create 25 percent of the gross national product? That's amazing, isn't it? We're the third largest city in the country, but we produce more than the second, fourth, and fifth largest cities combined."

Monterrey's history as an economic powerhouse started during the U.S. Civil War. Because of its geographic proximity to the United States, the city could help supply the voracious needs of the Confederacy. The capital earned during that time of expansion was invested in industrialization and Monterrey has never looked back.

The King hasn't looked back since he started his harangue. Nor has he looked around to notice that Bryan has practically gone into a hypoglycemic coma. "When it gets down to it, the story of Monterrey's success is directly tied to two families—the Garza and Sada clans. Well, they *were* two families. Over time they have intermarried to become one. Anyway, they are the people who founded the first large business in Monterrey, the Cuauhtémoc Brewery. You could say that they put Monterrey on the map."

The Garza-Sadas are legendary not just in the region, but throughout the country. The powerful, tightly knit group started with beer manufacturing and parlayed that into steel, glass, chemical, finance, and real estate enterprises. The family's stamp on Monterrey is so strong that their values have become those of the city. Described as a no-nonsense, socially conservative group, they have made ambition, profit, and education the pillars of Monterrey's development.

My friend Paco arrives at our table apologizing for his tardiness. He recognizes and acknowledges The King, who moves on to the next table. It's now 10 PM and the restaurant is just kicking into high gear. Paco, in a suit and tie, has come straight from work. "Casual day" is still unheard of in Mexico, even in informal Monterrey. I haven't seen Paco in over five years, but his looks are unchanged. Stocky and fit, he has managed to keep the physique that propelled him to star as quarterback at the city's most prestigious university. To that he has added a veneer of business professionalism.

"Hey *gringuita*, how's it going?" Paco greets me with a kiss on the cheek. We have known each other since graduate school, where we worked closely on a time-consuming project for Televisa, the Spanish-language television station.

Contacting Paco this morning had been a bit of a trick. The number I had for him in my address book was answered by somebody else's answering machine. I looked in the phone book under Francisco del Monte, the name he used in grad school. It wasn't that easy, however, because of the Mexican use of both mothers' and fathers' last names. I found a Francisco del Monte Reyes, Francisco del Monte Sada, Francisco del Monte Prieto and even a Francisco del Monte del Monte. There were too many. I needed another approach.

I remembered that he worked at a cement company called CEMEX, one of the industrial giants created by the Monterrey Group. I called their headquarters and tracked him down.

Paco is a typical product of upper-class Monterrey. He grew up here and has strong ties with the city, but that hasn't kept him from continually looking outward. After his undergraduate studies at Monterrey Tech, the distinguished school founded by the Garza-Sada family, Paco went to the United States to study international management at Thunderbird School in Arizona. That was where we met. We both spent the summer after graduation traveling. He covered Europe by train and I camped in national parks throughout the western United States. The following fall found us both looking for jobs.

My goal was a job in Mexico. I thought Monterrey would be a good place to start my search, because it was smaller than Mexico City and relatively close to home. It was a place where I felt comfortable. I stayed with Paco and his family for a few weeks to feel out the job market. I didn't have much success.

Paco, interviewing at the same time, was having much better luck. Monterrey's business community is a tight, highly educated group that doesn't need to hire foreigners. With the city's emphasis on education, they have a huge pool of talented locals from which to fill open positions and return favors for friends and relatives. Without the right contacts, I was shut out.

Paco landed a job with CEMEX in human resources. CEMEX, a model Monterrey business, is the third largest cement manufacturer in the world. They have plants spread across multiple continents and Paco has traveled to most of them. He recently spent eight months in the Philippines and Singapore working out the personnel requirements for CEMEX acquisitions in those countries.

Paco orders a Carta Blanca, another beer made by the local brewery. "Well, *gringuita*, since the last time I saw you, I have gotten married and had three children. What do you think about that?"

As we quickly catch up, it strikes me how much our paths have diverged. Five years ago we were pretty much at the same point in our lives. Now, he is the sole breadwinner and father of a growing family. His parents died in an auto accident a few years ago, so he is also guardian to his youngest sister, who is still in college. As the oldest sibling, he is now ultimately responsible not only for her, but also for his brother and another sister as well. I, on the other hand, quit my international business job three years ago and have spent that time traveling and writing. We are at completely opposite ends of the responsibility scale. I feel guilty and grateful at the same time.

The subject turns to dinner. It's 10:30 and finally time to order. Bryan, using the last of his strength, asks Paco, the archetypal Monterrey local, which cut of roasted kid he recommends.

He looks at Bryan with a grimace of distaste. "I have no idea. I hate *cabrito*."

After dinner Bryan and I walk across the city's Grand Plaza to our hotel. The plaza, covering more than 100 acres, is the third largest in the world after Moscow's Red Square and Mexico City's Zócalo. Rather than being one large, open space, it's really a series of separate plazas that have been joined together. It's as if they took the classic Mexican square, cathedral on one side and the municipal building on the other, and stretched it out over six blocks.

It's a luxury for us to be able to move about safely in a city of this size. Both Guadalajara and Mexico City currently suffer from dangerous crime problems due to the economic crisis. Walking the streets at midnight in either of those cities would be unthinkable. Paco explained to us over dinner that the city's powerful business community did not sit idly by when a rash of car thefts broke out in Monterrey a few years ago. They hired their own security forces and investigators, hunted down the ring, and "encouraged" them to get the hell out of town. There's been very little trouble ever since.

The Cuauhtémoc Brewery's executive boardroom is a dark-paneled chamber with a ponderous hardwood table and tall, swiveling leather chairs. In a classic Mexican business move, Bryan and I have been kept waiting here for over fifteen minutes. It's a little show of power that accompanies almost every meeting. The more important the executive, the more that executive feels the need to demonstrate his or her importance by making you wait.

There is an annual report sitting near the telephone. Bryan picks it up and begins to read about FEMSA, the business group to which the brewery belongs. FEMSA, a huge concern with over 41,000 employees, has played a key role in the economic growth and transformation of the region. Vertically integrated to supply the brewery, FEMSA's holdings include companies that produce bottles, caps, cans, cardboard boxes, labels, and malt. The Cuauhtémoc Brewery, the cornerstone of the group, is the second largest beer manufacturer in Mexico. With all of their brands they have captured 45 percent of the total market.

A clock on the wall, adorned with the familiar red "XX" that comprises the Dos Equis beer label, ticks loudly as the minutes pass. Having worked in Mexico for a number of years, we're both used to the waiting treatment. It's frustrating nevertheless.

The door bursts open and in rushes Soledad Lorano, FEMSA's Director of Investor Relations. A dynamo in her late forties, Soledad has short, dark hair and ivory skin. Her stylish navy suit is adorned with an expensive silk scarf. Like Paco, she exudes professionalism.

We ask Soledad for some information on Mexican beer drinking habits. She lives and breathes Cuauhtémoc, so the facts roll easily off her tongue.

"Well, it will probably interest you to know that on a national level, Mexicans drink forty-nine liters of beer per person per year. As a point of reference, the Czech Republic has the highest per capita consumption in the world at 161 liters. The United States averages eighty-three liters.

"Considering the income differential between Mexico and the United States, Mexico's consumption level is pretty respectable. The Mexican picture gets really interesting though, when you look at it on a regional basis. Here in the north, where it's good and hot, we average eighty liters per person, almost equal to the U.S. level. We *regiomontanos* love our beer."

Soledad, who oversees the writing of many external company communications, sounds like one of her reports when she speaks. "This is an exciting time for our industry. Over the next nine years, we will see an influx of more than sixteen million people reaching legal drinking age. The trick, of course, will be to get them to tap into our beer. With a portfolio of ten distinct brands, it shouldn't be too hard to offer them something they like."

While we're talking, Soledad's Palm Pilot begins to beep. She opens it, reads her message, and snaps it shut.

"My employees call me 'Cyber-granny.' I may be older, but I try to stay up with the times. I started working here as a secretary twenty-one years ago. I had just separated from my husband and needed a job. I had only been in college for my M.R.S. degree, so I didn't have a lot of options.

"After being here a while I saw that I should be doing the kinds of jobs that the people with degrees had. I went back to school, got my degree, and have even studied in the United States. You could say that I've grown along with both the brewery and the city."

Soledad goes on to tell us about Monterrey's development over the last thirty years. She highlights how provincial the city used to be by making fun of the hour that they dined. "When I was a little girl, this was such a backwater city that we ate dinner at 7 PM. Can you imagine? Like farmers! Now I rarely have my evening meal before 9:30 or 10 PM."

We ask her about her favorite of the Cuauhtémoc brands.

"Well, guess I end up drinking Indio the most. It makes sense that it's my favorite, because I fit the target of higher-income people in their thirties, forties, and fifties. Indio is a lager with caramel and malt undertones. It's great on a hot day because it's the brand with the highest drinkability. You might not know it, but drinkability isn't a subjective term. It's actually something that is measured in the beer business."

It strikes Bryan and me that "indio," meaning "Indian," is a very non-PC word for a beer brand. Mexican indigenous people view "indio" in much the same way that Native Americans in the United States view "Indian"—a word charged with negative connotations. We ask Soledad about the name.

"Well, originally it was called Cuauhtémoc Beer, named, like the brewery, after the Aztec warrior. As you know, Cuauhtémoc is one of Mexico's national heroes, a martyr who resisted the Spanish invaders after Montezuma was killed. He refused to surrender to the conquistadors and held out for months on an island in the middle of Lake Texcoco. He was ultimately captured while attempting to take his family to safety. The Spanish applied boiling oil to his feet, trying to force him to confess where he had hidden Montezuma's treasure. Cuauhtémoc stoically endured the torture, not divulging a word, which led to his eventual execution. He is now a symbol for resistance to outside meddling.

"Anyway, the beer had, and still has, a picture of Cuauhtémoc on the label. When the beer was introduced about a hundred years ago, instead of requesting the beer by name, customers used to ask for *El indio*, referring to the picture. Rather than fight it, we changed the brand to Indio."

Bryan and I walk across the street from the corporate headquarters to the Cuauhtémoc plant. Established in 1890, it's the oldest commercial brewery in Mexico. Founded by a group that included both Mr. Garza and Mr. Sada, Cuauhtémoc borrowed German brewing techniques to create its famous lagers.

A display near the waiting area outlines the history of beer in Mexico. The country's indigenous people enjoyed a non-alcoholic beverage resembling beer before the Spanish arrived. Called *sendecho*, Spaniard Orozco y Berra described it as "similar to the *bier* of the old Germans, but made from corn instead of barley." The first real beer in the country was brewed in 1544 by conquistador Alfonso Herrera. Beer production in Mexico was small and scattered for the next three hundred years, but in the mid-1800s immigrants from Switzerland and Germany began to found local breweries. It's the heritage of those lagers that are now enjoyed by millions of Mexicans every day.

Travelers to Mexico have long been fans of Cuauhtémoc beers. W.E. Carson journeyed to Mexico at the turn of the twentieth century and found that "Some very fair light lager beer, brewed by German firms at Monterrey and Toluca, is a very popular drink."

Carta Blanca was the company's first brand, brewed in 1890. Three years later, the beer won first prize at the Chicago World's Fair. It still enjoys a strong following in this part of Mexico. We see the Carta Blanca logo plastered on buildings, signs, and billboards at every turn.

The Mexican beer market was for many years entirely regional. The effect of that legacy lingers today. We're surprised to learn that brands that are strong in certain areas of the country are not even available in others, even though they are made and distributed by the same company.

Felipe, our guide, works at the brewery as part of his business internship for Monterrey Tech. Young and earnest, his generation will soon fill the hundreds of cubicles in the FEMSA tower next door. He eagerly goes through his spiel.

"Beer making is essentially the same worldwide. You start with toasted barley, which not only gives the beer its flavor, but also its color. To make a pale beer, the barley is lightly dried, but to make a dark one, the barley is roasted until it becomes almost chocolate-colored.

"The barley is then crushed and infused with boiling water. This produces wort, a sugary liquid. Hops, another plant, is then added to give flavor and to improve the keeping quality of the beer."

Felipe shows us a jar of hops. The inch-long green buds look like mini-pinecones. He encourages us to pick up a handful and smell them. Not content with the olfactory experience, I take a bite of one. Its bitterness launches my face into a spastic grimace.

"After the hops are added, the wort is boiled some more. Then yeast is included. The yeast causes fermentation, which is the conversion of sugars into alcohol. After that, you've got beer."

The making area, a glassed room of gargantuan vats and mazes of tubes, is strictly off limits. We are content to tour the bottling plant, one of the most efficient in Latin America. It's amazingly modern. One or two people are all that's needed to handle entire manufacturing lines. Felipe informs us that six million bottles of beer are filled here a day.

Bohemia is the brand being filled on the line we watch. Felipe mentions that it's his favorite.

"Bohemia is our super-premium beer. It's the only one we make using hops imported from Europe. The name 'Bohemia' refers to a brewing region in Czechoslovakia, which is where the hops comes from. This beer is aged the longest and has the highest alcohol content of all our beers. You could say it's for the most sophisticated beer drinkers in the country."

A worker walks by wearing a sharp polo shirt and jeans. He's young, neat, and trim. Even the line staff look professional here. We ask him which of the Cuauhtémoc brands he prefers.

"Pues, la Sol."

Felipe has already told us about Sol, the newest beer in the company's portfolio. He called it "a light lager." Both Felipe and Soledad have been using the word "lager" all day and I realize that I'm not sure what it means. Felipe explains. "Lager is a term that literally means 'beer conditioned by maturing in very cold storage.' I understand that 'lager' is a term for 'refrigeration' in German. Lagers were first made in Munich and then taken to Pilsen. The Munich lagers are traditionally dark, and the Pilsener lagers light. Most of the beers in Mexico, made to be drunk at cold temperatures, are Pilsener lagers."

Sol is a direct competitor to Corona, made by the country's other brewery, Grupo Modelo. Modelo, the market leader with a 53 percent share, battles with Cuauhtémoc across Mexico. There are some exceptions to the regional nature of Mexican beer, and Corona, a national player, is one of them. Cuauhtémoc has responded to Corona's countrywide appeal by launching Sol, a Corona knockoff, on a national level. Like Corona, Sol comes in a clear bottle with a painted label.

After our tour of the plant we retire to the company beer garden, a pleasant patio shaded by tall trees. The garden is another Cuauhtémoc tradition that has long been popular with tourists, as noted in *All the Best in Mexico* in 1949.

> It is not quite decent to mention Monterrey without offering a tribute to its famous Cuauhtémoc Brewery, largest in Mexico, which is a site of the city. Public tours are made through it at almost hourly intervals and the tourist is rewarded at the end by a free beer in the garden.

I order the highly drinkable Indio, while Bryan samples a Dos Equis. Dos Equis, the brand that adorned the clock in the company boardroom, is popular with young drinkers both nationwide and internationally. The lager, in its distinctive green bottle, is one of our favorite beers to accompany tequila. The bartender tells Bryan about the beer's name as he pours.

"Do you know what the two Xs stand for? This beer was introduced in 1900, the first year of the twentieth century. The Xs are the Roman symbols for 'twenty.' It was the beer for the new century. Maybe we should add an 'I' to the label now that we're in the twenty-first century, huh?"

The next morning finds us back on the Cuauhtémoc grounds. It's a hot, sunny day—the kind that beer company executives love. The higher the temperature the more beer they sell. We're not here for the beer, though. This century-old brewery offers much more than just fermenting barley and hops. In addition to the brewery, the Cuauhtémoc grounds include two museums. We're here to visit the Monterrey Art Museum.

Located in the oldest section of the brewery, the museum is housed in a five-floor neoclassical red brick building. Stately ivy covers much of the exterior. Inside, modern masterpieces hang among antique copper vats. The museum, founded by the Garza-Sada family in 1977, owns an impressive permanent collection of twentieth-century Latin American art. Wandering through its displays, we enjoy works by famous Mexican artists Rivera, Kahlo, Siqueiros, Orozco, and Tamayo.

We eavesdrop on a knowledgeable docent as she finishes up with a group of high school students.

"This museum focuses on modern art, but art in Mexico developed in four distinct periods. The first period, the pre-Hispanic era, spans almost two thousand years. Different tribes and the passing of centuries make it hard to make sweeping statements about this era, but there are a few commonalities, such as the art's highly religious nature. It's not designed to replicate the real world, but rather represent perfection.

"After the arrival of the Spanish, Mexican art entered a new phase. For almost four centuries it was under strong European influence, mainly Spanish, Flemish, and Italian. Of course, Mexican art of this period isn't just a copy of what was happening in Europe, but rather a synthesis of different European styles filtered through indigenous craftsmen. Its basis however, was always European.

"The third period began after the Revolution in 1910. It was then that art in this country became truly Mexican. The artists of this era, very nationalistic, revolutionary people, adopted fresh ideals of Mexican values. They incorporated the vital force of indigenous works in their new art, while at the same time belittling what they considered obsolete European standards. The muralist tradition, revived from pre-Hispanic civilizations, was modernized and refreshed. Many of the most famous Mexican artists, like Rivera and Siqueiros, are from this period. You saw their works in our permanent collection.

"In the fourth period, since the 1950s, our country's development has exposed us to outside factors. Our art has not been immune to these influences. It remains very Mexican, but it's freer, more open, than it was after the Revolution. We don't have to reject everything from abroad, but rather fuse it into our own tradition. Many of our temporary exhibits focus on works from this stage."

Talking to the docent after her tour, we are surprised to discover that Monterrey has a vibrant modern art scene, built from scratch in the last thirty years.

"At the beginning of the 1970s, Monterrey didn't have a single art gallery or museum. Imagine how provincial we were. Today, our art market competes with places like Mexico City and Dallas. It used to be that an artist had to leave here to make it internationally, but now cutting edge artists come to Monterrey to launch their careers.

"One man started the whole thing. His name is Guillermo Sepúlveda. You should talk to him. He brought art to Monterrey."

We find Sepúlveda in his gallery, Arte Actual Mexicana. Situated in part of Monterrey's best zip code, the del Valle neighborhood, the gallery is located not in retail space, but rather in a house. A sculpture in the front yard is the only clue that we've arrived at the correct address. We enter the gallery and hear Sepúlveda before we see him. His voice, deep and sexy, slips sensually around the art-covered walls. "*Bienvenidos*, welcome, to Arte Actual."

Sepúlveda appears from around a corner. A large man, he fits the image of a mover and shaker in the arts scene. His expensive white pima cotton shirt, made to be worn untucked, covers tailored black pants. Square-toed designer shoes in soft ebony leather click against the floor as he approaches. In his early sixties, Sepúlveda reminds me of a handsome, stylish Liberace.

He invites us upstairs to his office, a large room with two buff leather couches in one corner. Bryan and I sit in one, and he faces us on the other. As we sink into the furniture, he tells us how he became the founder of the Monterrey art scene.

"I was working at a bank, if you can believe it. As a serious young man in those days, my only option was serious business. But I lived and breathed aesthetics. Ever since I was a young boy out at my grandparents' ranch, my senses have been saturated. I remember the smells of the villages, the sounds of the church bells, the taste of the country food. Anyway, one day at work I read about a bank in Europe that was acquiring its own art collection. I showed the article to my boss and suggested we do the same thing here, focusing on Mexican artists. He liked the idea, but this was 1968 and we couldn't get support at the bank. He motivated me to follow through with the idea anyway, encouraging me to start my own gallery."

As Sepúlveda talks, he reclines across the couch, leaning toward Bryan and me, gradually becoming almost horizontal. "Monterrey is filled with thoughtful, educated collectors now, but that wasn't the case back then. When I went to Mexico City to study some galleries and learn the business, people in the capital just laughed at me. They said, 'Why bother with Monterrey? All you have there are uncultured cowboys, goats, and tortillas.'

"I thought differently, though. I noticed a similarity between the development of Monterrey and Chicago, with Monterrey about thirty to forty years behind. First, both cities survived the harsh landscape, then created giant industries, then amassed fortunes. Chicago, ahead of us, then started to buy art and eventually became a thriving center for the humanities. That's the future I saw for Monterrey."

Sepúlveda is now actually horizontal on the couch, a sybarite entertaining devoted listeners. "When I first opened the gallery thirty years ago, I knew I had to concentrate on the industrialists. They would become the patrons for the arts in this city, the sponsors to build the museums and finance the shows. Luckily, the business and social community here is very small and tight—the Garza-Sada connection, you know. It was easy for me to focus on the most influential people in town. Once I sold them on the idea, everybody else just followed their lead."

Sepúlveda handles a number of Mexican artists whose works range in price from $400 to $400,000. "For the first five years I concentrated 100 percent on local artists. After that, I expanded to cover all of Mexico, but I still have a soft spot for *regiomontanos*. Some of my first artists have now become very collectable, very respected. The value of their works has skyrocketed. At the same time, I am always looking for new talent. Discovery is a giant thrill.

"I used to always hang out with people older than myself, artists like Tamayo, but they have all died. Now I find myself making friends with the younger generation. We have thirteen universities here, amazing resources for fresh new ideas. I have a board of about twenty people from the ages of twenty-two to thirty-five. Many of them have studied abroad and been exposed to excellent art. They have much higher standards than their parents, and are very demanding and dynamic. I keep pieces in inventory that they can afford; I even let them buy on installment plans."

Sepúlveda suddenly sits up on the couch, moves to his feet, and motions for us to come along. We follow him down the hall to an inventory room with hundreds of paintings stored on shelves along the walls. "Here. It's much easier to show you the diversity than to try to explain it. Ever since the '80s there hasn't been an overriding ideology, such as the abstract, guiding galleries. Now there is a plurality, many different voices, and each with merits. That makes it much harder for collectors, though, because it's difficult for them to judge works without defined parameters. I find that I spend most of my time and effort educating my clients. One generalization I can make, however, is that art is becoming more figurative again. Many of my artists, like all Mexicans, are preoccupied with discovering their identity, looking to the past versus the unsure future."

Sepúlveda instructs an assistant to pull out a number of paintings, most of them around four feet by six feet in size. The range of techniques and styles is astonishing. The most disturbing, yet oddly compelling, is a huge mortuary scene focused on a cadaver in mid-autopsy. The body is slit up the middle and the top of its skull hangs open. The painting is realistic, with bright colors and soft brushwork. "This work is by Martha Pacheco. She's a genius. She'll be as big as Frida one day. It takes a very sophisticated collector to handle her work, though. Look at these. Now she's working on a series of portraits of people in mental institutions. These are the living dead. Look how masterly she shows their lack of hope, their marginalization. It's hard art, but it's amazing."

From there he turns to a large canvas showing a stylized person spreading tubes of paint over the top of his head. The figure is inside an obviously Mexican shack with a skeleton in the corner and lush countryside showing out the windows. The technique is loose and fast, with rich strokes and thick, lush paint. "Felimón Santiago is a true inspiration. He's from a small village in the state of Oaxaca. When I met him, he didn't know how to speak Spanish, only Zapotec, the indigenous language there. He has had no formal training, but look at his compositions—incredible."

Bryan lingers over these works, attracted to their style and themes. We look through some of the smaller paintings, hoping one of them will call our name, but the artist's best pieces are the large, rich oils that won't fit into our car or our budget.

Sepúlveda shows us a number of other works, all of staggeringly high quality. We're standing in a treasure trove of Mexican modern art. We are about to leave the room when he stops and comes back in. "Oh, I forgot to show you my latest find. He's from Jalisco. I was in a second-rate gallery in Guadalajara and saw some of his stuff. This young guy is brilliant. I saw his work and was flabbergasted. I bought five of his paintings and begged to be introduced. Look at that technique. He paints incredible scenes and then etches shapes into them, making for flowing contours and bringing harmony into the composition."

He shows us a small painting of a boy floating on his back underwater. Fish and seaweed swirl around his body, a sensual scene with dreamlike qualities. Painted over a deep red layer, the etchings, carved into the paint, seep crimson. It's beautiful. Bryan and I hold it and admire it. We're thinking the same thing, but afraid to say it. Finally Bryan breaks the silence.

"We should get it if you like it. It's really incredible."

We half-heartedly debate the idea, trying to be practical, but we both know that we're going to end up giving Arte Actual a sale.

From our hotel room, we can look across the Grand Plaza to the Monterrey Contemporary Art Museum, known as MARCO. Built in 1990, the striking building was designed by Mexico's most famous architect, Ricardo Legorreta. While its exhibits are noteworthy—large modern pieces and fascinating mixed media displays—the building itself is a masterpiece.

The woman at the MARCO information desk hands us a folder that outlines the history of Mexican architecture. Not surprisingly, the stages closely parallel those of Mexican painting. Before the Spanish arrived, indigenous people constructed great cities and monuments, many of which were concerned with the religious themes of death and the afterlife.

This was followed by four hundred years of European influence, mainly Italian and Spanish. Colonial architecture reached its zenith with the elaborate baroque-derived style known as Mexican Churrigueresque.

This era was followed by a period after the Revolution when the state constructed large utilitarian buildings. Their main purpose seemed to be to provide the walls and spaces for populist murals and sculptures.

It was in the 1950s that Mexican architecture really came into its own. By synthesizing the forms and hues of everyday Mexican culture with fresh approaches from abroad, Mexican architects created a new, dramatic style. Surprising elements such as reflecting pools, hidden gardens, freestanding walls, and unexpected colors created a uniquely Mexican school of construction and design.

Before we embarked on this Mexican adventure we spent quite a bit of time in Austin collecting background information. One of the books we found on Legorreta contained a foreword written by Hal Box, former dean of the University of Texas School of Architecture. Box wrote that Ricardo Legorreta offers a timeless yet modern architecture appropriate to a wide range of building types, and that Legoretta is able to achieve this from a point of view that is deeply rooted in the two millennia of Mexico's complex culture. In other words, Legorreta is an architect whose works have universal appeal while at the same time being rooted in Mexican settings. While his buildings satisfy the real world demands of function and budget, they are filled with mystery, surprise, humor, drama, and sensual richness.

We sought Box out in Austin to talk about Legorreta's designs. Speaking specifically about the MARCO building, Box raved. "Legorreta's use of color in that structure is just brilliant. It makes the paintings on the walls come alllliiiivvve."

His deep voice and thick Texas drawl appropriately animated the word *alive*.

"Most architects are afraid to use color in museums; they try to stay neutral so they don't overshadow the art. Legorreta is not at all timid. His clean, bold lines and vibrant colors are fantastic.

"There's a funny story about Legorreta and color. During the construction of the Hotel Camino Real in Ixtapa he saw a worker wearing blue pants. He loved the way the man's pants suited both his skin tones as well as his jungle-like surroundings. Legorreta decided that he must use that exact color somewhere in the hotel. It is now covering the walls of the presidential suite."

The workers who built MARCO must have been wearing a lot of bright clothing.

Monterrey's Bishop's Palace, known as the Obispado, was built in 1787, when Mexico's architectural styles were still heavily under European influence. A yellow church edifice erected high on a hill, the Obispado is one of Monterrey's best scenic landmarks. From here the purple desert walls of the Sierra Madre Oriental surround the city in bruised, toothy layers. Covering the valley floor below us are the tools of Monterrey's industrial might—tidy smokestacks, factories, and grain elevators that extend to the very edges of the mountains' sheer cliffs.

The Palace's thick adobe walls enclose a sunny central courtyard. Inside its rooms, a small regional history museum highlights the Mexican-American War. Although the people of Monterrey are more open to the United States than the rest of the country, neither they nor their fellow Mexicans can forget this conflict, having lost half their territory to the aggressive young nation to the north.

Swept under the rug by the U.S. school system, the invasion is branded into every Mexican's mind starting at an early age. It's as integral a part of Mexican history as George Washington and the Boston Tea Party are of U.S. history.

The conflict started with American annexation of Texas in 1845. Texas had won independence from Mexico eight years earlier, but had not been invited to join the United States until James Polk became president. Polk, basing his decision on the dictates of Manifest Destiny as well as bowing to political pressures to gain another slave state, issued an invitation for Texas to become part of the Union. This caused

Mexico, which had never recognized Texas's independence, to break off diplomatic relations with the United States.

The widely perceived right of the United States to extend its boundaries inspired Polk to send General Zachary Taylor to a contested section of Texas territory. Polk's desire was to bait Mexico into battle so that the United States could declare war on its neighbor to the south, allowing the United States to take possession of Mexican lands. Taylor's provocation had its intended effect. Shots were exchanged and the United States declared war on Mexico.

The American general marched across the desert to take Monterrey in a bloody battle. Taylor then used the Obispado as his headquarters during the American occupation of the city. While Taylor and his troops controlled Monterrey, other American generals conquered both New Mexico and California. It was from this strong position that Polk demanded that Mexico sell the occupied lands to the United States. Mexico refused. The bellicose American president then sent troops to Veracruz, on the Gulf of Mexico. From this coastal city, the U.S. infantry marched over the same path that Cortés followed to take Tenochtitlán.

With U.S. troops in their capital, Mexico was forced to sell territory to the United States, giving the latter possession of present-day California, New Mexico, Arizona, Utah, Nevada, Wyoming, and part of Colorado, as well as Texas. Ulysses S. Grant, a young lieutenant during the war with Mexico, reflected on the conflict at the end of his life: "I regard it [the United States-Mexico War] as one of the most unjust ever waged by a stronger against a weaker nation."

The staggering defeat scarred the Mexican psyche and led to lingering fear of further U.S. aggression. This distrust continues to mar U.S.-Mexico relations, although the expansion most feared by Mexicans today is economic and cultural rather than territorial.

We slink out of the museum down to El Tío's, a popular restaurant for traditional food of the north. Crowded with lunching *regiomontanos*, the restaurant offers all of our favorite dishes. We assuage our guilt with guacamole, spicy *chorizo* sausage, and *queso fundido*: thick, oozing melted cheese. Looking around the restaurant we notice that almost everybody is drinking beer and all of them are Cuauhtémoc brands. Not a Corona to be found—an amazing occurrence in Mexico. Monterrey supports its own.

The Cuauhtémoc Brewery grounds also accommodate the Mexican Baseball Hall of Fame. Opened in 1973, the Salón de la Fama del Beisbol Mexicano was the first museum in Monterrey. A statue of famous pitcher Fernando Valenzuela, with his traditional eyes-to-the-sky wind-up, greets visitors at the entrance.

The museum displays 150 years of Mexican baseball history from old gloves, uniforms, and game balls to biographical outlines of the country's most famous players. There is also a huge photo of Monterrey's peewee team, which won the Little League World Series three years ago.

We learn that baseball was first played in Mexico in 1847. American workers called to Mexico to build roads, telegraphs, and rail under the Porfirio Díaz dictatorship brought their favorite pastime with them. The game was spread from city to city as the rail lines advanced.

The Cuauhtémoc Brewery has been tied to baseball since 1939, when it sponsored its first Carta Blanca team in Monterrey. It's because of this relationship, still strong, that the Hall of Fame exists.

A room honoring the Hall's inductees is decorated with bronze plaques that feature relief sculptures of each member. We are surprised to see Americans Roy Campanella, Satchel Paige, and Josh Gibson among the inductees. Campanella, the second African American inducted into the U.S. Baseball Hall of Fame, was one of baseball's most popular players ever. How did he wind up catching in Mexico?

A display explains that the first Liga Mexicana was an outlaw circuit organized by Jorge Pascual in the mid-1930s. Pascual filled his teams with American Negro League stars, giving them a professional stage before they could break through the color barrier at home. Campanella played for the local Monterrey Sultans in 1942-43 before going on to star in the U.S. major leagues for the Brooklyn Dodgers. He was the Mexican League Most Valuable Player years before he won three National League MVP titles in the United States.

Today the Mexican League still offers a forum for a few players from the United States. Each club in the league is allowed five players from outside of Mexico. Many times these players are the stars of the team.

We talk about life as an "imported player" with Tony Barron, first baseman for the Monterrey Sultans, before their game against the Yucatán Lions. Tony's descriptions of his fifteen-year professional career sound like a geography lesson—Vero Beach, San Antonio,

Tacoma, Philadelphia, Montreal, Puerto Rico, the Dominican Republic, Venezuela. Only one time in this period did he spend two years in a row with the same team.

"Yeah, I've moved around quite a bit. But you know what? For me, the city where I live isn't my home, but rather the ballpark, and the ballpark is more or less the same everywhere you go. I love this game and I just need to be out there on the field. I live in hotels, but my real house is the stadium."

Barron, tall and muscular, is a handsome man with electric almond-shaped green eyes. A real life Crash Davis (the minor-league baseball player who was the main character of the movie *Bull Durham*), he loves his job and makes a good living. "Most of the imported players here are veterans like me. We've paid our dues in the minors, made it to the bigs a time or two, and are tired of fighting to get the numbers and then being overlooked. Here they treat us like stars, pay us well, and are just more relaxed about everything. It's a great gig."

I look up Barron's statistics the next day. During his years playing in the United States, he got called up to two major league teams, the Expos and the Phillies. While in the majors he hit a respectable .284, had 4 home runs and 24 RBIs, and made only 2 fielding errors—stats of which he can be proud.

"The only drawback is being away from my family. That gets hard. They come and see me when they can, but we end up spending a lot of time apart. My wife and nine-year-old daughter are here in Monterrey now. It's been great having them around. My son, he's fifteen, he's up in the United States staying with his grandmother—he said he'd rather play golf this summer. I miss him."

We ask him how much longer he envisions himself playing. "You know, I love this game so much I've always said that I'll play as long as somebody will pay me. There are guys in this league that are in their 40s, one guy who's 47. I'd hope that I have at least five more years in me. Then my dream would be to scout for a U.S. major league team, maybe covering the Pacific Northwest where my family lives. That would be great. I can't imagine just walking away from the game, though. It's too much a part of me."

Tony suddenly realizes the time. "Oh, man, I've got to get down to the field. It's been nice meeting you. Hope you all enjoy the game—and a few cold beers."

We assure him that we will.

When we walk out of the clubhouse offices, the game is about to start. The Sultans' ballpark, the best in the league, could pass for a major league stadium back home. With a real grass field, a fancy multimedia scoreboard, and multiple levels, the stadium transports us immediately to the United States. Well, not quite. While reminiscent of any ballpark in the United States, there are unmistakable Mexican touches. A live salsa band belts out tunes at the entrance, Carta Blanca beer is the biggest advertiser, and vendors hawk such Mexican snacks as pork rinds with hot sauce and onion rings with jalapeños.

We find our seats right behind home plate and wave to the beer vendor. He keeps his bottles of Carta Blanca buried in ice. After securing our tingling cold beer, we start in on the snacks. I go for potato chips with *picante* sauce while Bryan opts for a hotdog with *salsa mexicana*. The mayor throws out the first pitch and the game is underway.

Tony comes up to bat in the first inning with two outs and a man on second. Hired for his offense, he immediately produces with a hit to the gap that bounces over the fence and is ruled a double. Sultans 1, Lions 0. That sets the tone for the game. With some great defensive plays and strong offense, the Sultans' lead is extended inning by inning. Tony gets another RBI in the sixth.

It's a beautiful night and we watch the sunset reflect off the mountains ringing the stadium. Tony had complained to us earlier that the games here take forever, but this one flies by. During the seventh inning stretch, *Take Me Out to the Ballgame* booms over the loudspeakers, but Bryan and I seem to be the only ones singing. The Mexican ritual is to stand and wave one's arms during this traditional ballpark break.

The game ends with the Sultans' 6-1 victory. We loved the entire experience, a bicultural version of the U.S. classic. One could argue that the Monterrey adaptation, borrowed from the north and tweaked to fit into the *regiomontano* vision of the world, was in its own way better than the original—and a *regiomontano* would certainly agree.

Resources

Álvarez, José Rogelio, ed. *Enciclopedia de México*. México, DF: Compañía Editora de Enciclopedias de México, 1987.

Attoe, Wayne, ed. *The Architecture of Ricardo Legoretta*. Austin: University of Texas Press, 1990.

Carson, W. E. *Mexico*. New York: MacMillan Co., 1909.

CBS Sportsline online. Baseball Library.com, Mexican League. http://www.baseballlibrary.com.

Clark, Sydney. *All the Best in Mexico*. New York: Dodd, Mead & Co., 1949.

De Mente, Boyé Lafayette. *NTC's Dictionary of Mexican Cultural Code Words*. Lincolnwood, IL: NTC Publishing Group, 1996.

FEMSA Annual Report, 1998. Monterrey: FEMSA, 1999.

García Naranjo, Nemesio. *Industria en marcha*. Monterrey: Gobierno de Nuevo León, 1955.

Malkin, Elizabeth, and Richard Melcher. "Can Corona Beer Hang onto its Crown?" *Business Week*, June 17, 1995, 90B.

Metropolitan Museum of Art. *Mexico: Splendors of Thirty Centuries*. New York: Bullfinch Press, 1990.

Museum of Modern Art. *Twenty Centuries of Mexican Art*. New York: Trustees of MOMA, 1972.

Nelson, George, ed. *An Encyclopedic Dictionary of Mexico*. Cuernavaca: Centro para Retirados, 1975.

Reid, Michael. "Making It in Monterrey." *Economist* 345 (8046), December 6, 1997, S19-S25.

Riding, Alan. *Distant Neighbors*. New York: Vintage Books, 1989.

Sullivan, Edward J. *Latin American Art in the Twentieth Century*. London: Phaidon Press Limited, 1996.

Warner, Michael, ed. *Encyclopedia of Mexico, History, Society, Culture*. Chicago: Fitzroy Dearborn, 1997.

VERACRUZ

> In a country almost obsessed with introspection, Veracruz and the Gulf Coast are Mexico's windows to the world through which a great variety of influences have passed. Cortés himself founded Veracruz when he arrived there from Cuba in 1519. Later migrants settled in the area, giving the city a cosmopolitan and multiracial air that it retains to this day. The influence of Cuba, where ships would call en route from Spain to Mexico, is particularly felt. The vegetation, climate and even geographical shape of Cuba as well as the island's Afro-Iberian racial mixture are all repeated in Veracruz state. Cuba is also present in the way the locals speak Spanish, in the dark coffee and strong cigars, in the music and food and in the tradition of holding a noisy pre-Lenten carnival.
>
> —ALAN RIDING, *DISTANT NEIGHBORS* (281–2)

Becky and I reach the coastal city of Veracruz after a six-hour drive east from Mexico City. We timed our arrival to hit the last days of its pre-Lenten carnival celebration, which the city promotes as among the best in the world. This claim presents Veracruz as a debauched peer of bead-slinging New Orleans and samba-strutting Rio de Janeiro. As we head deeper into town we encounter scores of promotional banners with this year's carnival logo, a masked mermaid perched on a quarter moon.

Though we booked late, we lucked out in reserving a room in the Emporio Hotel overlooking the waterfront Malecón. The receptionist suggests we go for coffee next door at the century-old Parroquia Café while they finish preparing our room.

The walls of the Parroquia Café open with sliding doors so that the tables flow from the interior onto the sidewalk uninterrupted. The waiters wear white *guayaberas*. The loose cotton shirt, usually dandied up with a few pleats down the front, whispers "slow down and relax" like no other garment. *Guayaberas* are popular in muggy climates like that of Veracruz because the shirts billow outward, rarely clinging to a sweaty body.

The sticky climate and unhurried tempo is the antithesis of Monterrey, where we have just spent some time. It seems like a different country.

None of the *guayabera*-attired waiters pays attention to us. Each carries a tray with two silver pots on it. A patron next to us slurps down the last of his coffee from a tall, thick glass, then clangs a solicitous melody on it with his spoon. Almost immediately a waiter is at his side pouring a black stream from one pot, then a high column of steaming milk from the other. Becky and I clang our glasses simultaneously and waiters appear over each of our shoulders, gracing our glasses with the steaming mud.

As we sip our coffee, we listen to the mellow beats of marimba played on a wooden xylophone. Two musicians strike the lustrous cedar keys in harmony. A gray-haired man playing the high notes at the narrow end of the triangular instrument wields a pair of softheaded mallets in each hand. His sidekick bonks out the low notes with a pair of mallets in one hand and a single mallet in the other. Next to them, a percussionist scrapes a long teardrop gourd. Several of the numbers are familiar as mariachi songs, but played in these hollow, soothing tones, the music assumes a tropical guise. The elder marimba musician offers to play a request for us, so we ask him what one might consider a traditional song from Veracruz. We are surprised when he informs us that it is *La Bamba*, the folkloric tune that Ritchie Valens made internationally famous in the 1950s, then Los Lobos again in the 1980s.

"*La Bamba* is from Veracruz?" Becky asks incredulously.

The musician adjusts his glasses on his nose so he can get a better fix on the doubters. He sighs and then patiently begins, "La Bamba is a meaningful story of Veracruz." I interrupt him by sliding back one of the wooden chairs, inviting him to join us. Becky's authoritative *clink!* conjures waiters who pour alternate streams of black and white into our new friend's glass, which froths up into a velvety brown mix.

Vicente introduces himself by name, and then raises his glass in the air. "This *café con leche* is mulatto, the perfect drink for this mulatto town! *¡Mira, mira nada más!* It's the same color as I am, a mixture of black and white. *¡Mírame nada más!*"

He slurps in equal parts air and liquid to cool the drink. "You are skeptical of *La Bamba's* origin, but I swear to you it started here. It was during the time that the pirates attacked this city and looted it.

"On a hacienda near here lived the widow Doña Beatriz. She was middle-aged, not at all unattractive, mind you—in fact dignified, pretty, as many Spanish women remain, and underneath very sensuous. Doña Beatriz was a widow. That means her husband was dead—not her!" He chortles. "She had a lover named Malanga, a strong man, the type that is forged out of steel, as big as those freighters out in that bay, the type that men follow, the leader of the workers, the type that many women want, that many women fear that they will want. Malanga was a mulatto, you see."

Vicente sips his coffee, letting us ponder that for a moment, and then waves to his fellow musicians to take a break. "One perimeter of the hacienda was shoreline. The hacienda buildings were practically the only signs of civilization visible from the ocean except for this city. One day Malanga saw ships approaching that belonged to the pirate Lorencillo. He immediately ran to the big house to warn Doña Beatriz. He distributed weapons to the farm hands and advised her to take the women by wagon away from the coast where they would be safe. 'But what about you?' she argued, 'You are not marines.' Gallantly, Malanga replied, 'We are not marines, but to defend you, we will be.'

"The men positioned themselves on the beach with their old muskets and even brought down the little cannon that was used during the saints' days celebrations. They said a prayer and waited for their suicidal clash with the pirates. Rather than seek refuge, Doña Beatriz led the women to the beach, bringing additional ammunition. They were prepared to help the men, to die with them if necessary.

"As the ships drew nearer, all watched, shaking with fear, but facing death with courage. The ships tacked, changed directions, and simply sailed on to Veracruz without stopping at the hacienda.

"They celebrated the episode as though they had defeated Lornecillo's forces. A barrel of rum was uncorked and the musicians among them played. The man who sang was renowned for improvising lyrics. Of course he was asked to make up a verse about the day's valor. Everyone cheered and laughed heartily when he sang . . ." At this point, Vicente croons:

Yo no soy marinero.
Yo no soy marinero.
Por ti seré, por ti seré.

Vicente laughs the booming laugh of Malanga and calls his men over to play *La Bamba*. When the playful rendition ends, we shake hands with Vicente and cross the street to the waterfront.

Vendors shout from stalls that display coastal bric-a-brac and snacks. Among the ubiquitous shell creations are Jesus crucified on a conch shell and a Barbie doll mermaid with a fish tail constructed of hundreds of tiny shells. Others sell heavily sugared fruit sweets called *ates*, thick jams squared into finger food. A mango vendor skewers the luscious fruit with a stick, peels back its golden skin, then carves the pulpy flesh into petals so it resembles an exotic flower.

Where the line of stalls ends, the Malecón opens to a pier-embraced bay. Across the harbor the mighty port machines lever their steel-caged necks like giant seabirds ready to peck cargo from the docked freighters. Oil tankers, container ships, barges, and fishing boats swallow and belch goods via pipelines, inter-modal boxes, grain chutes, and seafood conveyors.

On the red-and gray-tiled boardwalk a crowd gathers around a group of young sun-baked men in damp shorts. Black hair plastered to their heads drips down to narrow torsos strung with taut cords of muscle. Each of the men has one cheek bulging with what I suspect is chewing tobacco or some similar substitute. They huddle around a patron and shout numbers at him, "*Cinco*!" "*Diez*!" The man tosses a ten-peso coin into the murky port water. Three of the eight boys leap from the edge into the bay five feet below. One of them surfaces holding the coin above his head. A few more coins are tossed and the boys perform the same recovery feat, done without the aid of a mask. Their eyes burn red from peering through the murky water. The crowd disbands, none wanting to assume the role of benefactor after the current one leaves.

Becky and I debate what exactly the swimmers have in their chipmunk cheeks. Tobacco? Bubble gum? Some kind of root? We approach the divers to ask them.

One inquires first, "You want to buy some *mota*?"

I respectfully decline the offer of marijuana, and then ask the oldest of them, "What are you chewing? Tobacco?"

He scoffs at me. "We do not chew tobacco. We are not chewing anything."

"Then what's in your mouth?"

The young man looks at me puzzled, and then inserts a thumb and finger into his mouth to extract a stack of fifteen coins from one of his cheeks.

From the balcony of our hotel room we see a colorful line of parade floats idle until their evening departure. On the bay side, the Venustiano Carranza lighthouse rises from a neoclassical government building. Two painters deepen their silhouettes as they whitewash the tower from an old-fashioned scaffold, which is nothing more than a long, narrow plank held aloft by two sets of ropes. Beyond the lighthouse is a pale office tower, a dozen stories tall, constructed to look like a high-rise oil platform. The national petroleum company, Pemex, occupies it. These two edifices are gawky aberrations in a skyline made up of compact colonial buildings.

To one side of the towers, at the end of the boardwalk, we can see a gargantuan inflatable Coke can near a stage with a banner that proclaims, "Rockola Coca-Cola." Our carnival program informs us that this is to be the stage for a concert after this evening's parade. Even now, seven hours beforehand, a line is forming in front of the cyclone fence that delineates the event area.

It is not surprising that Coca-Cola is a sponsor, considering how much Coke this country drinks. Mexico ranks first in the world in per capita consumption and second only to the United States in total consumption.

Along with Canada, Mexico was Coca-Cola's first export market back in 1898, just twelve years after an Atlanta pharmacist, John Pemberton, invented the drink. Pemberton concocted the caramel-colored syrup in his lab, with active ingredients in the controversial X-7 formula including cocaine from the coca leaf and the caffeine-rich extract of the kola nut. (The cocaine was removed from the formula in 1905 and the kola extract is now synthetic.) Like most of his creations, Pemberton touted his drink as a tonic for most common ailments, first distributing it by jug from his home to a local pharmacy. Pemberton sold the business after successfully commercializing the syrup in drugstore soda fountains. The newly incorporated Coca-Cola Company rapidly expanded sales to every state in the union and began looking outward to new markets like Mexico.

When I first moved to Mexico, it was impossible not to notice how much Coke the Mexicans drank. It was particularly apparent to me because I worked in the food and beverage industry. I wanted to learn what Mexicans ate and drank, so I spent a lot of time in grocery stores studying the shelves and noting who bought what. For example, the typical lunch of an *obrero*, a manual laborer, is often purchased in a supermarket at the mid-day break. One guy will be sent by a small group, say five construction workers, to the supermarket, where he buys a stack of tortillas, a few cans of tuna fish, a can of jalapeño chiles, and a two-liter bottle of Coke. The crew can eat this meal at minimal cost. As for evening consumption habits, at parties I observed with awe the prodigious flow of Coke mixed with rum to make Cuba Libre cocktails.

Though not the national drink, perhaps the most popular cocktail in Mexico is the Cuba Libre. Look around a crowded bar and you will see gallons of Cuba Libres being sucked down. Throw a party in Mexico City, and you'd better have a lot of Coke as mixer, because what Mexicans bring to contribute is rum. Nine out of ten guests will bring rum, almost exclusively Bacardi.

Charles H. Baker, in his *The Gentleman's Companion, An Exotic Drinking Book,* published in 1946, suggests how you should go about mixing a Cuba Libre:

The Cuba Libre—or "Free Cuba"—Analyzed and Improved

This native island concoction started by accident and has caught on everywhere. Last summer, for instance, we ran into 'Kooba Lee-brays' 5000 feet up in the North Carolina Mountains at High Hampton, the year before in Mexico City and Seattle. The only trouble with the drink is that it started by accident and without imagination, has been carried along by the ease of supply. Under any condition it is too sweet.

What's to do? After clinical experimenting for which our insurance carriers heartily dislike us, we tested several variations of the original, with the result: the improved Cuba Libre consists of 1 big jigger of Carta de Oro Bacardi, the juice of 1 small green lime, and the lime peel after squeezing. Put in a Tom Collins glass, muddle well to get oil worked up over side of the glass, add lots of ice lumps, fill up with a bottle of chilled Coca-Cola. Stir up once, and salud y pesetas! (27)

Though Baker states that the drink started by accident, a good argument can be made that it was fate that brought Bacardi and Coke together, at least at the historical juncture that gave the drink its name. To piece together the chronology, I grab a seat at an internet café and pay the eternity rate as the ancient phone lines labor to download

Bacardi's vivacious Web pages, which gives me time to piece together its history with my notes on rum and Cuba.

Christopher Columbus introduced sugarcane to the New World in 1493 on his second voyage. Sugarcane became a cash crop of the Caribbean islands as plantations sprang up to supply the Americas with sugar and molasses. Molasses is a syrupy derivative of cane juice that has been cooked and then crystallized in a centrifuge into dark brown syrup. To make rum, molasses is fermented into a simple alcohol, which is then distilled to concentrate it into hard liquor. Stanley Arthur, author of *Famous New Orleans Drinks and How to Mix 'Em*, conjectures that the word "rum" is derived from *rumbullion*, a West Indies term meaning "tumult" or "uproar." Rum became the drink of the high seas, prized by pirates and British naval officers alike. The custom of compensating British sailors with rum rations didn't end until 1970. Caribbean islands such as those of Barbados, Jamaica, and Puerto Rico continue to dominate the production of rum today.

My mood becomes buoyant when the Bacardi home page finally downloads, because Celia Cruz and Tito Puente tunes blast out of the computer speakers. Everyone in the café unconsciously taps their fingers and moves their bodies to the lively salsa tunes.

A fifteen-year-old Spaniard named Facundo Bacardi emigrated with his brothers to Cuba in 1829. Three decades later, in Santiago de Cuba, the town where Hernán Cortés governed as mayor before founding Veracruz, Facundo established Bacardi y Compañía as a maker of rums. He experimented with all aspects of the production process, introducing light rums as well as carefully aged sipping rums. Bacardi's attention to quality and product differentiation would make Bacardi the largest rum distiller in the world and one of the strongest companies in the food and beverage industry.

Attaining the status of industry leader would not come easily. Bacardi, like other companies, would have to confront Cuba's political turmoil. The consequences of the Spanish-American War and of Cuba's fight for freedom now come into play.

In 1895 Cubans finally began taking measures to gain independence from Spain, their colonial master of four centuries. Sensationalist newspapers stirred American sympathy for the Cubans by reporting on brutalities committed by the Spaniards in their attempt to halt the rebellion. The USS *Maine*, sent to Havana Harbor to protect U.S. citizens and property, was mysteriously sunk. This provoked formal support of Cuban independence by the U.S. Congress, and, in turn, a declaration of war by Spain on the United States. "Remember the Maine!" and "Free Cuba!" became the rallying cries of the U.S. public.

The U.S. military fought Spain on two main fronts, in Cuba and across the world in the Philippines. It would only require three months for the U.S. military, which included Theodore Roosevelt's Rough Riders, to defeat Spanish forces in Cuba. As a result of the war, Spain would cede control of Cuba, Guam, Puerto Rico, and the Philippines to the United States.

Now I mix one part Bacardi lore with two parts Cuban history, and a twist of intervention to concoct the legendary conclusion.

It was during the U.S. occupation of Cuba that a U.S. soldier, provisioned with supplies from home, allegedly mixed Bacardi and Coca-Cola together, christening it a Cuba Libre in honor of the battle cry "Free Cuba!"

The name Cuba Libre stuck and the drink grew in popularity. It became a fashionable drink, along with fruity daiquiris, in Havana's casinos, especially during the years of U.S. prohibition. And in 1944 the Andrews Sisters had a hit with the song "Rum and Coca-Cola."

There are subsequent chapters to Cuba's quest for freedom. The U.S.-supported puppet governments following independence made no attempt at social progress, condemning most Cubans to poverty. Fidel Castro, who planned his coup during exile in Mexico, won popular support when he led a mere force of one thousand into the capital in 1959. Castro's government increased the accessibility of health care and education to people in poverty, giving Cuba the highest rates of literacy and access to medical care in the region. Unfortunately, the strides were accomplished by a totalitarian regime that nationalized U.S. property and Cuban businesses to achieve its objectives.

Among the factories and holdings that Castro seized were those of the Bacardi Company. A century after the company's creation, the descendents of Facundo Bacardi fled their homeland to set up operations in Puerto Rico. The company still holds a claim against the Castro government for its assets.

Free Cuba remains an ambition unfulfilled.

In the evening Becky and I walk to the parade route in anticipation of witnessing the wild festivities such as those that wreak havoc in New Orleans and Rio. Certainly, alcohol will flow with abandon, women and she-men will flaunt breasts and behinds in skimpy attire, perhaps beads will be thrown, and who knows what sort of uniquely Mexican twists will contort the event?

We pick our way through the crowd to find vacant spots in the crude wooden spectator stands. Once seated, we quickly realize that the Veracruz carnival is a family affair. Nearly all of the onlookers pack together in family groups of four or more, and in many cases extend from newborns to grandparents. The crowd, composed of folks from surrounding provinces, is orderly and nearly alcohol free. The first participant in the procession to pass is the Suzy Veracruz Baton Twirlers. The next is a convertible transporting a young brunette crowned and sashed with glittering "Queen of Carnival" accessories. The event feels like a small-town parade.

The parade is calm in terms of antics, but acoustics are another matter. Each float supports a massive wall of speakers that make our hearts leap against our shirts in rhythm with the exploding bass. Beverage companies promoting their brands—Sol, Superior, Modelo, Corona, Dos Equis, and Presidente Brandy, sponsor many of the most extravagant floats.

Extravagance is a relative term, however. All of the floats employ a simple three-piece design. First comes the tractor, a green John Deere or red Ford, driven by the owner. The tractor pulls a flatbed trailer mounted with thematic scenery and dancers. The Dos Equis float, for example, features a huge papier-mâché spaceship around which young women in sultry, futuristic jumpsuits dance salsa. The caboose is a smaller trailer dedicated solely to the sound system. It lugs a generator and five-foot tall speakers stacked two high and three wide. The effect of one such system alone would be deafening, to say nothing of dozens of them cutting loose simultaneously.

The other big-spending sponsors include several soft drink companies like Coca-Cola, Pepsi, Peñafiel, as well as a handful of random corporations such as Sherman Williams paint. There are a few more spaceships, some nautical themed entrants, an Egyptian float, and a Hawaiian affair with hula girls in grass skirts. In the low-budget category, one participant drives a beat-up milk truck inexplicably garlanded in gold lamé.

Samba groups, accompanied by local marching bands, sway by in florid attire. Inevitably, a few dancers from each group arrive late. Those scurrying individuals, in the same wild getup that flocked by earlier, zigzag through the floats and other marchers in order to catch the group. A dozen Brazilian performers were imported, perhaps to legitimize the event. Sparkling in sequined leotards and glitter-encrusted skin, they glide past while gyrating their hips in a bewitchingly distinctive manner, a trait that surely someday will be isolated as an attribute unique to Brazilian DNA.

Our carnival program states that the holiday is thought to have originated as a pagan celebration in ancient Rome that was later adopted as a Christian holiday. The word "carnival" comes from Latin, *carnem levare*, which means "to take away or remove meat." This coincides with the fact that carnival is the final festivity before the commencement of the austere forty days of Lent, during which Roman Catholics abstain from eating meat. The New Orleans moniker of Mardi Gras, French for Fat Tuesday, refers to the custom of using all the fats in the home before Lent.

The carnival of Veracruz began in 1866 during the reign of Emperor Maximiliano, who was enthroned in Mexico by Napoleon III. The mayor of Veracruz at that time was a Frenchman. He enacted the holiday by throwing masquerade parties in the old customs house and theater. Even after the French were expelled, the tradition continued and even grew in popularity.

We head for our hotel as the tail of the parade thunders past. An entrance line for the Rockola Coca-Cola concert wraps around the block even though the concert has already started. We opt to watch it from our room. It is a great vantage point and there are no lines for the bathroom.

On Tuesday night we make our way along the Malecón to the central plaza. While walking down the pedestrian street that leads toward the central plaza someone shouts at us, "*Güero, güera!*" This friendly nickname means "blond," but is also used for anyone who has light brown or blond hair, fair skin, or even blue or green eyes. I have been addressed as *güero* in Mexico nearly as often as with my own name, as has Becky, so we automatically turn toward the person speaking to us. It is then that we notice that he isn't looking at us. He continues to shout in rapid fashion, "*Güero, güera, güero, güera* . . ." He is a tout employed by the ice cream parlor. The competition directly across the walkway uses the same call. The summons was originally targeted at foreigners visiting the port, but now is used as an ice cream announcement for all prospective clients, regardless of nationality or hair color.

Curiosity draws us into the muggy ice cream parlor, a maelstrom of waving arms, barked flavors, and tiny wooden spoons dipping into frozen treats. This is a survival-of-the-boldest situation, so I draw a competitive breath and bellow for a scoop of lime and a scoop of mango. Italian ice it isn't, but after enduring the sauna-like crush to get it we are happy to have the frozen relief.

Los Portales, as the town's central plaza is known, is called such for the stone archways linked together as though following the path of a bouncing ball. Along the plaza perimeter, patrons squeeze in among tightly fitted tables. We thread ourselves through the tables, unavoidably bumping into diners' chairs, checking out their seafood cocktails and fish preparations along the way. From our seat we can see the lush tropical tangle of plaza trees coifed into harmony by astute gardeners. Across the way, floodlights illuminate the church's orange creamsicle roof and blue-tiled dome.

A temporary stage has been set up for the carnival in front of the municipal building. We are in a prime position to watch the entertainment as soon as it starts. Meanwhile several marimba bands play in front of our tables. Behind us a rotund harp-strumming woman has infiltrated the dining area. Her gelatinous arms taper into plump pink fingers that flutter and leap across the strings. She leans forward into a trio of men to sing coy, ribald verses for their ears, flashing her gold-capped teeth to deliver spicy jabs to which the men react with raucous bursts of approval.

The first of the vendors approaches our table, and during the course of an hour will offer us candy, compact discs, watches, assorted nuts, a shoe shine, umbrellas, cigarettes, cigars, hammocks, wooden combs, magic tricks, refrigerator magnets, intricately carved ships, dolls, herbal medicines, balloons, cassette tapes, lottery tickets, belt buckles, whisk brooms, copper pots, rag dolls, coat racks, amber paperweights with scorpions inside, and blood pressure measurement.

Our waiter serves Becky a perspiring beer and I receive a Cuba Libre *a la Campechana*, meaning that mineral water has been added to dilute the sweetness. A quick look around shows that most people are ordering beers. Their tables are crowded with brown, green, and clear bottles that the waiters use as a sort of abacus, sorting and counting them on each table to determine how much the patrons owe. Other patrons request bottles of rum, which arrive with several soft drinks. Ordering a bottle of hard liquor for a table is quite common in Mexico, particularly in nightclubs, where it is done more often than asking for individual drinks.

People accumulate in the plaza to listen to a geriatric eleven-man orchestra equipped with trumpets, clarinets, violins, drums, and a trombone. A dancing area has been set up in front of the stage where several senior couples chat amiably as they wait for the music to begin. At the beginning of the song, each couple holds hands and faces the stage. Simultaneously, cued by a beat in the opening, the man and woman in each pair slide to face one another, then stop. Once again signaled by a beat in the music, the couples all begin to move as gracefully as royal ball attendees to the smooth, singular rhythm of *danzón*.

As the conductor intensifies the tempo, I sip my Cuba Libre and taste Mexico City. I moved to that unwieldy megalopolis because my savings account, which I was using to fund the office I set up in Guadalajara, ran dry. The other partners in our loose trading company experiment were not generating sales, either. I was put to work for a trial period of a few months in a Mexican partner's office.

Ramón, a cigar-smoking Humphrey Bogart knockoff, became my Mexican business mentor. Part one of my training consisted of his brutally hacking at my sales letters and converting them from translations of concise American commercial prose into flowery, verbose Spanish business poetry. For example, each letter ended with "Thank you for your kindness in reading this communication and please allow me to take advantage of this opportunity to send you, my esteemed associate, a warm embrace. I close with dearest regards, always at your service, attentively [signature]." The openings to these letters and nearly every paragraph were equally warm and gushy. It is impossible to write a one-page memo, an unquestioned edict in American business, with such an inordinate amount of courtesy.

Part two of my training centered on the following insight: "You know what your problem is? You think like a *gringo*."

To think less like a *gringo,* I intentionally stayed away from my own kind. I did business with Mexicans, made friends with Mexicans, watched Mexican movies, went to every gallery, governmental palace, and museum I could find with paintings by the Mexican muralists, and in order to date Mexicans, I learned to dance. At one of the first parties I attended (where the only drink option was a Cuba Libre, by the way), I positioned myself against a wall to hang out and look cool, as per my previous party training. The problem was that leaning against the wall was not gaining me a lot of interaction with anyone, especially not with the young women who were busy having the time of their lives dancing salsa with the guys who knew how—which was every one of them except me.

The experience I had had up to this point, grade school square dancing and the disco-style arms-akimbo shuffle step, would not help much. Dire circumstances—social hermitage—required that I take drastic action and seek out dance instruction. Entering a dance studio made me feel as self-conscious as if I had walked through the busy streets in a tutu to get there. I stammered and stuttered about my deficiency, signed up for a spot in the evening group, and ultimately got the deed done. Not only did they teach salsa, but they also threw in steps for merengue, cumbia, and *danzón.*

My Spanish improved, I became more comfortable with the culture, but my sales totaled a disheartening *nada.* Our small organization was trying to sell agricultural commodities dominated by a few big companies and we simply couldn't compete. I made plans to head back to the United States in debt and dismay. Days before I planned to leave, I found an ad in the English-language paper for a job as sales representative for a U.S. trading company. I badgered the owner at his hotel with a barrage of phone calls until he was convinced that I was salesperson material, though desperate was a more apt description. I negotiated Ramón in the deal as an agent. Within a few months, we made our first sale, ensuring my continued residence in Mexico. It struck me as bizarre that, after having tried to sell basic foodstuffs like soybeans and rice, my first contract was for five truckloads of baby corn—that miniature gourmet corn-on-the-cob.

Back in the plaza, Becky and I head toward the area where a half dozen couples are dancing. Becky is naturally coordinated; she began dancing salsa without a single lesson. However, she is apprehensive about learning new steps. This is particularly the case now, even though I encourage her with the input, "It's easy. Most of it is the box step." She declines, preferring to watch the flowing pageantry.

Men wear light suits with debonair hats. Silky dresses drape from the shoulders of women who unfold Chinese fans between each number. Their posture is erect while they dance. With a tapping foot, Becky picks up the rhythm, which is interrupted every so often by an abrupt silence. The dancers pause mid-song like stately European statues, then glide anew when the music resumes.

A new band takes the stage, invigorating the crowd with feverish salsa music and other rambunctious tropical rhythms. Becky and I squeeze into the dance area, twisting, buffeting, spinning, and jostling until our shirts are soaked with sweat. We step to the side of the stage for a breather. The conductor of the *danzón* orchestra is there watching the gyrating mob, so we take the opportunity to compliment him on his group's performance. He tells us that if we want to hear more *danzón*, we should go to the Plazuela La Campaña tomorrow night. He is Maestro Bernardo and his group has played there every Wednesday night for thirty years.

We spend most of Ash Wednesday submerged in the hotel pool to escape the oppressive humidity. For lunch we drive out along the coastline to the small town of Boca del Río for a tasty seafood meal. Becky comments on how pristine the coastal highway used to be. As we pass it, we stare accusingly at the newly built Wal-Mart store as the perpetrator of the development, while wondering if there is anything inside we might need.

In the evening, the streets leading to Portales Square are crowded with families. Most have visited the cathedral, as smudges of ash on their foreheads attest. Everyone is waiting for the burial procession of San Juan de Carnaval, the carnival king, signifying the end of the celebration. A team of police cars leads the parade, clearing the way for the official mourners. Fireworks explode overhead as the first-prize-winning samba group dances by in hot pink and white. Two dozen women dressed and veiled in black dab their eyes with black hankies, yet manage to wave, smile, and laugh a lot. Such is the lamentation of San Juan's harem of widows. A platoon of men attired in black robes with black conical caps forms the next contingent. Behind them on a float is the coffin of San Juan. The only discernible parts of him are one hand holding a beer can and the other hand saluting the crowd.

The Veracruz carnival ends, but our evening hasn't. Asking directions along the way, we walk a few blocks to find the small hidden square, Plazuela La Campana. No street noise is heard because only two narrow walkways lead to it. Old men play chess on boards painted directly onto stone tables. Palm trees and flowers overflow from the gardens. A fountain bubbles near the namesake bell that looks much like the yoked Liberty Bell. Pastel walls and colonial buildings encase the entire plaza. Two businesses remain active at this hour, an open-walled billiards hall on one side of the plaza, and on the other, a taco restaurant that serves food and drink to those sitting at the folding tables set up in front of the bandstand.

Maestro Bernardo's band is finishing up a set as we arrive. The conductor sees us and shuffles over to our table. His body is severely bent at the waist, even when he walks, and his slacks are pulled up around his gaunt body all the way to his chest. His remaining hair is combed back in a dignified manner and thick black glasses pinch his ears. Most of the men in his group are about his age, seventy-three or even a decade older, so he informs us.

"Not as many young people are interested in *danzón* as they used to be. I started playing this music when I was young. Let's see, I got my first trumpet when I was fourteen. I don't have that one anymore, though. I set it on the road for a moment and a bus flattened it! The one I use now, I've had for twenty years."

When we ask him about the origin of *danzón*, he explains, "It came from Havana to Veracruz in the late 1890s, about the time your countrymen helped Cuba gain independence from Spain. Cuban musicians came to Mexico and played here. They started with the *contradanza*. Do you know this music?"

We shake our heads "no."

He beats a long, knotted finger on the table like a conductor's baton and sings rhythmic puffs, "Pim, pom, pim, pim, pom!" He searches our faces for comprehension, finding none. "That one is *contradanza*."

"The *contradanza*, it evolved into *danzón*. That is what we learned to play. At one time, in the '40s and '50s every club in Mexico City played *danzón*. I traveled with my group to New York and Paris and played those cities. Those were better days. If you were good enough, regardless of the circumstances, they would not let you starve. They'd discreetly lend you a hand—hire you for a gig.

"Now I think Veracruz is the only place where *danzón* is heard anymore. They rarely play it in Mexico City, and I think not at all in Cuba. That's okay. Look around you here—this plaza looks like Havana, doesn't it? It's up to us to carry on the tradition."

I walk the maestro back to the stage so I can get his card, and then watch him lead his group into a number. When I return to our table, Becky is not there. I spot her on the dance floor with a gray-haired gentleman outfitted in a light blue seersucker suit and a dashing hat. She makes a "help me" face of desperation over his shoulder, but I can't do anything for her. She is already engaged in a fluid, sweeping box step of a graceful *danzón*.

Resources

Arthur, Stanley. *Famous New Orleans Drinks*. Gretna: Pelican Press/ Harmonson, 1949.

Baker, Charles. *The Gentleman's Companion*. New York: Crown Publishers, 1946.

Bethell, Leslie. *Cuba: A Short History*. New York: Cambridge University Press, 1993.

Ober, Frederick. *Travels in Mexico*. Boston: Estes and Lauriat, 1883.

Pendergrast, Mark. *For God, Country, and Coca-Cola*. New York: Scribners, 1993.

Riding, Alan. *Distant Neighbors*. New York: Vintage Books, 1989.

Verti, Sebastián. *Tradiciones mexicanas*. México, DF: Editorial Diana, 1993.

MARGARITA

TEHUACÁN AND TAXCO

Bryan coaxes the car forward as he squints through the brown haze surrounding us. Dust clouds swirling like angry phantoms scour our hood with abrasive grit. Even with our headlights on, visibility fades to zero after about fifty feet. The air conditioning filter can only do so much. Our eyes water. We cough and sneeze. Dried grasses and plastic garbage propelled on a carpet of blowing dirt rocket into the side of the car.

It was a muggy, still day when we left Veracruz this morning. The wind began to pick up as we climbed out of the jungle onto Mexico's central plateau. Now we're an hour outside of Tehuacán and in the center of a brownout. It's just past one in the afternoon, but it looks like nightfall.

It will be better when we get to Tehuacán. Known as a city of mineral springs and mineral water, it will be an oasis compared to the parched, hostile landscape we're driving through now. Tehuacán used to attract spa-goers from around the world. *Terry's Guide to Mexico*, a bible for travelers in the 1930s and 1940s, hails the mineral waters in Tehuacán as refreshing and "efficacious in curing liver and kidney disorders." If we can make it through this dust storm without getting smashed by an oncoming truck or flying debris, we should be in a completely different environment.

All across Mexico, but particularly in the central region, people simply ask for *un Tehuacán* when they want a bottle of carbonated water. I remember my first attempt to use the term. Wanting to sound like a local, I replaced my usual mineral water order, *agua con gas*, with my new word. Unfortunately, I added two extra syllables, and ordered *un Teotihuacán*. Teotihuacán is the name of the famous ruins outside of Mexico City. I was ordering bottles of pyramids.

We keep driving and the wind keeps howling. Thirty minutes later on the outskirts of town my spirits, already teetering, begin to plummet. The land, as dry and scabby as it was twenty miles back, looks as if it has been robbed of its last nutrients. Cyclones of forever-lost topsoil continue to buffet the car. The chalky cement factory we pass at Tehuacán's entrance blends perfectly into the blowing, suffocating wall of brown and gray. A slash of green cutting across the stingy valley below us is the only sign that this land is habitable. This isn't what the birthplace of the margarita is supposed to be like.

How could the margarita, that zingy, refreshing, good-time cocktail, come from a place like this? Margaritas are an almost mythical

Mexican drink with the power to transport a person from a cold, dark bar in Cincinnati to a sunny, carefree place south of the border. One of the most popular cocktails in the United States, its ingredients—earthy tequila, tart lime, soothing citrus, and marine salt—represent the flavors of Mexico. It almost seems as if the margarita, with its elemental completeness, has been around since this land was formed. That isn't the case, of course. In fact, margaritas have taken their strong hold on the imagination in less than one hundred years.

A handful of different people claim to have invented the drink. Bryan and I are here to peel back the layers of legend and confusion to unearth the drink's origin. Candidates that we've rejected due to the dates of their assertions include Enrique Bastante, a cocktail world champion who says he invented the drink for Margarita "Rita" Hayworth in 1945, and an American socialite named Margaret Sames, who insists that she concocted the beverage in Acapulco in 1948 during a string of wild Christmas parties.

Chronologically Tehuacán's claim comes first. According to legend, a man named Danny Negrete invented a drink for his girlfriend Margarita in 1936. She had a penchant for salt, adding a few dashes to everything, including her cocktails. I guess she was either sodium deficient or working on a high blood pressure disaster. He came up with a drink she liked and named it after her. An article in *Texas Monthly* placed Negrete as manager of the Crespo Hotel in Puebla, Mexico.

All we had to do was drive to Puebla, a town about an hour from Mexico City, find the Crespo Hotel, and dig around for señor Negrete or anybody who had known him. Unfortunately, I couldn't find any information about a Crespo Hotel in Puebla. A search in Mexico travel guides from the last seventy years came up with nothing.

Then one day, while deep in the stacks of the Nettie Lee Benson Latin America Library at the University of Texas, I thumbed through a travelogue, *Mexican Interlude*, published in 1936. A line jumped out at me.

> Our plan was to go on down to Tehuacán, to the Garci-Crespo Hotel where there are enormous mineral baths and the bottling plant whose fizzy water we had carefully been drinking ever since we came to Mexico.

Of course! Puebla was not only the name of a city, but also a Mexican state. And, Garci-Crespo, the hotel, was also the name of a brand of mineral water Bryan and I had been drinking for years. It was produced in Tehuacán, Puebla.

I looked for an entry on Tehuacán in a current guidebook. Nothing. I tried another. No Tehuacán. I restarted my search from the early years, looking in Frances Toor's 1938 *Motorist Guide to Mexico*. Bingo. Hailing Tehuacán as a delightful vacation retreat, Toor singles out the Garci-Crespo Spa as the best hotel in town. I followed the declining state of the hotel through guidebook entries from subsequent years until the trail went cold. By 1960 there was no mention at all of the Garci-Crespo. The new Hotel Spa Peñafiel, with expansive grounds and swimming pools, became the resort of choice. By 1970 Tehuacán entries disappeared completely. My hopeful deduction, as Peñafiel is another well-known brand of mineral water from Tehuacán, is that the dying Garci-Crespo had been converted into the Hotel Peñafiel. We would just have to go there to see for ourselves.

Now, as we make our way through the dust storm past unpainted, windowless cement houses, I think I must have made a mistake. How could any hotels, other than those that rent rooms by the hour, attract enough visitors to stay open here? Where are the green hills with frolicking wildlife? Aren't wild streams and crystalline air supposed to be prerequisites for mineral water operations? The only stream we see entering town is filled with tired women huddled into hunchbacks, washing clothes in a barely trickling creek clogged with garbage.

The scenery improves in the heart of town. A few tree-lined streets and graceful old squares hint at the town's past as a resort destination. Most of the buildings in this section of the city are at least painted, although a disproportionate number display the splashing Peñafiel mineral water logo.

Small stores and bars all over Mexico are decorated with different manufacturers' logos painted directly onto sides of buildings. Generally it's beer companies that spend significant amounts of their advertising budgets coating the exteriors of establishments. The usual agreement involves a new coat of paint over the entire wall in exchange for the logo display. The proprietor gets part of his shop painted for free, and the manufacturer doesn't have to pay for billboard space. In Tehuacán, Peñafiel and Garci-Crespo don't let you forget that you are in the land of mineral water. I suppose they have to paint so many walls here because it's such an incongruous place to produce anything purified.

We pull over in front of one of the Peñafiel-decorated stores to ask directions to the Peñafiel Hotel. A look of recognition on the woman's face leads us to believe that the hotel indeed exists. A long set of instructions sends us through the crowded and dirty commercial district downtown, where additional guidance from other pedestrians steers us into a more residential zone.

An approachable-looking woman stands outside in the wind futilely sweeping her sidewalk. We ask her if we're on the right track to the Hotel Peñafiel.

"Well, you're on the right track," she laughs in a gravelly voice, "But you're about twenty years too late. What used to be the Hotel Peñafiel is now the Euro-American University. There's a nice hotel next to it if you're looking for a place to stay. You can visit the university, though. The building and grounds are beautiful. My daughter studies tourism there. She's writing her thesis right now on ways to bring travelers back to Tehuacán."

"Good luck on that one," we both think while we smile at the progenitor of this optimistic young student. Isn't it a cruel oxymoron for this town's university to offer such a major?

"Do you happen to know if the building now housing the university used to be the Hotel Garci-Crespo before it was the Hotel Peñafiel?"

"*Sí*," she expels in an elongated, rising note. "But that was about seventy years ago." An exaggerated gesture backward past her pale ear accompanies this sentence.

We ask her about the once famous mineral springs even though neither one of us has a liver or kidney disorder, or at least we didn't before we started our travels for this book. She pauses and lowers her voice. "There are still some baths at San Lorenzo just up the road. But they are for, well, you know—the middle class."

The tone of her voice leaves no doubt that "middle class" is a euphemism for "people below my station." This from a woman sweeping her own sidewalk, something that neither Bryan nor I have ever seen an upper-class Mexican do. Not interested in getting into a class discussion, we quickly change the subject. We ask if she's ever heard that the margarita was invented here.

"Ha, ha! No, I've never heard of that. We're famous for our water, not any margarita. Who knows? Ha, ha."

The school's gates are locked. A gardener informs us that it closes at lunchtime on Saturday, but will reopen in a few hours. We try the hotel next door, built on what was obviously part of the original spa grounds, for our own meal. Once inside the entrance of the hotel, it's much easier to imagine the Tehuacán of old, but even the high walls aren't a complete barricade against the rumbling of hulking semis loaded with bottled water. Protected from the wind and grit, we sit in a grassy courtyard by the pool. Table umbrellas shield smartly dressed patrons from the glaring sun. All seven of the town's elite, minus the woman we talked to outside her house, are dining here with us.

I request *un Tehuacán*. Contemplating my order, I query our waiter about how people from Tehuacán ask for mineral water.

"Well, they order mineral water, *agua con gas*, or a specific brand, like a Peñafiel or San Lorenzo or something like that. Nobody here says '*un Tehuacán*.' That's only people from out of town."

He pauses for a second and then continues. "There is one thing we kind of call a Tehuacán, but we really call it a *Tehuacanazo*, a big-time Tehuacán. The PRG, which is like your FBI or CIA, I guess, uses mineral water to force confessions from people. They shake the bottle to get it very gassy and then spray it up a person's nose. Sometimes they even put chile powder in the water to make it really sting. It doesn't leave any marks or bruises, but imagine how much that must hurt. It's kind of unfortunate, but that's a *Tehuacanazo*."

Bryan and I both involuntarily squinch our noses. Bryan asks if he's ever heard of anything about the margarita being invented here.

"*Puueesss* . . ." the waiter looks up at an imaginary point while racking the far recesses of his brain. "The truth is . . ."

We both lean forward.

"No. Ha, ha!"

So much for local lore, or locals for that matter, helping us out.

Bryan orders a margarita. There are many different variations on the margarita recipe, but the basic ingredients are fixed—tequila, orange liqueur, and lime juice. A true margarita connoisseur, however, is very finicky about these ingredients. I have been a margarita snob for a long time and have a standard spiel that I give my friends when they ask about what makes a good margarita.

I tell them that the best tequila to use is a 100-percent agave, unaged *blanco*. This gives the drink a bite that combines perfectly with the tartness of the lime. Sometimes people like a smoother taste, so in that case I'll suggest using a slightly aged *reposado*, but the gold hue of *reposado* makes the drink cloudy compared to the clear freshness you get with a white or silver tequila. Some people request special margaritas using *añejo*, aged tequila, but I tell them that that's just a poor use of good tequila.

I'm also picky about the type of orange liqueur I use. Triple Sec is a good standard, but I prefer the balanced flavor of Cointreau, a premium brand. Cointreau, or Controy here in Mexico, is stronger than Triple Sec, though, so I have to watch that the orange flavor doesn't overwhelm the rest of the drink. Some restaurants make their "top shelf" margaritas with Grand Marnier, a blend of orange liqueur and cognac. That's fine every once in a while, but the cognac flavor is a departure from the true original. I prefer to stick with Cointreau.

The crux of the entire drink, however, is the lime juice. I tell my friends to use small yellow-green key limes, not their big, dry, acidic Persian counterparts usually found in U.S. supermarkets. The lime juice must be freshly squeezed, of course. In fact, I'll go so far as to say that if you can't find key limes, forget the margarita and just drink tequila straight.

I also prefer to drink margaritas "up," which means shaken with cracked ice and then strained. If it's particularly hot, I'll reluctantly approve serving the drink on the rocks. Although admitting their popularity, I advise against drinking frozen margaritas because they get too watery as they melt.

My ultimate margarita recipe varies depending on the tartness of the limes or my whims of the day, but my standard departure point is two parts tequila to one part Cointreau to one part lime. It never fails to get a party going.

Bryan and I almost never order margaritas in the United States because they are often made from a mix, are very sweet, or both. In Mexico, however, where mixes are rarely used, we can be more confident about what will arrive at the table. Unless we're in Tehuacán. Bryan takes a sip of his drink and makes a face. Too sweet. They must be using a mix. There is no way the margarita can be from next door.

The façade of the university resembles the Alamo. Set back from the road, surrounded by violently purple jacaranda trees, the large beige building still looks like a resort hotel. Blue and white tiles decorate its base, while vivid azalea and bougainvillea bushes brighten the grounds. Amazingly, the hotel lobby has been left almost intact. A large wrought-iron chandelier hangs down from thick brown vigas. Intricate white molding highlights rows of archways. Tehuacán was once known as a marble carving area. Perhaps as a tribute, or because it would just be too heavy to move, the ponderous marble reception desk remains in place.

A large conference room toward the back of the lobby was once the restaurant. Exquisite leaded windows, stained at the tops, arch around the room in oversized iterations. Looking through them we see the top of the Peñafiel plant next door, built on what were once the hotel's mineral springs.

It is rare to be able to wander around unannounced in any Mexican edifice. Even modest office buildings have guards in the lobby requiring people to sign in before entering the elevator. Two administrators approach us. We relay our mission. They look at each other and then the taller one, middle-aged and wearing Sansabelt slacks, starts to laugh.

"Margarita? Invented here? Ha, ha! I've never heard of that and I study our local history."

The shorter one just chuckles.

"You're more than welcome to go in the bar and see if you can find anything."

The shorter one chuckles again.

Why does everybody think this is so funny?

The bar is now part of the cafeteria, which is closed, so the room is dark. Muted light trickles in through wooden doors ornamented with heavy etched glass. The wooden counter, inlaid with single rows of blue and yellow talavera tile, shines from the years of elbows bent at its surface. Behind it a large mirror reflects a reversed image of twelve small tables. Octagonal red and green tiles cover the ceiling and below them runs a border of off-white ceramic shields.

Bryan leans on the counter to place an order with an imaginary Danny Negrete.

"I'll have one of those new drinks you invented for your girlfriend. It's world famous now and called the margarita."

I swear I hear the room echo, "Ha, ha!"

We originally found the competing theories about the margarita's origin a bit startling. It soon became clear, however, that the drink was destined to be invented. It even seems plausible that it could have been created by more than one person around the same time. Tequila, salt, and lime have gone together for a few hundred years, although until relatively recently tequila was taken straight, preceded by a lick of salt and followed by a squeeze of lime. Tequila cocktails were unheard of. *The Gentleman's Companion* describes a 1937 attempt to find an alternative to slamming a shot of tequila in Mexico:

> This process [slamming] not only being a definite menace to the gullet and possible fire risk through lighted matches, we began going on a hunt for some way to mix tequila. We were greeted with raised eyebrows, expressions of commiseration for waning sanity, open distrust.

The writers of *The Gentlemen's Companion* could not have been alone in their desire to find a way to mix tequila. People would logically experiment with known cocktail recipes, substituting tequila for other liquors. A natural cocktail to imitate would have been the Sidecar. Created in Harry's Bar in Paris around the turn of the nineteenth century, the Sidecar was a drink popular with the world traveling elite. Served blended and strained in a glass with the rim frosted in sugar, the Sidecar was made of brandy, orange liqueur, lime, and a little sugar. Knowing that tequila combines well with the sharp taste of sodium, even a creatively challenged drink mixer could have substituted tequila for brandy and salt for sugar to come up with what is now known as the margarita. The similarity between the drinks seems too close to be coincidence. Or is it?

Pancho Morales told *Texas Monthly* that he invented the margarita at a bar called Tommy's Place in 1942 in Juárez, Mexico, and that it had nothing to do with a Sidecar. As he remembers it, a lady came in and asked for a Magnolia. Too proud to say that he didn't know the exact recipe, he improvised. Remembering that the Magnolia contained Cointreau and lime, he mixed a drink using tequila as the liquor. When the lady complained that it wasn't what she ordered, he covered his tracks by saying that he thought she had ordered a Margarita. (He stayed in the flower family as *margarita* is the word for "daisy" in Spanish.) According to Pancho, she decided that it tasted good anyway, and so the drink was born.

It was Vern Underwood who helped make the drink famous by marketing it in the United States. Underwood was the exclusive importer of José Cuervo tequila in California. In 1953 sales were slow everywhere except at one restaurant in Los Angeles called The Tail o' the Cock. Underwood investigated. The head bartender there, Johnny Durlesser, was duplicating a tequila cocktail that a customer named Margaret had tried in Mexico. He had dubbed it the Margarita. Hoping the drink's popularity would spread, Underwood began marketing it around the state with the slogan "Margarita: It's more than a girl's name." Not too catchy, but it obviously worked. The question remains, however: Where in Mexico did the customer named Margaret first try the drink?

All the Best in Mexico, published in 1949, provides a clue. When discussing what to drink in Mexico City, the author states that tequila is so inexpensive that sporty spenders are ashamed to order it. He cites a single exception, however: a famous tequila Collins named the Berta. Calling it "an established feature of life" in Mexico, he lists the ingredients as tequila, lime juice, and honey, describing the taste as resembling that of a daiquiri.

I quickly turn to the next chapter, where I read that Berta's Bar, where she held forth like a "stout brown priestess of Bacchus," was the life of the Taxco evening. Although the book was written in the late 1940s, the drink, having spread to different cities and being so well known, must have been invented years earlier.

Joseph Jackson's *Mexican Interlude*, published in 1936, confirms my hunch. The author declares that no visitor to Taxco should miss Doña Berta's *tequila-limonada*. Cortés de Figueroa's *Taxco, the Enchanted City* gives even more details:

> Downtown, where things are a bit more informal and have more local color, is the world-famous cantina of Madam Berta. This estimable señora is known as Doña Berta by all and sundry, and has occupied her little corner bistro by the church for some odd forty years. Her claim to fame is a drink of her own invention, known as a tequila-limonada or as a Berta.
>
> It tastes like a delicious soft drink but after two or three, one receives a big surprise! There is nothing like it in the whole elbow-bending world!

Who hasn't received the same big surprise when standing up after drinking a few margaritas? A reproduction of Berta's drink recipe was printed in *The Gentleman's Companion*. It called for tequila, lime juice, orange bitters, and sugar. These ingredients were stirred in a Collins glass with lots of small ice cubes and then topped off with mineral water. I begin to believe that the Berta, made in Taxco, was the original source of the Tail o' the Cock's special cocktail—the drink that was reproduced, renamed, and marketed in the United States as the margarita.

A final reference convinces me that the Berta is the source. It sends us running to Taxco.

The traffic-filled road from Mexico City has us tired and frazzled as we near the end of our four-hour drive. Taxco is located at 6,000 feet in the heart of the Sierra Madre. My strongest memory of a previous visit to Taxco fourteen years earlier is of extreme nausea after enduring what seemed like hundreds of hairpin turns on the back of an old bus. Bryan assures me that a toll road has been built since then, so the ride will be much smoother now. We pay our tariff for the spur that branches off the main Mexico City-Acapulco highway and soon find ourselves laughing in spite of our motion sickness. The much-hyped toll road, while better than the old route, is a twisted threadlike passage through the mountains.

In Taxco, thousands of white buildings, all with red tile roofs, cling to the terrain in a jumble of intersecting plains. Clogged with the traffic of buses, microbuses, and Herbie-the-Love-Bug taxis, the main artery into town freezes into gridlock. All the taxis are painted white in keeping with the town color scheme. Even the traffic police follow the code. Dressed in tan pants and white shirts, all they need is a single red tile on top of each khaki hat to camouflage themselves completely.

Navigating the narrow cobblestone streets, we search in vain for our hotel. This is the only town in Mexico where pedestrians not only have the right of way, but also put great faith in drivers' clairvoyance. We constantly slam on our brakes to avoid crunching people who walk obliviously out of doorways and into the street without pausing to glance at oncoming traffic. Vendors display their wares to the very edge of constricted alleyways that are only wide enough to accommodate a single car at a time. Our lumbering sport utility vehicle is a burden. Pulling in both sets of side mirrors, we generally have only inches to spare. Occasionally we turn a corner to face a menacing line-up of six white Volkswagen Bugs bearing down on us. We are then required to maneuver the complicated corridors in reverse until we find a spot wide enough for them to pass.

We arrive at the Hotel Victoria Rancho Taxco exhausted. Parking our car, we resolve not to use it again until we leave. When we get to our room, I open my files and read aloud from Joseph Henry Jackson's *Mexican Interlude*.

> Taxco is not a town to drive about in. After you have accomplished the not inconsiderable feat of guiding your car once through its twisted alleyways to your hotel—especially if it happens to be the new Rancho Taxco, to which we had to ascend practically every steep street in the place—you are glad enough to forget you have a car and use your legs.

Bryan jokingly accuses me of withholding insider information. How could I have known that six decades later nothing had changed?

The plaza is the center of life in most small towns in Mexico. Taxco, a city of 90,000, seems to have forgotten that it isn't small anymore. Looking around, it's easy to see why. The cobblestone streets, white adobe buildings, and red tile roofs probably look much as they did over two hundred years ago. On the other hand, the constant noise and squeeze of traffic everywhere you walk is a not-so-subtle reminder that the town has outgrown itself. There's just no graceful way to accommodate more and more cars and people in such a tightly constricted area.

All of the writings about Berta's Bar describe it as being located on a little corner next to the cathedral. We scan the buildings around the square. I'm embarrassed to admit it, but my heartbeat actually quickens a bit because we're finally here at what could be the Mecca of Margarita.

"There it is. That tiny two-story building right there. It's not just next to the cathedral, it's practically part of it."

Bryan points toward a diminutive sugar cube of a structure just a few feet from the wrought-iron fence that surrounds the church. "Bar Berta" painted directly onto the side of the white building in small, simple black letters is the only sign marking our most important Taxco landmark. The petite building is adorned with a few pairs of green shutters upstairs and a tightly shut green door. Closed! How could it be closed? It's just a few minutes past eight on a Thursday night. Isn't it a bar? Oh, my God, what if it's been shut down?

Bryan sees my face fall and goes to get information from a ripened old man selling children's toys on Berta's front steps. He comes back with the news that Berta's closes every night at eight because of its close proximity to the church.

We turn to study the church. The pink granite edifice dominates the landscape of downtown. Two ornately decorated bell towers, designed to imitate Chinese woodcarvings, frame a baroque façade that competes with the towers in its elaborate adornment. Behind them hovers a single blue and yellow tile-covered dome.

The Parroquia, or parish church, is just one of Taxco's indelible physical legacies created by miner José de la Borda. A Frenchman, Borda immigrated to Mexico in the early 1700s to live with his uncle and learn the mining business. In 1747 he discovered a bonanza vein of silver that would forever change the face of Taxco. Although he worked the mine for only nine years, Borda made a fortune. Part of this fortune financed the Parroquia.

We walk across to the plaza, built by Borda as well. Indian laurel trees shake with the rustles and screeches of birds descending to roost for the night. About sixty forest-green wrought-iron benches surround a white octagonal bandstand flaming with bougainvillea around its base. Although most of the benches are still occupied, movement around the plaza slows as area shops and stands close for the evening. The appetizing smell of sizzling meat is revealed to be the not-so-tempting treat of hotdogs wrapped with bacon in the type of countertop cooker found in movie theaters. Translucent puffs of cotton candy, lit from underneath by a single strong bulb, glow neon pink. A semi-permanent cart leaned against the church fence doesn't seem to have the same restrictions as Berta's. Its proprietor hawks *cantaritos*, an unappealing drink made of tequila and Squirt, to the passing crowd.

Borda didn't stop at building the church, but also reconstructed most of the houses in town. Taxco's unique style is no accident. Longing for the scenery from the country of his birth, he had the typical mud and thatch huts of Taxco rebuilt into stucco and adobe houses topped with red tile roofs. He also cobbled all the streets with stone, built a community aqueduct and fountain, and erected a huge home for himself on one side of the plaza adjacent to the Parroquia.

We wander away from the plaza and back up to our sprawling hotel. Old travel guides heartily endorsed the establishment, citing such luxuries as large terraces, romantic views, and Simmons mattresses. While the hotel's glory has faded, the terraces and views remain superb. From our balcony we look down through seven levels of bougainvillea and folded white buildings to the Parroquia.

Ours is the only car in the parking lot, although it appears that two or three of the hotel's hundred-odd rooms might be occupied. We stop at the restaurant. The lights are out, so we wander back toward the kitchen to see if it's open. The long industrial galley, designed to feed legions of demanding guests, seems ridiculous given the hotel's current occupancy. The cook and the waiter, conversing under a single lamp, jump up when we enter. Amid profuse apologies, the waiter begs us to go back to the restaurant where he will serve us with all of his professionalism and training.

We decide to have sandwiches and margaritas sent up to our patio. We pull ourselves up four flights of crooked outdoor stairs to our room. Our waiter appears with dinner, which he sets up on our round patio table. The margaritas are excellent. Crisp, cool, and tangy, they have nothing in common with the sweet concoction we were served in Tehuacán. We have a good feeling about our quest as we look down at the lights of town.

We picked this hotel not because of the views, but because part of it was designed by one of Taxco's most important twentieth-century residents, an American named William Spratling. I have brought his out-of-print autobiography with me to Mexico. Spratling's life story is fascinating. As an architecture professor at Tulane he was an active member of the New Orleans artist colony, hanging around and even rooming with literary greats like Sherwood Anderson, John Dos Passos, and William Faulkner.

He moved to Mexico in 1929 with a contract to write a book about the country. He deftly put his fingers on the pulse of Bohemian Mexico while managing to surround himself with money and power. Quickly working his way into the highest circles, he won over people like Dwight Morrow, the U.S. ambassador to Mexico, and muralist Diego Rivera. With commission money from Diego Rivera for a job that

Spratling had negotiated, Spratling bought a little house in Taxco. I'm sure neither Spratling nor Taxco's residents had any idea of the impact this move would bring upon the city.

One day in 1931 Morrow made a comment to Spratling about Taxco's history as a source of silver. He thought it was a shame that none of the silver was ever used to create an industry or economy for Taxco. Spratling agreed. As an experiment he brought two goldsmiths in from a neighboring town to make Spratling-designed silver jewelry. That little experiment is what supports Taxco's economy today.

I lie in bed contemplating Taxco and silver while trying to ignore the muffled barks of dogs and the roar of distant microbuses through my earplugs. There must be over one hundred silver stores in the central section of the city alone. Some of them offer works by famous Taxco designers and others offer copies of the same pieces in varying degrees of quality. I find the plethora of silver objects absolutely numbing.

I've felt the same way since my first visit to Taxco. It was my third day as a summer student at a language school in Cuernavaca. I had been to Mexico many times with my parents, but this was my first solo visit to the interior. I was nineteen years old and full of enthusiasm despite my nervousness. I was on my own in the country that had fascinated me since childhood. I wanted to explore everything. The school offered different outings after class every day and I signed up for all of them, including the trip to Taxco.

We arrived in town on a rainy afternoon. Shopping alone, I entered my first store and was astounded by the variety. Row after row of necklaces, rings, earrings, money clips, spoons, key chains, flatware, picture frames, and candelabras glimmered into infinity off mirrored counters and walls. I saw five necklaces I liked, four rings, and a few sets of earrings. I couldn't buy at the first store I set foot in. My instincts told me to look around for other designs, better prices, more variety. I went in the next store and saw more of the same, then the next and saw the same again. By the time I had been in five stores I couldn't even remember what I had liked in the first place. I ended up not buying anything. When I got back to the bus everybody was chatting and laughing and comparing their purchases. I remember having a sad, out-of-place feeling as I sat silently and without a keepsake for myself or anybody with whom I could share it.

The next morning the restaurant fills with the glare of the rising sun. Two waitresses lean on a high chest and look down on the city. This appears to be their daily sentry post. We've noticed that people in Taxco spend a lot of time observing other people from above. Single long braids flecked with gray split the backs of their white pinafore uniforms. One points her chin in the direction of a house just below the hotel.

"*Mira, comadre*, it looks like Sergio bought a new hose to water his plants."

"You know what, *comadre*, I think you're right, but he's watering his plants later than usual today."

"You're right, you're right, *comadre*. He must have gotten up late today."

"*Ayyyy sí, comadre*. Maybe a party last night."

Our attention is drawn to a loud group of four middle-aged, slightly overweight Anglo-Americans. Three of them have that somewhat bewildered look of novice Mexico travelers, with sunburns and new clothes. The fourth obviously organized the trip. She directs her energy to instructing the others about what and how to order, even though the menu is in both English and Spanish.

They may not be seasoned travelers, but they are definitely veteran shoppers. Every other sentence is about silver. Two of them chant prices per gram in the same mumbled tone usually reserved for the Lord's Prayer. Showing minimal interest in the culture around them, their conversation revolves around whether or not one of them should buy a set of flatware and a candelabrum. They are down here on a silver-buying bender.

Spratling started all of this. In 1935 he moved his growing operation to a building just up from the plaza. The shop, Las Delicias, offered not only silver, but also weavings, tin and copperware, and furniture. He called it a four-ring circus.

The newly completed road from Mexico City to Acapulco went straight through Taxco. Many travelers began to schedule a few hours on their way to the beach to do a little shopping with Spratling, who could be a raconteur and charmer when so moved. He had a big ego, but was always entertaining. He liked to be in the center of things, but kept everybody in stitches (and booze) while he was on stage. He soon developed quite a following. Some of his fans extended their stays for months or even years, creating a large expatriate colony. One observer of the time quipped, "It remains uncertain whether they are painters who have gone there to drink or drinkers who have gone there to paint." These were ripe conditions for margarita invention. Word about Taxco spread quickly and soon it was a required stop on the Mexico circuit. It still is for any dedicated shopper.

After Spratling completed a design he would hand it over to one of his silversmiths. New artisans were trained in the shop through an apprentice system that Spratling established from the beginning. Any boy that demonstrated desire was allowed to join, and those that showed aptitude stayed and learned directly from the *maestros*. Over time many of these men opened shops of their own, most with Spratling's blessing and even assistance. Some of them grew to become world-renowned designers in their own right.

Only of few of Spratling's apprentices are still working. If a boy was in his late teens when he started with Spratling in the mid-1930s, he would be in his late eighties now. Antonio Castillo is known as one of Spratling's most successful trainees. Señor Castillo has invited us to stop by his ranch outside of town and we're looking forward to the visit even though it means using our car.

Driving through the video game gauntlet of narrow alleyways and heedless pedestrians, we notice that we need gas. In addition to being oversized, our car is a glutton. It takes a long road trip for a car to earn a name and ours just has—El Gordo. *Gordo* literally means "fat" in Spanish, but it doesn't carry the same negative connotation that our slimness-obsessed society places on the word. It is often used as a friendly nickname or even a term of endearment. We christen *El* Gordo with a splash of Tehuacán water at the gas station and then head out to meet Castillo.

Castillo's ranch is about ten serpentine miles south of town. No longer on any toll road, we come face to face with rural Mexico. A donkey wanders down the middle of the road trailing a red lead rope. We ponder whether it will make it through the day. A stray dog trots by daintily carrying some indistinguishable flattened and sun-dried road kill. Around another blind curve we narrowly avoid a pregnant cow munching scrabbly grass on the almost nonexistent shoulder. We are running a little late, so I call ahead to let Castillo know.

"Oh, I'm afraid Mr. Castillo can't see you now," his wife says apologetically, "He had to go to the hospital to see the doctor unexpectedly this morning."

Bummer. This sounds terrible, but our first reaction is that we need him as a resource. He can't get sick on us. His wife offers to reschedule the visit. His illness must not be too serious if his wife is at home and is making new appointments for him. We pick a day later in the week.

Trying to trace a drink that is probably about sixty-five years old is difficult when many of the primary sources are no longer around. Sr. Castillo, at eighty-three, is potentially a rich and interesting source of information. We wish him good health.

Spratling's business boomed during World War II. American department stores, cut off from their European sources of luxury merchandise, turned to Taxco to purchase jewelry and silver objects to stock their display cases. Neiman-Marcus, Bonwit Teller, and Saks Fifth Avenue were all customers. Demand was practically insatiable and the only restriction on Spratling's growth was his limited capital. He followed advice to sell part of his company to outside investors in order to raise funds for expansion. To Spratling's dismay his investors took over management of the company, relegating him to what he considered a clerk-like position. They brought in a financier who bought controlling interest in the company and summarily ran it into the ground to get a tax break. After almost fifteen years of operation, Spratling's Las Delicias closed its doors.

Always a survivor, Spratling moved out to his ranch in Taxco Viejo and opened a scaled-down silver workshop. We are almost there, so we decide to stop by Spratling's ranch to see what, if anything, is going on. We almost miss the large wrought-iron gate decorated with the Spratling seal as we twist around a curve, but manage to pull in at the last minute. Thanks to a small stream that runs along the property, the foliage is verdant and abundant compared to the desiccated landscape we passed to get here. A young boy directs us down a cobblestone driveway. We pass numerous simple white buildings highlighted with royal blue trim and five different shades of blossoming bougainvillea. The spaces between the buildings are infused with flowers and greenery. We park El Gordo in a lot in back.

Spratling was known as a bit of a daredevil, sailing his boats and flying his small plane off on bold adventures. He survived a couple of plane wrecks, including one that forced him to spend the night on the side of a mountain in subzero temperatures. It was a routine drive, however, that ended up taking his life. In August 1967 he was headed to the airport in nearby Iguala. It was about five o'clock in the morning. He rounded a corner in the dark and failed to see a tree that had fallen across the road during the night. His car smashed directly into the trunk. He lay there for two hours before anybody passed by. They rushed him to the hospital in Iguala, but were too late to save his life.

When Spratling died, Taxco shut down for two days of official mourning. A procession carried his coffin through town and hundreds of people turned out to grieve for this man who had brought so much prosperity to their lives. Many of the silver shops, staggered by the weight of his legacy, closed for the entire week.

Spratling has been dead now for over thirty years. We can't imagine what will be happening out at his ranch. We know that his designs were bought by an Italian and are still being produced today, so our hope is to see some of them.

We walk down an outdoor corridor into a thick-walled adobe building. A pregnant girl about seventeen years old greets us at the door. Stepping around her—which is no small task—we see two rooms laid out like a museum. Silver objects shine against rich backgrounds of crushed black velvet. The lights are low, but small beams focus on individual pieces.

We hear the whoosh of a blowtorch through the open door on the other side of the showroom and step outside into a courtyard. A tile roof shades old wooden tables cluttered with rusty instruments. There are three people in the workshop, but nobody is talking. It feels as if we've stepped into the middle of a shrine. A woman in her early twenties delicately handles a bracelet of simple overlapping silver ovals. She shapes the ovals with a thin, pointed tool and a slim torch. On the table next to her a grizzled man with thick glasses works a larger torch over five long, thin silver slats that glow white at the ends. Inside a glassed room a young man with a modern rat-tail haircut is lost in the tunes of his Walkman. He is diligently soldering the two halves of little silver balls.

We notice a shelf stacked with molds and walk over to examine some of them. They are direct links to Spratling himself. Looking over the designs while I hold the heavy models, I am struck by their pre-Columbian motifs. These themes were common in his pieces because he often turned to ancient designs for inspiration and ideas.

We wander back into the showroom to study some of the finished pieces. Most of them are unique even today. Spratling had very set ideas about silver design. His mantra was "simplicity, surface, and definition." As we study the pieces, we're overcome with the desire to buy a set of flatware. The heavy pieces feel good in our hands. The price tag, however, reflecting both the value of the Spratling name as well as the artistry involved in handmade pieces, is heftier than we can afford.

Later in the week we return along the same route for our appointment with Antonio Castillo, the former Spratling apprentice. We pull through the gates and are enveloped in a world of green spliced with blazes of color and tropical fruit. We follow a young woman past the family house, a white adobe building adorned with murals, masks, sculptures, and hundreds of potted plants, to a large garden. A river flows along one side, spilling over a small dam in a melodic waterfall. Five men, pruning in sync to a fast Latin rhythm, tend the explosion of colorful flowers and shrubs.

The woman points through a doorway and we walk inside a small on-site store and office. The white walls are covered with photos, framed newspaper articles, letters, and shelves displaying various awards. A long counter covered in pink cloth runs the length of the room and a few glass cases sit in front of the counter.

When we finally meet Castillo I feel terrible about my original selfish thoughts. He stands smiling in the center of the room, leaning slightly on one of the display cases. His eyes, however, grab and hold our attention. Warm, frank, and welcoming, he seems sincerely pleased to be meeting with us. At just over five feet tall, with gleaming white teeth and beautiful smooth skin, age has not diminished his handsome features. His gray cotton *guayabera* almost perfectly matches the color of his only slightly receding slicked-back hair and dapper little mustache. A polished malachite stone hangs on a silver chain around his neck.

I ran across a photo of him in a travel book about Taxco while we were doing our research in Austin. In the photo he is gently hammering a sliver of necklace in Spratling's Las Delicias workshop. His thick, wavy black hair, deep black eyes, and flawless complexion couldn't have hurt sales with foreign women.

We introduce ourselves and he says that we've arrived at just the right moment because he's going over some of his favorite pieces. His voice is soft and his language formal. One of the things he shows us is a silver necklace from which is dangling a round, flat stone. The stone has some engravings and a small circle carved into its center. We're puzzled over the piece until he explains that the stone is an ear disc, inserted into a stretched lobe and thus worn by the indigenous people of the region before the Conquest. Its wearer would stick a pencil-sized rod into the small carved circle to leverage the disc into the tight skin of the lobe. Round beads carved from the same stone as the ear disc decorate the necklace.

I'm as fascinated by his hands as I am by the jewelry. His frail skin is almost transparent and he caresses the silver pieces as if they were part of his family. The tone of his voice indicates that he's attached to the necklace. "It's completely unique," he says over and over as his slightly quivering fingers adjust the pendant on its pink cloth background. "You'll never find something like this in Taxco."

We move over to sit with him at his desk. His assistant, a young woman in her twenties, unobtrusively gives him her arm as we walk across the room. We talk about his fascinating life in the six decades since he first walked through Spratling's door. His attentive gaze is fixed on our faces.

An aunt had originally sent him to Spratling to learn English, but young Castillo was also interested in the silversmithing going on around him. Soon he and three of his brothers were Spratling apprentices.

"Oh, was he *exijente*, demanding," Castillo chuckles in his gentle voice. "He was a great person, but he was strict. He was a perfectionist, that's all. He would design a piece and give it to one of us to create. We'd bring it to him and half the time he'd say, '*Ay chingado*. That's not the way I drew it. You tried to make it pretty, didn't you? Make it ugly just like my drawing. Don't try to improve it, just make it ugly like you see it on the paper.'"

The strong phrase "*Ay chingado,*" which can translate a number of ways depending on the tone, but basically means "screw this," sounds strange coming out of Castillo's mouth. Spratling's rough language clashes with Castillo's quiet dignity.

"He always kept his designs so simple that, especially as boys, we thought we could make them a little better with a flourish here and there. Over time I finally learned to appreciate them. It helped me become a better designer.

"One day my brothers and I, we were always very close, we decided to start our own shop. We were a little scared to tell Sr. Spratling, but finally we did. He didn't want us to leave, but when he saw that we were determined, he said OK. Many times when somebody left they would make things that looked almost exactly like Spratling designs. We didn't do that. We had our own designs. That made him happy and we stayed very good friends over the years."

In Spratling's autobiography he tells about a strike that took place at the Las Delicias workshop. We ask Castillo what he remembers about the incident.

"Some of the silversmiths were being influenced by outside forces to make excessive demands. One of the things they said they wanted was ten restrooms. Why did we need ten restrooms? We barely used the four we had. They wanted to make a union. I studied the issues and thought they were making crazy demands. The shop was divided. I went to Sr. Spratling and told him I thought these were silly issues. We were having a meeting the next night and he told me that I should speak my mind at the meeting.

"I stood up the next night and said that I thought these demands were putting the whole shop at risk. I explained why and then I told the people who agreed with me to step forward. Most did and soon we were back to work."

Spratling recalled this as an "act of courage and integrity, qualities that have added world prestige to Castillo Silver."

While we're talking a worker from next door brings in a piece for Castillo's inspection. He holds it, studies it, turns it right and left. He softly instructs the worker to make a change, explaining his reasoning in detail. I can't help comparing his gentle words to Spratling's "*Ay chingado.*"

He speaks about the satisfaction of his profession.

"My favorite thing is the creativity. I love to pick up a stone and think about how to work with it, how it will fit best in a piece. I always think of a specific person when I am designing a work and imagine how it will look on that person. Take this, for example."

He pulls a stone out of his front pocket and rubs it gently, almost reverently. It's a pre-Columbian piece that he will incorporate into one of his works.

"My daughter bought this and gave it to me a few days ago. She knows that I love pre-Columbian jewelry. I've been thinking since then about the best way to show its properties, how to set it off. I just remembered some other stones I have from an ancient necklace and I am trying to decide if they can work together."

As he talks he looks at the stone as he might a child, wondering what it will become. He seems to want to guide it to become the best that it can be, but it's almost as if he believes that the ultimate responsibility is up to the stone itself.

Always curious about a designer's personal jewelry, we ask Castillo about a ring he wears. He explains that the pattern, a stylized version of a parrot's head in profile, was created by his brother Chato. It won first place in a countrywide design competition many years ago. As he talks he lifts his shirt to show his belt buckle, which features the same design. His pants are not unzipped, but the cloth over the zipper is slightly folded back. He smoothes the cloth, embarrassed over what he perceives as an impropriety. He says that he made the belt over fifty years ago and then later made the ring to match. He wears them both every day.

The worker brings the unfinished piece back. Castillo studies it again and makes another change. Although his manner is distinct, he appears to be just as much a perfectionist as Spratling was.

Bryan asks Castillo if he has an apprentice system. Castillo proudly nods and explains that he's taught almost 200 people to work silver. His apprentices start with him when they are about fifteen years old. They go to school in the morning and then to the shop in the afternoon. It's men like Castillo who not only kept Spratling's dream alive, but expanded and improved upon it. Spratling worked with silver in Taxco for thirty-six years. Castillo has been doing it for sixty-three years. We ask if there's any one student that he's particularly proud of, and he beams, "My daughter."

Castillo's daughter Emilia is an amazing artist. Two-time winner of the prestigious Taxco Presidential Award, she has taken silver work to another level. By developing a technique to fuse silver to porcelain she has created objects that are both unique and beautiful. Graceful and smooth ceramic plates, bowls, and vases shimmer with hundreds of gleaming silver fish or stars. The effect is stunning.

He invites us to follow his employee next door. *Talleres de Los Castillo* (the Castillos' workshop) is painted at the beginning of a long white wall, broken by at least twenty arched entries. We walk into an extended open space with natural light flowing in through the curved doorways and windows. Multiple worktables painted royal blue hold pieces in different states of completion. Radios fill the room with competing tunes. If Spratling's shop was a shrine, this is a revival.

We've heard from the experts over and over again during our time in Taxco that the single most important thing to look for in a piece of silver jewelry is that it be handmade. Many of the shops in town sell pieces stamped out by machines, but here, as well as down the highway at Spratling's, each item is carefully created by hand.

We go back to the store to spend more time with Castillo. Eventually we ask him about Berta's. He sits back in his chair and his smiling eyes crinkle at the edges.

"You know, before, when Taxco wasn't so busy, nobody drove on that side of the plaza. Doña Berta used to set up chairs and even a few tables in the street in front of her bar. It was the place everybody went. Doña Berta was already older by then, but she kept a tight grip on things.

"Sr. Spratling used to go there every afternoon. I mean *every* afternoon. We would meet him over there and drink Bertas. They were so cheap. They only cost five *centavos*. We had lots of good times."

Visitors never knew what famous Mexican artists or international socialites might be there at Berta's mingling with the poets, authors, writers, painters, and pretenders. One thing is for sure: they were all drinking. In *Beyond the Mexique Bay,* Aldous Huxley sarcastically recalls the time:

> Taxco is a sort of Mexican Saint-Paul largely inhabited by artists and by those camp followers of the arts whose main contribution to the cause of Intellectual Beauty consists in being partially or completely drunk for several hours each day.

Bryan and I look around the store to see if there is anything that catches our attention. Bryan has never worn any type of jewelry, and I usually keep mine small and simple. Today I am wearing a single ring on my left hand and that's it. No watch, no necklace, no earrings. To Sr. Castillo I must look naked.

Most of Castillo's pieces are heavier and chunkier than I would ever wear. Spratling wrote that the key design elements for silver are "surface and body, plus a good convincing weight." Castillo seems to agree. Even though it's not my style, we want to buy something. Once we get to know an artist we like to have a reminder of time spent with him. Especially with somebody as sincere and interesting as Castillo.

We ask him about a pendant in silver and lapis that looks like a type of beetle. We've heard about the *jumil*, an insect that people in the Taxco area eat with regularity. Sure enough, that's what it is. He begins to tell us about the bug.

"Do you know about the *jumil* festival? It's in November. The first Monday after *día de los muertos*, Day of the Dead, on November first. People go into the mountains to collect the bugs and then they make a salsa out of them. It's a good salsa; you should try it. It's high in iodine. Some people even eat them plain. Lots of iodine."

We ask if the *jumiles* are available year-round. His assistant, who is a nurse, says that there is a specific season for the bugs. It has just started because she saw some in the market in Taxco yesterday for the first time in a few months.

As unique as the *jumil* pendant is, I can't see myself wearing a big blue-and-silver beetle around my neck.

When we get back to Taxco we head straight to the market. We have decided to ask our new friends in the kitchen to make us some *jumil* salsa. We enter the market and start asking around for the bugs. We are sent deeper and deeper into the fray. Cutting through the meat section, I concentrate on keeping my gaze low and holding my breath. Nothing will ruin your appetite for insects like fly-covered entrails.

We finally arrive at a stand selling tortillas and herbs. We ask for *jumiles* and the woman pulls out a small plastic bag. The bag is moving. The bugs are *alive*. For some reason I expected them to be dead. There are about thirty brownish insects in the bag, along with some leaves for them to munch on. Each *jumil* is about half an inch long, disturbingly beetle-like in its slightly triangular shape. We ask our vendor about making the salsa.

"You need to buy *tomatillos* and serrano peppers. Roast the peppers and tomatoes and then throw them and the bugs in the blender. It's a great salsa. And really high in iodine."

It has been made very clear that *jumiles* are an excellent source of iodine, a deficiency of it being the single most common cause of preventable mental retardation and brain damage in the world. A *jumil* a year leaves nothing to fear.

We buy the bag of bugs for twenty cents and walk across the aisle to a vegetable stand to buy the tomatoes and peppers for another thirty-five cents. We arrive at the kitchen of our hotel with our supplies in hand. The cook smiles and says he'd be happy to make some salsa. Looking around the restaurant we are quite sure we're not taking him away from any other work.

"I love *jumil* salsa," he enthuses through a mouth missing a canine tooth. "It's so much fun in November when we go up in the mountains to catch them. We go in the morning and set up picnics. Everybody from town is up there. They run special buses all day. We have great barbecues with fresh *jumil* salsa. They're very high in iodine, you know."

We indicate that we've heard rumor of such.

"Oh, yes, very high in iodine. Some people just throw them on the grill and eat them roasted, but I like them in the salsa. Relatives come down from the United States for the festival. Some of them dry out the *jumiles* and take them back in a powder so that they can have *jumil* salsa all year. You should do that too."

I ask him if he puts the bugs into the blender alive and his reply is positive. Yuck. The salsa is ready a few hours later, after it has cooked and the flavors have mingled. It looks like a regular green salsa, only it's flecked with lots of black spots. I'm convinced that the black spots are little bug legs and wings, but Bryan thinks they are bits of charred tomatoes and chiles from the grill. The cook hands us each a heated corn tortilla and we dig in. The salsa has a sharp, almost metallic undertaste, but is pretty good. We fill a couple more tortillas and tell him to take the rest home to his family—so that they can get their iodine.

When Berta's Bar is open, the small doorway and bright green shutters around the windows upstairs give the building the appearance of a startled little face. The bar inside is rib high and about eight feet long. Three men prop themselves against it while sitting on tall green stools. Behind it a wooden cabinet holds glasses and bottles of liquor.

A large picture of Berta hangs on the wall to the right of the cabinet. In it she stands behind the bar, pouring her famous drink. She looks more like a Sunday school teacher than a bartender. Her hair is pinned up in a bun and she wears a conservative dress.

We wedge ourselves into the little remaining space at the bar and ask innocently if there are any special drinks here. The bartender proudly announces that we must try the Berta, invented here over sixty years ago. After ordering two Bertas we ask the bartender about the drink's namesake. She died before he was born, so he directs us to Don Séptimo.

Before we can watch our drinks being made, Don Séptimo invites us up a narrow set of stairs to a small green table on the newly built second floor. I bend to sit down and am surprised as I continue down, down before hitting the seat. All the chairs in the bar are only about a foot off the floor. The tables are all equally low. It's like a daycare center. I find it quite humorous for three grown people to be having a conversation with their knees up around their ears.

Don Séptimo, about sixty years old, is extremely serious about any information he imparts. He wears tan polyester pants and a plaid polyester shirt halfway unbuttoned to reveal four silver chains: a silver crucifix, an Indian head, a brown rock, and a silver coin hang in a tangle of chest hair at the end of the chains.

Don Séptimo has a bit of a speech impediment, so we both have to lean forward and concentrate to understand him. I realize by watching his front teeth move while he talks that the lisp is due to an ill-fitting plate. I'm mesmerized by the wriggling teeth and find it hard to focus on what he's saying.

He talks to us about Berta. According to Séptimo, Doña Berta Estrada Gómez opened the bar in 1930 when she was thirty-two years old. Doña Berta was a good Creole, a Catholic woman who went to church every day. She was also strong-charactered, *muy fuerte*, and wouldn't stand for nonsense in her bar. After reading about all the drunken gringos in Taxco who regularly liquored up here, I wonder what her definition of nonsense was.

Don Séptimo then states matter-of-factly that "she died young," *se murió joven*. Bryan and I look at each other in confusion. If she died young, who's that gray-haired lady in that picture on the wall? It pains Séptimo to have to remind us that "died young" is a euphemism for spinsters who had never "known" a man.

Ah yes, a sainted virgin—of course. What Don Séptimo is saying is that although Berta lived to old age, she maintained the high moral status that Mexican society associates with virginity. As explained by

Octavio Paz in his book *Labyrinth of Solitude*, the macho element in Mexican culture views any "opening up" as evidence of vulnerability. Any unmarried woman who has lost her virginity is stereotypically seen as inferior, weak, and untrustworthy. Of unmarried women, only those who have never "known" a man can stand high on the pedestal to represent purity, honor, and decency—women like Berta.

Don Séptimo tells us we need to talk to Don Pineda, the current owner of the bar and Berta's cousin. Don Pineda has a jewelry store across the plaza on the other side of the church. Suddenly, Don Séptimo jumps up and walks downstairs, leaving us sitting in our baby chairs. We watch him cross in front of the church and disappear into a store.

In the meantime our drinks have arrived. Served over ice and topped off with mineral water, the mysterious liquid inside our Collins glasses beckons. It's the moment of the tasting, the reason we're here. We toast what we hope is the origin of the margarita and bring the glasses to our lips.

Right at that moment Séptimo returns with Don Pineda. We put our glasses down and struggle out of our Playskool furniture. Don Pineda looks to be in his seventies. Slender and shrunken, he's wearing thick gray suspenders over a starched blue polyester outfit. The smell of a minty mouthwash accompanies him whenever he speaks.

It turns out that he is not Berta's cousin. In fact, his knowledge of Berta is overshadowed by the fact that he prefers to talk about himself. We soon understand why he has ordered a beer. Every time he makes what he considers an important statement, he picks up his glass and says, "*Salud.*" Etiquette demands that we hoist our much stronger Bertas to our lips and return his toast. After our first sip of the Berta we look at each other excitedly, but cannot interrupt Don Pineda. He has launched into a complicated story about the Parroquia's clock. The anecdote involves a German-Swiss, Big Ben, copies of telegrams from 1976 that he pulls out of his pocket, town controversy, and the BBC, *salud.* The gist of the story is that the clock is *el hermano de Big Ben*, Big Ben's brother, *salud*, and he is its sponsor, *salud*, because he paid for it to be repaired, *salud.* Bryan and I think this is all well and good except that the damn thing doesn't work, *salud.*

The tequila infuses our surroundings with exceptional effulgence. Our Berthas taste unmistakably like margaritas, just a little fizzier. Don Pineda excuses himself to retire to his house and we practically run downstairs. Pushing our way to the bar, we order two more Bertas and stand there to watch them being made.

We follow a mental checklist. Tequila, lime juice, and orange liqueur are the flavors we need. The bartender fills a Collins glass with ice and pours in a liberal shot of José Cuervo white tequila. Check. An equal amount of fresh lime juice follows. Check. He then pulls a mason jar out from underneath the bar counter and dribbles in an equal amount of some secret ingredient. This is topped off with a bit of mineral water and stirred. What's in the jar? We need our last check mark.

Again we are directed to Don Séptimo. "That's Berta's special honey. It has eucalyptus and orange leaves. When she first started making the drink it was before Taxco had electricity. She had to cook the honey at home over a wood-burning fire."

Orange liqueur sounds like a good substitute for orange leaves and honey thinned with a little mineral water to me. Check. That's it. We've found it. Bertha's Bar, 1931. Hollywood movie stars and Texas socialites, step aside. If justice had been served, Jimmy Buffett would be crooning, "Wasting away again in Berthaville."

I think about William Spratling and his lasting influence on almost everything that's famous about Taxco today. The reference that sent us running to Taxco in the first place was from his autobiography. How could it not be?

> I took him [John Dos Passos] to Berta's Cantina where . . . I had Berta prepare him a tall lemonade with a hefty slug of tequila in it. This was a sort of tequila collins and it proved so delicious a drink that gradually all our friends became addicted. Actually this concoction later became known as a 'Berta,' a drink which is now universally in demand all over Mexico, even in the fanciest bars. Recently, perhaps in order to lose sights of its humble origin, the drink has become famous as a 'Marguerita.'

Vintage Spratling. *Salud.*

Resources

Baker, Charles. *The Gentleman's Companion.* New York: Crown Publishers, 1946.

"Barroom Brawl." *Texas Monthly,* July 1991.

Castrejón Diez, Jaime. *Santa Prisca Taxco.* México: Editorial Santa Prisca, 1998.

Clark, Sydney. *All the Best in Mexico.* New York: Dodd, Mead, & Co., 1949.

Cooper, Brad. "The Man Who Invented the Margarita." *Texas Monthly,* October 1974, 76-78.

Cortés de Figueroa, Leslie. *Taxco, the Enchanted City.* México, DF: Editorial Fischgrund, 1950.

Foscue, Edwin Jay. *Taxco, Mexico's Silver City.* Dallas: University Press, 1947.

Huxley, Aldous. *Beyond the Mexique Bay.* New York: Harper and Brothers, 1934.

Jackson, Joseph Henry. *Mexican Interlude.* New York: MacMillan, 1936.

Jacobsen, Richard. "Opposition Governors Try to Kill Time Change." *The News,* March 28, 2000, 3.

Mark, Joan. *The Silver Gringo: William Spratling and Taxco.* Albuquerque: University of New Mexico Press, 2000.

Martin, Paul, ed. *World Encyclopedia of Cocktails.* London: St. Edmundsbury Press, 1997.

Paz, Octavio. *The Labyrinth of Solitude.* New York: Grove Press, 1961.

Sharpe, Patricia. "Viva Tequila." *Texas Monthly,* August 1995, 74-79.

Spratling, William. *Little Mexico.* New York: Jonathan Cape & Harrison Smith, 1932.

Terry, T. Philip. *Terry's Guide to Mexico.* Boston: Houghton Mifflin, 1932.

Tiano, Jack. *American Bartender's School Guide to Drinks.* New York: Rutledge Press, 1981.

Toor, Frances. *Motorist Guide to Mexico.* Mexico City: Frances Toor Studios, 1938.

Wilhelm, John. *Guide to All Mexico.* New York: McGraw-Hill, 1959.

Top: A field of blue agave awaits harvest under the shadow of Mt. Tequila.

Left: Valente Nieto Real shapes a pot, called a *cántaro*, which is traditionally used to hold either water or mezcal.

Right: Among Taxco's picturesque hills can be found Berta's Bar, the birthplace of the margarita.

Below: After agaves are harvested, their hearts, the *piñas*, are steamed to transform their starches into sugars. These sugars are released in their juice when they are crushed. By double-distilling the agave juice, tequila is produced.

Above: After the smoked and crushed *maguey* hearts ferment, the liquid seen here, called *mosto*, is transferred in plastic buckets to the distillation still.

Left: After distillation, tequila must be aged in oak for a minimum of two months to be called *reposado.* The huge oak casks at the José Cuervo plant show the size of the Cuervo operation.

Top: Many people erroneously believe that tequila has a worm in the bottom of the bottle. Only mezcal has the worm, and only a single type of mezcal—*mezcal de gusano.*

Right: This statue in the José Cuervo plant freezes a *jimador* in mid-stroke as he shaves the leaves off an agave plant with his finely sharpened *coa.*

UPSIDE-DOWN MARGARITA

CANCÚN AND HOLBOX ISLANDS

Taxi, señor?" the white-uniformed driver at the head of the taxi queue outside of our hotel asks politely.

"*No, gracias*," I say.

"Hey lady, you want Maya tour?" rasps a woman a few steps later.

Becky replies, "*No, gracias*."

In a beat we hear, "*¡Hola, chicos!* Information?" from the next doorway.

We dodge the gauntlet of shills en route to Cancún's buffed torso, the Forum by the Sea Mall, a spiraling shopping center that seduces with showy attire and a cool interior. Inside is the resort's hottest disco, Coco Bongo, the throbbing heart of the lanky isle. Its thundering bass pulsates and broils, Bahboom! Bahboom! Bahboom! Below the midriff, vines and palms surrounding the vibrant Rainforest Cafe create a tuft of wild tropical foliage. Just in front of this the three-story-high Hard Rock Cafe guitar juts upward, angling away from the mall's belly.

On this lanky swath of limestone and sand rages a fragment of the modern Bacchanalian festival honoring the passing of winter. Thousands of college students from across the United States make a pilgrimage to Cancún to cut loose and imbibe amid the euphoric revelry of spring break.

Evening has snuck up on the Forum's beach bar. Swimwear soaks up the billow of sweat like petite hankies as the youths jostle and whoop in this generation's version of *Beach Blanket Bingo*. Their wrists are banded with multicolored fluorescent plastic bracelets, one of which grants them all-you-can-drink rights at this venue, while the rest are merit badges from a glorious haze. Most of the revelers cart around three-foot-long drinking glasses known as *yardas*, from which they quaff effervescent beers and syrupy cocktails. Spontaneous hoots prove epidemic and echo throughout the crowd. The partygoers chug up and down like pistons energized by rap, hip-hop, Latino pop, and steroidal dance beats. Lateral movements are not so consistently fluid. When a mission requires crossing the sand, all semblance of balance disappears and numb, rubbery limbs knock over plastic chairs and tables.

A DJ equipped with a high-powered microphone and spotlight interrupts the music with an exuberant report: "He's going up, up, up, and away!"

The spotlight beam swerves from the frenetic troupe of dancers to a bubble-shaped rock a few feet from shore. On it a couple gropes and slurps, not at all oblivious to their exhibitionism. The eager buck maneuvers a caressing hand up his companion's white halter top and upon hearing the play-by-play raises his free hand in a victory salute. The young woman reacts by pushing him off abruptly with seeming indignity. After wobbling to a sitting position, she squints into the probing beam. She gives the crowd a sloppy smile, then dives tongue-first back into the passion.

The spotlight darts to another nearby rock protruding from the shallow Caribbean water. Here a stocky young man is armed with two flashlights that shoot out stiff, glowing strands of fluorescent light, one green and the other purple. His pudgy form gyrates and jukes in eloquent, physics-mocking choreography. His arms weave like wrestling snakes, synchronized to the rapidly paced music. The crowd shouts in admiration, which elicits a smile from the dancer, his teeth glowing radioactive green from the liquid fluorescent stick nestled in his mouth.

"He's going down for the count!" The spotlight ogles the amorous couple again.

The young woman lies motionless except for rocking hips as the young man kisses his way up her thighs toward the hem of her miniskirt. The crowd cheers as though she is a sacrificial virgin. Suddenly the young woman startles. She pulls her knees deftly toward her chest. Then with a decisive thrust of her feet, she launches her lover into the water. She staggers to stand up, but can't maintain her balance and belly flops into the foamy waves herself.

Meanwhile, the throng that had been dancing on the beach invades Gropers' Rock to collectively usurp the spotlight. Blazing, exalted, the revelers jump, undulate, and shimmy as waves splash up around them.

Cancún is a seven-mile long island off the snout of the Yucatán Peninsula, but separation from the mainland is so negligible that many people don't even realize that it's not connected. The island, only a kilometer wide for the most part, forms a slender rectangular track around the Nichupte Lagoon. On the short ends of the rectangle are two narrow waterways crossed by bridges spanning only a few hundred yards, which can be missed in a blink.

A beach in Cancún.

The Spanish were the first Europeans to see the island. Though several Mayan structures were visible from the ocean, the conquistadors shunned Cancún, opting to set up base on the island of Cozumel. Other than hosting a few coconut plantations and a temporary military airport during World War II, Cancún remained unpopulated for 450 years.

That changed dramatically in 1968 when Banco de México concluded that an aggressive tourism strategy would generate badly needed foreign revenue. After a thorough study of Mexico's geography, the central bank identified Cancún's powdery white sand and calm blue Caribbean water as the perfect oasis to be developed. With a $22 million loan from the Inter-American Bank, the Mexican government built an airport, a golf course, and roads as well as other infrastructure. By 1974 direct flights from Mexico had been established and migrant workers had populated Cancún City, located on the mainland near the island's northern link. The first hotels were erected, among them the Camino Real and the Aristos, both still in operation, and it appeared that the project was well on its way to meeting its 5,000-hotel-room objective.

Today Cancún boasts 26,000 rooms in about 100 hotels. This might seem like hospitality overkill, but during this month of spring break the island is booked to 100 percent capacity. This is a mixed blessing for hoteliers, who appreciate the revenue but prefer their island to be known as the family-friendly spot it is the other fifty weeks per year. Flights here from the United States are as cheap and convenient as the one we took from Mexico City. The three million visitors per year bring in more than $2 billion, evidence that at least one international bank loan to Latin America was not squandered.

Giant gleaming hotels blockade the beach that runs along the outside perimeter of the island. Driving on the island's two-lane road, you will never see the ocean. You get several views of the lagoon, which is the very plain sister of a beauty queen as far as waterscapes go. Most of the restaurants, malls, and travel services occupy the lagoon side. Every imaginable multinational food chain is present—McDonald's, Burger King, Domino's, Outback, Planet Hollywood—as well as a handful of successful Mexican chains, the most prominent of which is the Anderson Group, owners of Mexican beach resort cornerstones Señor Frog's and Carlos & Charlie's.

This small island abruptly impaled with hundreds of international hotels and chain restaurants in no way resembles any other place in Mexico, except similarly planned beach resorts such as Ixtapa and Huatulco, which were targeted and built to Cancún specifications. Foreigners who come here get an English-speaking locale with a slight Mexican accent. It is an ideal gringo version of the country, one that caters to south-of-the-border fantasies—a Pancho Villa theme park, an upside-down Mexico.

The first time I had an upside-down margarita was in a resort town. It doesn't really matter which one; take your pick. The bar was packed, the music was American rock'n'roll, women showed off their tans and painted toenails, and the men brandished biceps and beer bellies. We were all slamming straight shots of tequila, slamming them harder and faster than any Mexican desperado we could imagine. We were macho, all of us, even the women. Lick the salt! Slam the shot! Suck the lime! Shout your craziest *grito*! Ayyyyy-yiiiii-yaaaaiiiii-aaaaaay!

A Mexican waitress approached our group in cut-offs that burrowed into her lower concavities and tiny bikini triangles that strained to cover her upper convexities. She was armed with a bottle of tequila in one hand and a bottle of margarita mix in the other. She danced me into a barber's chair (Where the hell did that come from? I must be *borracho*!) Thunk! The chair dropped to a backward tilt past ninety degrees as the woman climbed onto a short stool just behind my head. A stream of tequila fell five feet into my mouth. A stream of margarita mix followed. Some of the beverage splashed on my face, but it didn't matter because soon two triangular bikini-top napkins absorbed the excess. The woman was blowing a whistle and furiously shaking my head to mix the two parts into one.

Only later would I learn by observation that Mexicans don't drink this way. I've never seen a Mexican slam a straight shot of tequila, never seen one shoot a fizzy tequila and soda-pop *mopet* (mix tequila and Sprite in a shot glass, slam it on the counter, then swig before it overflows), nor have I seen one endure the inane, self-incited whiplash of an upside-down margarita. I'm sure there is the occasional oddball Mexican who does, but in reality these rites are created specifically for gringo titillation.

Although I've been to the Yucatán Peninsula several times, I have never been to Cancún. I either sought out the then barely developed beach town of Playa del Carmen for relaxation, or Cozumel for diving. Though I've stayed a few nights in resort hotels on the Mexican Pacific, I've also managed to avoid those instead by heading to surf beaches where palm thatch huts are the norm. Becky came to Cancún as a preteen with her family when there were only a handful of hotels and hundreds of coconut palms. She fondly tells me about chasing enormous iguanas from the beach into the tropical foliage leaving the perfect folds of sand indented with tail tracks and footprints.

We hit the beach as soon as we can drop our bags and change clothes. Our hotel features a series of linking pools sashed with lush gardens. At the far end of the last pool a water aerobics class splashes to hypnotic dance music that has been allotted a miserly portion of lyrics. The words repeat over and over during the song, and in fact, continue to do so long after, because no matter how much the music offends your tastes, the damned songs are so catchy that you find yourself singing them later in the day.

I'm excited to snorkel. That's what I really liked about Cozumel. While the diving there was first class, even better than the Great Barrier Reef in my opinion, what I found particularly enchanting was that you could go for a quick dip in front of your hotel, just to cool off, and marvel at hundreds of exotic fish while snorkeling.

I'm as giddy as a five-year-old boy as we walk on blinding white sand toward Caribbean water that is a more brilliant blue than the swimming pool. I strap on fins and a mask and plug a snorkel into my mouth as Becky leisurely spreads sun block on her body. Not me; I'm off, tripping over my flippers all the way to the water, dunking into its sparkling clear coolness and opening my eyes like a fish to peer through the glass and see . . . sand. There is only sand, no sea life. A half hour of kicking earns me sightings of a couple of pipefish as well as a sunburned back.

Becky has slipped into a novel. She lies on a reclining chair half shaded by the palm-thatched beach umbrella, but I can't sit still. I decide to check the activity list to see when beach volleyball begins. The activity director, Francisco, advises me that the game will start in about forty-five minutes. He has typical Mayan features, as far as I can grossly generalize—short black hair, dark brown skin with a bronze gloss, a wide arrowhead nose, and a brilliant smile. He is young and quite fit, but he is shorter than I am so I can't imagine he will be a demon on the volleyball court. I learn that Francisco is from an inland village that he visits every weekend so he can keep in touch with his family and keep tabs on his video arcade business.

I ask him about the impact the Cancún resort development has had on the locals. "For me, for us, all of the Mayan people, I think it's an excellent thing. Do you know how much people earn working in my village? Two dollars a day."

"I know this damages, kills the flora and fauna," he says, gesturing to a trio of passing jet skiers and swinging his hand so the arc includes the hotel, his employer, "but we need the work, and we work hard. We deserve a good standard of living like anybody else. For us Cancún is the United States. We are like the Mexicans in the north who cross the border to work for the gringos, except we don't need a *coyote* to sneak us here."

On the way back to our spot on the beach, I'm distracted by the commotion surrounding four dazzling sculpted, oiled goddesses in glittering bikinis. A photographer peers at them through the lens of a tripod-based camera so simple that it looks like a Kodak Instamatic even though it is cutting-edge digital. Each of these American beauties exhibits a lot of exotically toned skin from distinct origins—Asian, African, European, and East Indian. The current spring break shoot, which now captures the girls sprawling on top of a huge colorful beach ball imprinted with the logo "bikini.com," is a joint venture between that company and MTV. All of the girls, it is difficult not to notice, have invested in unnaturally round artificial breasts. They're cannonballs loaded into slingshots—tools of the trade, I suppose.

These women did not ascend to become bikini.com supermodels, their official title, based on their physical attributes alone. During and after the photo shoot they are extremely patient and interactive with their admirers, even when one happens to be a loud, balding, middle-aged man whose back is a hilly battleground of fat orange freckles and body hair. They pose for a photo with him and flirt and laugh with others in the crowd. They seem to have a fabulous time kicking the beach ball to a boxer. The dog is obsessed with trying to bite the ball, but instead bops it with his nose whenever he tries to sink in his teeth, flattening it when he finally does.

I ask one of the supermodels, the Asian American, Lola, what she has been doing with her free time in Cancún. She laughs. "Sleeping as much as possible. This is exhausting work." I can tell by the tone in her voice that it must be true.

Francisco, the hotel's activity director, is lacking in stature but possesses confounding spin on his serves and finesse on his dink shots. He sweeps up the volleyball court with my sorry butt while Becky logs some time on an exercise bike in the hotel gym.

I finish with my game before she returns, so I force myself to wring some contentment from this paradise by ordering a frosty Corona. Soon the otherworldly ocean entrances me. I decide that its color is neither blue nor green, though it often seems like one or the other. When I compare it to a green palm frond fluttering overhead, the water is blue, but when I compare it to the sky, the water is green. As I walk toward it I perceive electric blue like a neon light, but when my toes splash into the water the sun's reflection off the sand makes it a sparkling green opal. Beyond the buoy line of the swimming area the ocean is striped like a blueberry and blackberry parfait. A huge regatta of Laser sailboats, protruding from the water like shark teeth, cruises toward Isla de Mujeres.

The walk along the beach from our hotel to Fat Tuesday's takes us past numerous high-rise hotels. The beaches in front of them are an unkempt dormitory strewn with sun-tanning college students. We are surprised to pass a section of private homes, really mansions that look like mutant huts and stodgy structures that forgot to leave neoclassical architecture behind in the big city along with the starched long-sleeved shirts. These are obviously owned by Mexican families because the teenagers that pertain to them lounge out front. Even though the beach here is a broad and lengthy band, about fifteen teens squeeze together on three towels. They exchange friendly catcalls with their friends just offshore, who occupy gleaming ski boats and jet skis. Someday very soon, the players in the hotel industry will offer a bundle of cash for these homes so that they will have somewhere to construct the thousand rooms they do each year.

As we near the ferry dock, we come upon the *playa popular*. Used this way, the term *popular* in Spanish is a euphemism for "nonexclusive," which I suppose is my own euphemism for "poor." Whenever a Mexican refers to a neighborhood as a *colonia popular*, you can be sure it is one that everyone would like to move out of, not into. An amazingly well conceived law in Mexico is that none of the ocean beaches can be private. This is a very good thing. At lakes where no such law applies, public access simply does not exist; the wealthy alone are able to swim. Even though all of Cancún's beaches are public, the majority of locals come to this spot. I assume they just feel more comfortable here or come here because it's the closest beach to town.

FAT TUESDAY'S is spelled out in huge purple letters above the back of the building so you can see it from the beach. There is no way you could miss it anyway, with the music blaring and the impromptu roars erupting from the crowd. Fat Tuesday's is *the* daytime spot. Most of the patrons have on as little clothing as possible; there are bare-chested guys in shorts, girls in shorts and bikini tops, and everyone in sport sandals.

Most Mexicans will not wear sandals in public, except at the beach or in a gymnasium shower, for fear of looking *indio,* like an Indian, (a racist term with added classist insult; saying this is an efficient way of being a total jerk). On this trip I couldn't find my sandals in one of our hotel rooms so I checked with the maid. When she showed me where she put them she referred to them as *huaraches*. This term suggests a couple of straps of leather attached to a flat piece of rubber, usually from an old car tire. Just by coming to Mexico my high-priced, state-of-the-art sandals—extreme sportswear utilized by all the best rafting guides, as the salesman informed me—had been reduced to the status of *huaraches*. My feet are duly humbled.

Fat Tuesday's is hopping. The scantily attired throng masses into a small amphitheater-like dance area to sweat and grind in the sunshine. Occasionally the DJ tosses in a retro tune like one of the old hits from "Grease" or a Village People song. These are our folk songs if you think about it. They're the ones that everyone knows the words to, and that rally the crowd to the dance floor and tabletops.

The drinks here are frozen daiquiris that spin around and around in a row of miniature blending machines. The spectacular colors represent flavors such as Blue Demon, 180 Octane, Purple Passion, and Tropical Itch. These are sucked down in *yarda* glasses until the drinker incurs the wrath of brain freeze.

Today's events in the amphitheater, not intended for mature audiences, include a wet boxer contest for male competitors, a wet T-shirt contest for female contestants, and hottest kiss for both. The most entertaining competition, however, is the swimsuit swap. A guy wearing shorts and a T-shirt and a girl wearing a bikini team up. Competing against other couples, they dash to the ocean, submerging deep enough to shield themselves, then swap clothes. The surprise is that the women are sufficiently competent, through years of experience, to accomplish the task without compromising themselves at all. The men, however, do not fit in the bikini pieces, so they feebly try to cover themselves on the podium by crossing their arms and legs over their bodies. If you see a husky guy in a tiny bikini cower in such a modest, defensive pose, it makes you laugh.

On the way out of the Fat Tuesday's we stop by the temporary tattoo booth to check out the designs. These bold tattoos last several days and initially look quite authentic. The skulls are menacing, the belly button lace is sexy, and the hearts are sappy. We decide that the temporary tattoo is the perfect symbol for Cancún. Here you can desert your inhibitions, dance with abandon, and unleash primal screams.

You can always go back to your old self, routine, and society in a few days when the ink fades.

One might consider imprinting oneself with a tattoo while in Cancún a centuries-old fashion statement. Friar Diego De Landa reported in his comprehensive study of Mayan customs in 1566:

> The women pierce the cartilage of the nose within, to take a stone of amber for adornment. They also pierce the ears for rings in the manner of their husbands; they too tattoo the body from the waist up, the patterns being more delicate and beautiful than those of the men.

Look around any bar in Cancún and you realize that styles persevere.

ancún has changed, however, at least from the point of view of architecture. It has grown taller with age.

When Thomas Gann visited in 1924, he encountered

> great numbers of ruined temples and buildings all along the coast of Cancuen, together with innumerable mounds, probably burial-places of the caciques and chief priests of the ancient inhabitants. There was no attempt at centralizing the main buildings and raising them on platforms as at Tuluum. On the contrary, they seemed to have been dumped down anyhow, and strung out over probably a couple of miles of coast.

A few of the ruins survived the tourism development. One small set is on the grounds of the Sheraton Hotel. The ruins we decide to visit, El Rey, are surrounded by the César Park golf course.

"Taxi, señor?"

"Hey, lady, you want Maya tour?"

"*¡Hola, chicos!* Information?

The ruins are spread out over a narrow lawn of manicured grass. As you look down the green concourse, light gray structures in various stages of crumble line either side. Beyond the end of the field, a brilliant white pyramid rises up completely intact, taller even than those in Chichén Itzá and Tulum, but another look reveals it to be the Hilton. Beefy iguanas, camouflaged on the limestone blocks, warm their bodies in the sun.

In his book, *In an Unknown Land*, Gann describes his visit to these ruins.

> It was here, that we came across the best preserved building on the island, known grandiloquently to the laborers—the only people who had seen it—as "El Palacio del Rey." Just between the doors, stood—or rather squatted—the stucco figure of the King of Cancuen which gave the building its name. Unfortunately a mischievous Mexican peon had, with labour incomprehensible in one of his class—except when engaged in some work of iconoclasm—pried the king loose and tumbled him down on the ground, smashing the limbs and lower part of the body beyond hope of repair, but fortunately leaving the head and head-dress very little injured.
>
> The Mexican, we were informed, had died very painfully within two weeks of his act of vandalism, his death being looked upon by the other laborers as a direct visitation of the wrath of the ancient god for desecration of his sanctuary; and who shall say that his death, however brought about, was undeserved?
>
> Undeterred by the fate of the Mexican, I arranged with the (plantation) manager to have the head brought over to the landing by some of the laborers, from whence, on my return, I could carry it away on the Lilian Y, as I greatly feared that it might be smashed by some of the Indians, or carried off by a curio hunter. To this he was quite agreeable, and, in fact, rather pleased at getting rid of a relic with such a sinister reputation, not without some slight pecuniary profit to himself. Unfortunately, I was unable to call at the island on the return journey owing to contrary winds and tides, so presumably El Rey still rules over his ancient kingdom of Cuncuen.

In fact, El Rey does rule over his ancient kingdom, or at least his severed head does, from the archeological museum in the Cancún Convention Center.

At night Cancún's two lanes clog with traffic. For those lodged in hotels at the south end of the island, a high opportunity cost is the time-consuming commute into the party center of Cancún. Fortunately, there are cheap buses that run up and down the strip, and that cost less than a buck per ride. Another great thing about these buses is that they are BYOB. Just hop on with a six-pack and not only will you stay refreshed for the length of the ride, but you'll also make several friends. This custom turns the public transport into a tavern on wheels. Bottles are freely uncapped and cigarette smoke thickens the air.

The pick-up scene is quite active on the buses. Becky listens to a freshman brag about how many E-mail addresses he has acquired on the trip. I am watching a crew-cut lad with a thick neck meet a young lady from a town near his. When she mentions where she attended high school he informs her that he went to a nearby school. He then tells her exactly how many touchdowns he scored against her school. Since she is a junior in college such a feat fails to impress her. He continues to insist on informing her of how many touchdowns he chalked up against any other school that can be worked into the conversation. If her reaction is a trend, he will be held scoreless this evening.

I stand squashed in the aisle among fifty other perspiring souls, but Becky is lucky enough to snag a seat. She is staring sleepily outside when the full upper torso of a limber college youth lunges into the bus through her window. He begins to fall from the slowly moving vehicle, but hangs there long enough to shout, "You're beautiful! Get off the bus!"

She does get off the bus, eventually—both of us do—but it is farther down the road, directly in front of the glowing Hard Rock guitar. Across the street DADY'O is spelled out in gargantuan fiberglass block letters designed to look like chiseled granite. A half-hour wait in line and $20 each earns us bright orange all-you-can-drink plastic bands strapped around our wrists. It is just before 10 PM, fairly early by disco standards, so we can move relatively unobstructed upstairs to over look six other levels of dance floors.

We zip through the drink line without a problem for the first round, but as soon as we finish our first flimsy plastic cups of beer the bar line represents about a fifteen-minute wait. The dance floor is now jammed to capacity, and every inch of space in this flashing, smoking, lights-a-whirl disco is wall-to-wall bodies. You simply can't move without parting two or more bodies with your hands, elbows, or hips. This means that the dancing going on here doesn't require intricate knowledge of steps. Solo dancers get most of their movement from their knees and arms while couples rely on their pelvises.

In fact, most of the people in this disco are not dancing. There is not enough room or desire. The disco population is divided into two groups—the spectators and entertainers. The spectators mostly dress in the casual unisex outfit of shorts and T-shirts, but may even venture to put on a nice shirt and slacks or a skirt. The entertainers arrive in costume. You can tell they've spent hours in preparation. One woman is in a pink negligee, glittery pink eye shadow, and pink pumps. A guy who looks like a Latin American pop singer shakes by in a plastic chain-mail shirt that reveals most of his slender upper torso, tight stretch slacks, and short, spiky hair. Everyone watches these over-the-top poseurs when they are near because they came to *be* noticed.

A woman approaches with fifty plastic medical syringes laced around her neck, each with an individual cord. She sucks a "blue shot" consisting of vodka, lime, and curaçao into one syringe from a plastic container that she wears strapped to her waist. She shoots the concoction into a patron's mouth, blows a whistle, shakes the person's head against her bosom and then awards the patient the hypodermic syringe by necklacing it over his head like an Olympic medal. One freckly redhead wears as many syringes as Mark Spitz wore medals. He looks about fourteen, but is really twenty-three. It turns that out he is a welder from Boston, and like many of the spring breakers we meet, he is not on break from college at all, but simply timed his vacation to coincide with peak fellowship. He tells us, "I came here to party. This is awesome. I'm coming back every year until I die."

Suddenly a lad who introduces himself as Oliver appears at our table. He is convivial and plump. An orange Clemson baseball cap propped backward on his head floats on a mass of curly brown hair. A waitress comes by with a tray of beers, so I offer her a tip to get a round for all of us.

Oliver grins appreciatively. "Wow. That's great. Thanks, bro'. Now I don't have to wait in line."

We explore the economics of the all-you-can-drink deal using some of Oliver's business administration course material. Because there are a few bars that serve beers for as little as a buck, you have to drink twenty beers here to get your twenty-dollar cover charge worth. Let's say you are dedicated enough to go back to the end of the fifteen-minute line as soon as you are served a beer and drink it in line. With this strategy you'll end up spending about five hours just to break even.

We also figure out that if you want to drink so much that you break the house, that you actually cost the disco money, you are out of luck. There are simply not enough hours in the day. The house always wins.

But what if you don't wait in line? What if you tip the waiter twenty-five cents a beer, and you can get as many beers as fast as you want, what's the break-even number? Oliver's brain whirs.

"Twenty-seven beers," he says as he calls the waiter over, "I ain't buying a college education for nothing."

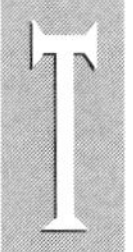oday we decide to rent a car from an agency down the block and drive seventy kilometers south to Xcaret eco-archeological theme park (pronounced "shkaret").

"Taxi, señor?"

"Hey, lady, you want Maya tour?"

"*¡Hola, chicos!* Information?

The drive through the jungle is on a smoothly paved highway, one that I remembered from the airplane looking like a white zipper on a velvety green evening dress. We pull into the huge Xcaret parking lot. Unlike most visitors who hear about the park from relentless touts, my first contact was in *Archaeology* magazine. Angela M.H. Schuster, a senior editor, wrote about the heretical concept of building a theme park around ancient Mayan ruins. As odd as it sounds, she gave Xcaret a thumbs-up. Schuster's take on it was that the trading post ruins, dating back to the late post-classical period in 1400 AD, were not significant enough to attract in-depth research or tourism otherwise. There are hundreds of ruins like these scattered around the Yucatán peninsula that are completely ignored. Schuster surmised that any negative impact of the unorthodox theme park is outweighed by the educational benefits for children and families who would spend time there learning about Mayan culture.

The activities in the park are inspired by either ecology or culture. The ecological activities include swimming with dolphins in an ocean water pool, snorkeling in giant tide pools brimming with colorful sea life, and walking along a self-guided botanical trail. The cultural activities include visiting a replicated Mayan village, attending an exhibition of the Papantla Flyers dance, and, of course, a stroll through the ruins. The most popular attraction, a swim through the underground rivers, is a combination of the themes. The meandering waist-high river, at times disappearing completely underground, is accessible to snorkelers.

The theme park isn't cheap, so between the cost of the tickets and the rental car we've invested a fair chunk of change. I convinced Becky to come here for the sole purpose of watching an exhibition of the ancient ball court game. During our travels in Mexico over the years we have visited countless pre-Hispanic ruins, many of which included a ball court. Imagine a narrow clay tennis court, without the lines or net, but complete with sideline grandstands. The seats and steps of the grandstands have been filled in with cement and covered with stucco to make a smooth slope. At the top of the slope on either side is a stone ring mounted vertically like hoops that an animal might jump through, not horizontally like a basketball hoop.

Guides and guidebooks told us that the game was played with a solid rubber ball that was shot through the high-mounted hoops by using only the hips. No matter how hard we tried, we could not visualize how the game was actually played.

After the ceremonial burning of incense, a group of eight players adorned in faux jaguar furs ready themselves on either end of the playing field. A solid rubber ball, slightly bigger than a cantaloupe, is tossed by one team to the other, somewhat like a football kickoff. As the ball bounces toward him, a man on the receiving team drops to all fours, butt toward the ground, and swings his hip like a pendulum. Smack! He whacks the ball with his forward facing hip. Becky groans vicariously with pain. This is a solid rubber ball weighing nine pounds, not one filled with air. A player on the other team returns the ball by running at it, dropping to his butt and skidding toward it sideways. His hip strikes the ball to send it back.

The trick of getting the ball to bounce up onto the high slope along the sides of the field is one of timing. The players hit the ball downward when it is on the up-bounce, so the ball will gain the necessary lift. Once it is on the stucco slope the two opposing players work together, bouncing the ball to one another, often scraping the bare skin of their legs and butts along the cementlike surface until one of them gets a shot at the hoop, through which the ball can barely fit.

A half-hour of exhibition play passes without a score. I am fascinated by the effort and impressed by the athletic ability of these scraped and scarred players. I am thinking to myself that since this is even a slower scoring game than soccer—the ball has barely touched the rim of the hoop—the mostly American crowd will get antsy and leave. To the contrary, every single spectator is on the edge of his or her seat, twisting and scooting, trying to help the players get the ball through the hoop with body English. Finally, a cheer explodes as the ball loops around the inside of the thick hoop and drops through to the other side.

Later that evening we walk from our hotel toward Señor Frog's.

"Taxi, señor?"

"Hey, lady, you want Maya tour?"

"*¡Hola, chicos!* Information?"

Señor Frog's is the classic animated Mexican resort bar and grill. As we enter the bar, Mardi Gras beads are tossed around our necks by the host so that we are festively attired. Pink, green, and yellow *yarda* glasses hang down from above the bar like neon stalactites. The lanky glasses are imprinted with the jovial Señor Frog's logo, and in hot pink letters, "Here comes trouble." Sawdust is scattered across the floor to absorb drink spills. On every conceivable wall and ceiling space are big signs with silly sayings such as "Hemingway never ate here."

Hemingway was a smart guy. If you stick to the burgers and sandwiches in a place like this, you're OK, but we make the mistake of going Mexican. One thing we figured out about Cancún is that hands-down it consistently serves the blandest Mexican food in the entire country. If you eat on the Cancún resort strip, I suggest going to one of the good Italian restaurants.

People crowd the dance floor and an emcee leads everyone in antics between songs. He announces that a bottle of Herradura *reposado* tequila will be awarded to the winner of a beer drinking contest. Before I can turn to Becky and comment that it is an excellent prize, she is on the stage lined up with four college-aged men. The amount of beer to be drunk, it turns out, will be a *yarda* glassful. An additional stipulation is that the last-place finisher has to take a trip down the water slide. A transparent plastic waterslide tube runs right across the ceiling of the restaurant, then drops into the dark waters of the lagoon. Becky looks through the back window at the bottom of the slide. The area immediately below the slide is cordoned off with a cargo net, in which floats a trash potpourri. Her face pales as she surveys the consequences.

"On your marks, get set . . . Go!"

The two guys to Becky's left are no mere amateurs. They lock their throats like open manholes and pour the beer down in a two-man race for first place. Becky is battling the guy on her immediate right gulp for gulp. A shirt and pants that are too neatly pressed constrict the last guy. He is not accustomed to such radical consumption, so whenever beer splashes on him he jumps backward with consternation that he is sullying his clothing. The dandy is dead meat. Meanwhile, Becky resurrects her college beer chugging skills in time to edge out her rival to show.

While Becky burps over the next couple of minutes, we watch a family from the Midwest with amusement. The mother has agreed to buy her teenage kids mini-*yardas* filled with sex-on-the-beach. The sixteen-year-old engages in the ritual with gusto. His shier fourteen-year-old-brother does fine drinking the mini-*yarda*, but blushes redder than his drink when the waitress serving him applies her signature sign-off treatment. She gently pinches his nipples, then runs her fingers down the middle of his chest, down his stomach, stopping just below the belt line, all the while blowing a whistle.

When the emcee orders everyone to dance on the chairs, we obey. A group of a dozen Kansas girls push their chairs to one side of the table, and then jump up to dance for a photo op. The photographer delivers the glossy eight-by-tens to them a few songs later. They are uniformly blonde with blue eyes, their tanned shoulders enticingly bare except for a few lacy straps. These are the vixens who motivate the male contingent to venture to this island.

Jessica, a senior studying physiology at the University of Kansas, wears a lithe, flowery sundress. The front half of her hair is braided into cornrows, which seems appropriate for this fair-haired country girl. I want to talk to her because she seems so absorbed by the photo of her group. Between her comments she flashes a gorgeous smile that highlights angular cheekbones and a Greek nose. She tells me that most of the girls in her group know each other from high school or college or through a common friend who organized the trip.

I prod her for some intriguing details of the girls' time in Cancún. She offers, "We've met a lot of guys. You know, I'm really surprised how nice they are. We stuck together, but would have been OK anyway with these guys. We stayed up dancing with them most of the night in their room, then just before sunrise we went down to the beach and cranked up the boom box. It was really great, dancing there on the beach with them, flirting, but we switched dance partners all the time so it didn't feel like there were any . . . obligations. We just had fun.

"We went shopping one day. You know, it's almost hard to do here, when you see people begging on the street. It makes you realize how lucky you are—and spoiled." Then to herself, "What can we do to help them?"

Picking up her previous thought, she continues, "We had a good time at our hotel pool. There were always a lot of activities there. Oh, yeah, we went on the Booze Cruise to Isla de Mujeres. That was pretty fun, the dinner they made was good, but I don't know, we didn't really like the dirty games. I mean, they should have some way for you to come back early if you're not into those."

Her eyes drift to the photo again. I can't blame her for being distracted by the image. The photo is resplendent, an evocative keepsake. It seems like something Rafael would have wanted to paint. These are modern goddesses with tans that make the smiles whiter and eyes yet bigger and bluer and the hair absolutely silken. They are illuminated by the halo of youth.

I ask, "What do you think you will remember when you look at that photo ten years from now?"

Without hesitation Jessica responds, "That we had at least a week of our lives together, just us, away from everything else, no work or relationships or hassles. No rules. You can do almost anything you want in Cancún, like walk around the streets with a beer. But at the same time it's safe. The music, the sun, that water, that incredible blue water alone would do it, the excitement every night before going out, the freedom, good friends—how often do you get all of that at once?"

ecky said it was the swimming pool aerobics music that finally pushed her over the edge, but for me I think it was

"Taxi, señor?"

"Hey, lady, you want Maya tour?"

"*¡Hola, chicos!* Information?"

Regardless, we are fleeing Cancún's spring breakers and tequila poppers and sex-on-the-beach and activity organizers and *yarda* glasses and annoying T-shirts that say things like "It's not a beer belly, it's a fuel tank for a sex machine."

Unfortunately, our taxi driver, who will control our fate for at least three hours, is an absolute lunatic. He insists on speaking pidgin Spanish with us, using infinitive verbs even though we conjugate all of ours. The worst part is that every time we pass an animal of any sort, he points to it, says the name in Spanish, and in English if he can think of it, then makes the animal noise for the next several minutes.

"*Pato*, duck, quack, quack, quack, quack . . ."

"*Vaca*, cow, mooooooooooo . . ."

We are on a *libre* highway that runs through numerous villages. Each town has three or four sets of enormous speed bumps that double the normal travel time of our 100-mile drive. There are eighty-three speed bumps along the way, an impressive number, even for Mexico. Because traffic lights, speed limit signs, and highway police are completely ineffective, speed bumps, called *topes* in Spanish, are really the only thing that works in the Mexican traffic system. Today we are happy that the *topes* exist even though we hit our heads on the roof of the car every time we buck over one. The *topes* are doing their job of slowing down potentially dangerous vehicles, which is what we consider ours to be, because our driver is now a *perro*, dog, bark, bark, bark, bark.

We know nothing about Holbox Island except that it is undeveloped and a long way from Cancún. When a fishing skiff picks us up at the dock, we warily board, noting that the water isn't so spectacular here. The gray and choppy wash reminds me of the ocean during stormy days in the Pacific Northwest. Fifteen minutes from shore, we realize there aren't any life jackets on board, nor is the boat equipped with anything that could serve as one. We do have a plan, however. If we capsize we will throw our daypacks overboard, dig out our C-shaped travel neck pillows, inflate them, recline comfortably on our backs, and kick toward shore. No kidding, that is our plan as the fiberglass boat launches across the hollow of a wave, smashing into the crest of the next.

Holbox is now clearly in view, but the water's cloudy scowl is unaltered. This concerns us because we are on the protected side of the island, which faces the mainland, while our hotel beach is exposed to the Gulf of Mexico. As we round the point of the island the water begins an amazing transformation to translucent emerald green. We pass a congregation of fishing boats moored just offshore from a small thatch-roofed village, its white beach unfurling endlessly.

As the eight huts that comprise our hotel emerge from the edge of the jungle like brown mushroom caps, the captain cuts the engine to drop anchor a good twenty feet from shore. Soon a playful rottweiler named Rufus splashes toward us along with two portly porters who wade through the crystalline knee-deep water to retrieve our bags.

We have some time to explore the beach before sunset. It is a work in progress. Compact, fine white sand is massaged by small waves that deposit a two-yard wide necklace of seashells along the shoreline. The seashells have accumulated in layers up to six inches deep. Most of the billions are clam and scallop-type shells, ranging in size from lentil to half-dollar, but retaining that perfect point-break shape. The minorities include pink razor clams, horseshoe crab shells that look like brown alien spaceships, and spiraling conches that you can find voluptuous and whole with a bit of searching. The rays of the sunset play on these shells as if they are monkey bars and merry-go-rounds, swinging from wafer edges, squeezing through cracks, sliding down ridges, trampolining off curves, and hiding in shadowy scoops.

There are fewer stars in the nighttime sky than shells on the beach, the perfect amount to identify constellations without the clutter of the Milky Way. We ignore the bear, the dogs, and the rabbit of the Greeks to search for the jaguar, the peccary, and the shark of the Maya.

Over the next four days our agenda plays out exactly as scheduled. Nothing happens—serene, azure, elusive nothing.

Resources

Cruz, Alicia. "The Thousand and One Faces of Cancún." *Urban Anthropology* 25 (1996).

De Landa, Diego. *Yucatan Before and After the Conquest: Relación de las Cosas de Yucatán.* 1566. Translated by William Gates. New York: Dover Publications, 1978.

Gann, Thomas. *In an Unknown Land.* New York: Charles Scribner's Sons, 1924.

Price, Niko. "Spring Break Hedonism Has Home on Sandy Beaches of Quintana Roo." Associated Press, March 27, 2000.

Schuster, Angela M. H. "Faux Maya." *Archaeology,* January/February 1999, 18.

MICHELADA

ACAPULCO

unset, the denouement of the day, is an appropriate hour to arrive in this once-famed oceanside destination. Although now in the twilight of its popularity, there was a time when it was almost inconceivable for the rich and famous to venture anywhere else for fun in the sun. Acapulco, the jet-set getaway, burned in its brilliance.

During the 1950s and 1960s, everyone wanted to share a piece of beach and romance with the famous couples gracing the covers of *Life* magazine. With a reputation for unleashing passion, Acapulco was also considered the height of honeymoon chic. JFK and Jackie, Henry Kissinger, Brigitte Bardot, and Elizabeth Taylor all spent their first days of marital union in these warm Pacific breezes. As is often the case, the rich congregated and the commoners soon followed. My friends' parents, an ex-boss, and even my own mom and dad traveled the busy path from the altar straight to Acapulco.

My parents arrived here on June 26, 1965, the day after their Houston wedding. I have been listening to stories about that week for my entire life. Fairy tales of private swimming pools, floating hibiscus, magic breakfast boxes, and sailing in Acapulco Bay are woven into the fabric of my childhood mythology.

Before Bryan and I came to Mexico, we stopped by my parents' home in Austin. It took a little searching, but we managed to dig up their album of honeymoon photos, pictures I hadn't seen in over twenty years. The slim gold brocade album cover creaked as I opened it. One of the photos fell into my lap. I picked up the small 3x3 and squinted at the form inside the white trim border. The picture had started to fade, but I was shocked to discover my thirty-year-old brother sailing a boat in Acapulco Bay in 1965, four years before he was born. No, it wasn't my brother, it was my dad leaning back against the tiller in his Ray-Ban Wayfarers. The resemblance was unsettling. Other photos included shots of my parents tanning at the beach, relaxing over lunch at a seaside restaurant, leaning on the balcony of their hotel room, and standing with arms draped around a bathing suit-clad Mexican teenager. We have come to Acapulco to go inside those photos and retrace my parents' steps.

It is impossible to consider Acapulco's heyday, or honeymoons, without taking into account the famous Las Brisas resort. It was, and continues to be, the top choice for Acapulco-bound newlyweds. A sprawling complex of white *casitas*, petite cakes with pink roofs, Las

Brisas clings to a hillside above Acapulco Bay. My parents stayed at Las Brisas, which is why we find ourselves here thirty-five years later.

As we pull into the hotel after our five-hour drive from Mexico City, an army of staff, all dressed in pink and white, scurries to check us in. A woman in a salmon-colored shirt hands us terrycloth towels laced with icy frost, while another offers us slushy rose-tinted frozen margaritas. A young man dressed like a candy striper presents a thick packet of welcome material. Eventually another bellboy loads us into a pink and white jeep. We wind up, up, and around the mountainside before arriving at our home for the week.

Our *casita* is identical to the mythical one described by my mother. The tiny white houses in Frank Lloyd Wright minimalist style are tucked into the contours of the hills and surrounded by greenery. Palm trees, laurels, bougainvillea, and acres of hibiscus spring out of the soil. We enter the front gate and walk down to our deck, insured privacy by a tall white wall. A diminutive swimming pool, private to our *casita*, teeters on the edge of a cliff looking over the bay. Fifteen graceful hibiscus flowers float on the pool's surface in a languidly choreographed water ballet. We enter our spacious pink and white room to find it covered in flowers as well. *Tulipanes*, hibiscus, are the signature of Las Brisas. We discover them scattered on room service trays and bathroom towel racks, in drinks, and on counters and pillows during our entire stay.

The bellboy shows us the "magic box" of my family lore. The box, built into our wall, is accessible via pink doors from both inside and outside the room. Every morning a silent messenger will deliver fresh fruit, a thermos of hot coffee, and Mexican pastries into the box before we wake. Bryan won't have to search for his morning coffee, an enchanting thought for both of us.

I had heard about Las Brisas's profusion of pink, but even so was unprepared for the ubiquitousness of its use. We are surrounded by it at every turn: pink pool umbrellas, pink chairs, pink pillowcases, pink towels. In spite of all the pink, it's hard to call Las Brisas tacky. The quirky color scheme is an idiosyncrasy, odd in relation to the quality of the installations and the excellent service.

Room service arrives in a pink jeep. The waiter sets our table by the pool with linens, candles, and flowers. He then places a pair of icy mugs along with two huge orbs full of seafood on the table.

We sit in front of our feast, glasses in hand. Acapulco Bay is coated with the roseate gauze of dusk. Our drinks, called *micheladas*, prickle our throats. Uniquely Mexican, the *michelada* is made from beer, lime juice, salt, and other spices. It is an extremely popular warm-weather drink downed in copious amounts on the beaches of Acapulco, the same beaches that we see spreading below us from our cliffside retreat.

To accompany our drinks we have ordered *vuelva a la vida*, a Mexican seafood specialty. Its name translates as "return to life." In addition to being an excellent dish, it is a common Mexican hangover cure. A farrago of seafood, cocktail sauce, onions, avocados, and olives, it is traditionally served for lunch after a night of drinking. Some people even add vodka to the cocktail sauce for a bit of hair-of-the-dog effect. The gargantuan goblets in front of us, easily able to hold a softball or even a cantaloupe, are packed with octopus, abalone, and calamari.

Night falls as we eat. Across the bay, individual buildings and roads blur into a shimmering incandescent wall. Although Acapulco is a large city past its pristine prime, the beauty of the scene after dark has only improved as the municipality has grown. The flickering lights in town, searing white, orange, and blue, are Sirius, Betelgeuse, and Spica reflected thousands of times on the mountain below. Following my parents' honeymoon footsteps isn't too arduous a task when it includes this view and a private pool. We've been on the road for weeks now and are due a little pampering. Las Brisas is just what we need for our personal revival—*vuelva a la vida*.

The saffron rays of sunrise ignite the undeveloped hillside that splashes down to the bay below us. Squirrels, hummingbirds, woodpeckers, and ostentatious magpie jays distract me in my yoga poses. With flowing topknots and sensuous long blue tails, a pair of the jays whirls above our deck busily erecting a nest in the top of a palm. After breakfast from the magic box, I pull out a color copy of one of Mom and Dad's honeymoon photos. Taken of their *casita*, the picture includes a pink jeep in the foreground and Acapulco Bay beyond. There are no high-rises on the other side of the bay. I look up to compare it with the scene before me. Hundreds of tall white condos deface the beaches of town. Another glance at the picture shows virgin hills towering above the city. Today, buildings have clawed their way up to precarious heights. Las Brisas hasn't changed much, but the town sure has.

Acapulco is not the sexy young thing she used to be. The name of the city comes from the Nahuatl word that means "place of dense reeds." That should be modified today to translate as "place of dense buildings." A twenty-minute ride on a dangerous narrow road drops us down to the city at the ocean's shore. Our cab driver is a mountain of a man, all neck and jowls from our point of view in the backseat. His meaty earlobes flap as he talks.

"Acapulco has changed in the last fifteen years. You used to be able to drive down this main street and see the ocean. Now all you see are buildings. All those people from Mexico City want apartments on the shore, but now we, the people from Acapulco, can't see the beach."

He's right. As we pass through the heart of town we see condos, restaurants, bars, and nightclubs, but not much beach. Acapulco is a city with almost two million residents, which gives it a decidedly un-resort-like feel. It is loud and crowded with traffic, but at the same time, it's real. Pharmacies, taco stands, small stores, and simple restaurants are as common to see on the streets as boutiques and souvenir shops. Many locals enjoy lives only remotely connected to the tourist trade, something that is hard to imagine in planned Mexican resorts like Ixtapa or Cancún.

At Hornitos Beach the ocean is still visible from the main thoroughfare. The sand is crowded with Mexico City residents escaping the metropolis for the weekend. There are some foreigners, but Acapulco is primarily a destination for Mexicans these days. Sunbathers fry in the morning sun, an outdoor market of sizzling meat. Browned toddlers waddle toward the sea like fat little kabobs.

Bars along the beach sell seafood and drinks. Seeing all of the frosty glasses filled with *micheladas* whets our thirst and tempts us into ordering two of the cold brewed concoctions. I try to picture my parents here. One of their honeymoon photos shows my mom standing on this beach with a huge shopping bag. She wears white pumps, an elegant green sundress, and a white scarf over her springy bouffant hairdo. Pumps and elegance would be decidedly out of place on this stretch of sand today.

Relatively few Americans vacation in Acapulco. Bryan has been here only once before, during his shoestring travel days, and he hated it. He rented a cheap room in the heart of town and was so disgusted after one day that he jumped in his car and escaped to Puerto Escondido the next morning—too many people, cars, and buildings, and too much noise and grime.

That hasn't always been the case. When the burgeoning jet set discovered Acapulco in the 1940s, the town was an unspoiled Eden. That elite group of world travelers eventually brought the resort to the height of its fame and glory. In Acapulco those pleasure seekers found soft, sandy beaches, exuberant jungle, and colorful culture. From their front doors they could lounge in the warm waves, sail lazily around the bay, and dine on succulent seafood brought in by local divers. The same people who entertained each other in Palm Springs and Ibiza now gathered for cocktail parties in large houses along Acapulco's shores.

Acapulco's real growth began with the inauguration of direct international air service in the mid-1960s. Droves of pale-skinned tourists descended onto its beaches while innovations like discos, parasailing, swim-up bars, hotels shaped like pyramids, and cliff diving were born. Coinciding with the 1960s trend toward self-gratification, Acapulco became a hotbed of sex and sensuality. Anaïs Nin wrote:

> In Acapulco no one ever thought of profession, titles, background, or past history. Everyone lived in the present and looked at each other with an appreciation of appearance only as one looked at the sea, the mountains, lagoons, birds, animals, flowers . . . all blended into an object for the pursuit of pleasure. *(Collages: A Novel)*

By the early 1970s, unchecked growth choked the city. Pollution contaminated the waters of the bay, still a working port. No longer difficult or expensive to reach, Acapulco lost its cachet with the jet set. Recently developed virgin beaches along Mexico's Pacific and Caribbean coasts drew travelers away from the tired city that Acapulco had become.

For some people, however, Acapulco still offers something that can't be found in cookie-cutter resorts. The city's glamour, although faded, continues to shine in certain settings. Something about the decades of decadence rubs off in the balmy nights and sensual breezes. One of those settings is Las Brisas. In addition to the *casitas* of the hotel, Las Brisas encompasses an exclusive neighborhood of multimillion-dollar homes. I first experienced the engaging side of Acapulco at one of the houses in this complex.

My visits to Acapulco have been entirely different from Bryan's quickly aborted trip. After striking out on a job search in Monterrey, I drove south to Mexico City to look for employment. Through a daisy chain of contacts I met a headhunter who referred me to an American company wanting to hire a country manager in Mexico City. The company, Jergens, was looking for a Mexican male. It took five interviews and a lot of persuading, but they ended up hiring me, a blond *gringa*. The exclusive distributor for Jergens in Mexico at the time was an important family-owned food company. My new office was in its headquarters. I started my job a week before their annual sales conference in Acapulco.

At the end of the conference's first day I found myself part of a small group invited to the owners' gigantic hillside mansion in Las Brisas for cocktails. We pulled through the gated entrance and the driver pointed out homes of famous personalities like Luis Miguel, Placido Domingo, and even the shah of Iran. A spectacular sunset tie-dyed the waters of the bay as we arrived at the house. The centerpiece of the home was an ancient laurel tree whose roots and branches spread in elongated limbs to hug and shelter the villa. An expansive patio dangled over the Pacific Ocean like a box perched on a fireplace mantle. We peered down at the house below, rented at the time by Imelda Marcos. As if on cue, the queen of footwear strolled out onto her own deck to admire the evening pyrotechnics.

It was here that I first tasted a *michelada*. A waiter in a white jacket came around with a tray of icy mugs rimmed with salt. The amber beverage inside the glass, served over ice, had flicks of red pepper floating in its foamy head. I tentatively took a sip. Lime, chile pepper, beer, and other spices hit my tongue at a refreshingly cool temperature. A soft breeze ruffled my hair, candles flickered, and violet shafts filtered across our party. The drink, exotic and exciting, combined perfectly with the surreal setting. Seven days earlier I had been pinching pennies as an unemployed graduate, but that night I was rubbing elbows with Mexico's elite.

Many Mexicans, especially those from Mexico City, still love Acapulco. The closest beach to the country's capital is connected to the metropolis by a fast, smooth toll road. Cut through entire sections of mountains and featuring massive suspension bridges, the highway is not only fast, it's one of the world's most expensive per kilometer.

The route from Mexico City to Acapulco covers 416 kilometers and costs eighty dollars per vehicle.

On weekends and holidays the Mexico City social scene is simply transferred to the homes and condos of Acapulco. The same people who socialize at the jockey club in Mexico City trade sailing tips at the yacht club here. Members of private resorts, they spend their mornings sleeping, their afternoons tanning, and their nights entertaining or being entertained at expensive dinners. The younger crowd continues on after dinner to fashionable dance clubs until five or six in the morning. Although not a part of that crowd, I've caught glimpses of that side of Acapulco while here on business.

Bryan has been so negative about Acapulco that I'm happy to have the chance to share my side of the city. A Suburban transports us down to La Concha, Las Brisas's waterfront club. Two immense rock-lined pools filled with seawater echo the curves of the bay. A freshwater pool, set above the other two, cascades into waterfalls. Tall palms and banks of hibiscus ring the club like a lei. White tents shade patrons from the sizzling afternoon sun as they relax in their pink-cushioned lounge chairs.

One of my parents' photos shows Dad at this same beach club. He's wearing little swim trunks and a red and white-striped collared shirt that obviously came as a two-piece set. He would never wear something like that today—his mother must have bought the outfit. Mom's finger blocks the entire bottom left quarter of the photo. Bryan walks over to the same spot where my father was standing and I snap a photo, intentionally covering part of the lens with my finger.

We enter one of the deep seawater pools via a pink-and-white diving board. To our surprise the pool teems with sea life. Rockfish, schools of angelfish, and scuttling crabs distract us from the monotony of our laps.

Cocktail hour starts as soon as our exercise is over. Our waiter, Julio César, brings us two icy *micheladas*. I love certain Mexican names and Julio César is one that always makes me smile. I try to picture one of my friends sending a card announcing the birth of her new son, Julius Caesar. No pressure for that kid to make something of himself. *¡Pobre!*

Dodging floating hibiscus flowers in the freshwater pool, I swim up to the bar and order another round. Gonzalo, the bartender, has worked at Las Brisas since before my parents honeymooned here. Today his black hair is graying at the temples, but he still cuts a fine figure in his starched pink shirt. His smooth face, permanently tanned from decades spent poolside, has few of the wrinkles commonly associated with years in the sun.

I ask him about *micheladas*.

"Well, people have been drinking beer and lime over ice at the beach since before I was a little kid. The drink didn't really have a name, though. Then, about the time I started working here, *chilangos* started calling them *micheladas*. The name just stuck."

Gonzalo asks me what brand of beer I prefer. "I always ask my clients what kind of beer they want in their *micheladas*. If they don't care or if they leave it up to me, I use Corona because it's nice and light. That's kind of the point on a hot day, isn't it? Most people request Corona anyway."

Not wanting to break tradition, I ask for mine made with Corona.

"Do you know that *chela* is the slang word that people from Mexico City use for "beer?" *Chelada* is a play on the words *chela* and *helada*. If somebody asks for a *chelada* I serve him a beer over ice with lime.

"A *michelada* is a *chelada* with salt and spices. *Michelada* means 'My *chelada*.' Maybe somebody came up with a special spicy version of the *chelada* and started calling it his *chelada* and that version just spread across the country."

I watch Gonzalo make my drink. He takes a chilled beer mug out of the freezer, runs a lime around the rim and dips it in a mixture of salt and chile powder. He then puts some ice cubes in the mug along with a healthy shot of fresh lime juice and a couple of dashes each of soy sauce, chile pepper, and Tabasco. He pours a Corona over the mixture, stirs it with a few quick flicks of his wrist, and pushes the drink toward me with a flourish.

I take a sip—ahhh, Acapulco. This is the only place where I drink *micheladas*. Wondering if any celebrities share my Acapulco-*michelada* connection, I ask Gonzalo about some of the people he's served here over the years.

"One of the people I remember best is Neil Armstrong. NASA sent the astronauts down here with their wives and kids right before they went up to the moon. I took a picture with Mr. Armstrong. It's hanging in my house. The other day there was a TV special on the moon walk and I called my kids into the room so that they could see Mr. Armstrong on television and on our wall at the same time."

"There have been hundreds of famous people here . . . too many for me to remember. Frank Sinatra, Dean Martin, Natalie Wood, Brigitte Bardot . . . "

His voice trails off for a second and then he looks at me with extreme earnestness. "Brigitte Bardot is *the* most beautiful woman. I will never, ever, ever forget her."

He may never forget Brigitte, but he certainly can't recall what she drank. He can't remember what type of drink anybody ordered.

"Wait, I do remember one thing. Ringo Starr was here and it looked like he was studying a movie script or something. He sat under that tent over there all day reading lots of pages. The whole time he was over there he kept ordering pitchers of lemonade."

Lemonade? Of all the hundreds of thousands of drinks that Gonzalo has served in over three decades all he can come up with is lemonade? *Gracias*, Gonzalo.

"Once in the early '70s, I was called away from work here to be a bartender at a special dinner party at a private house up the hill. It was President Johnson and Ladybird, from the United States, dining with Mexican president Miguel Alemán. Johnson and Alemán were both out of office, and it wasn't an official meeting, so it was kept a secret. I had to swear not to tell anybody. I prepared their drinks for them."

Ladybird Johnson is an Acapulco regular. She has stayed at a private home in Las Brisas almost every year for a quarter of a century. While we were doing our research in Austin, we spoke to her about her love affair with this city by the bay. Luci, her younger daughter, joined us for the conversation.

Ladybird, a wonderful communicator, had honed her skills during decades in the public eye. Her sentences, delivered in a soft Texas drawl, have a poetic timbre. "My fondest memories of Acapulco are from the years after Lyndon left the presidency. We spent four wonderful Januarys there. Those were very special times."

Luci laughs. "My father, before that, was almost incapable of taking a vacation. When I was growing up he took two—total—that I can remember. Vacation was something people did to irritate him, something his staff seemed to be doing when he needed them."

Ladybird enthuses, "It's the memories of those times, and the view, that entice me to Acapulco. I've been back almost every winter since then. I go with a group of friends and we enjoy fine meals and good conversation while we take in that marvelous, stunning view. I always stay at Las Brisas because of the vistas. I am just enraptured by them."

Luci adds, "We try to get her to take more vacations with us, but she insists on going to Acapulco. It's a place of romantic memories for her, one of the only places she truly vacationed with my father.

"My father left office on January 19, 1969 and died four years later on January 22, 1973. They had very little time, so I know my mother thinks back on those years often. They were scheduled to leave for Acapulco on January 23, 1973, but his death intervened. My mother's bag was already packed for the trip."

At my prompting, Ladybird affectionately lists her favorite Mexican food and drinks. "Well, I just love margaritas. I prefer mine with salt and not much ice. I've never tried a *michelada*, but I'm an aficionado of the Mexicans' liberal use of lime on everything. Oh, and the fresh fruits and juices are just divine.

"You know, life is filled with 'aren't you glads' and 'if onlys.' Many of my 'aren't you glads' came from my visits to Mexico. What a wonderful time of romantic exploration. Once Arthur Crim [President of United Artists] found a naturalist in Acapulco and we went off to a village where we learned every tree, vine, and flower. Oh, and the fruit. While we were there some children shimmied up the tall palms to break off coconuts and toss them down. We split them open and delighted in the milk . . . it was so good, so sweet.

"Acapulco, oh, Acapulco. Most of all, I just adore the views; I think about what it must have been like to be the first European who sailed into that majestic harbor and looked up and saw that stunning sight. Oh, Acapulco."

I too am enthralled by Acapulco's views. The scene from Madeiras restaurant in particular is one of the finest in the city. The lights of the town covering the hills are a gentle wave of phosphorescence about to break into the bay below us. Acapulco is unique among beautiful ports of the world in that there is no distinctive central cluster of buildings that identifies the city—especially at night. The large condos and hotels along the beach are so simply lit that they don't even catch the eye. Instead, thousands of individual lights create a pointillistic study of the hills' curves. This restaurant is an Acapulco institution for wealthy Mexicans, especially those with houses in nearby Las Brisas.

Although the restaurant, open to the gentle evening breeze, is not formal, the dress code is casual elegant. Before dinner I pulled my dress out of the bottom of my suitcase to find it a wrinkled little ball. To my surprise, I found an iron and ironing board—pink and white, no less—in our closet. This is a new phenomenon in Mexican hotels. Five years ago an iron was impossible to come by even in the best establishments. You simply had to pay for your clothes to be pressed by the laundry service. Upper-class Mexicans think themselves above any manual labor. Why learn to iron, cook, or clean when you have maids, cooks, and gardeners to do everything for you from the time you are born? Having an iron in a hotel closet was seen as a waste of resources. Most Mexican businessmen probably wouldn't even know how to turn one on.

The last time I was at this restaurant was before the country's most recent peso devaluation. It was a heady time to be doing business in Mexico. The economy was booming and the country had a sense of can-do optimism rare in such a fatalistic land. A bigwig from Jergens's parent company was visiting to meet our Mexican distributor and discuss a possible joint venture. The distributor gave their important guest the royal treatment and I was lucky enough to be along for the ride. We flew in their private jet to visit manufacturing plants around the country and ended up in Acapulco for the weekend. Of course, we dined at Madeiras.

Between Las Brisas, La Concha, and Madeiras, Bryan is starting to view our weekend in Acapulco in a whole new light.

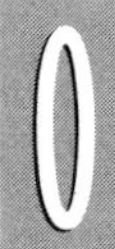

f all the ingredients in a *michelada*, I found soy sauce the most peculiar until I considered that Acapulco has been connected directly to the Orient for almost 450 years. This morning I picked up the flyer that came with breakfast to read:

> Did you know that those involved in the colonial trade between Manila and Acapulco in the seventeenth and eighteenth centuries became fantastically rich? Cargoes aboard each ship were valued at what today would amount to tens of millions of dollars, and before long, pirates infested the waters not far from shore. Among the better-known buccaneers was England's Sir Francis Drake.

Spain, having colonized the Philippines, used Manila as its Far East base of operations. In 1579 it designated Acapulco its New World base. By exclusively utilizing these two ports, the country was able to consolidate and control trade between Asia and the Americas.

The famous Spanish galleons that transported the merchandise weighed more than two tons each and were shaped in a way that made them hard to board from another ship—hard, but not impossible. The loaded ships were prime targets for English and Dutch pirates. The buccaneers would attempt to capture the heavily loaded vessels as the ships were about to enter Acapulco Bay. After one too many successful pirate attacks, Spain built Fort San Diego to protect her port.

The fort is positioned near the heart of downtown Acapulco. The original structure, built in 1615, was destroyed by an earthquake in 1776. It was reconstructed a few years later and has survived intact ever since.

We walk onto the grounds and inquire about the museum only to find out that it's closed for upgrading. Seeking additional information about the fort and the Manila galleons, we meet with the museum's director. He walks us across the fort's main courtyard to introduce us to the museum's information manager. We are led into what used to be a type of ammunition storeroom. Today it's a decrepit office. Paint, probably full of lead, is peeling off the thick walls in foot-long strips. Five old desks hide among a jumble of boxes and broken furniture. We are introduced to a sullen man named Alberto. As soon as the director turns to go out the door, Alberto makes a face, sticks out his tongue, and performs an exaggerated curtsy—a move stolen from the repertoire of a five-year-old child.

Alberto wears jeans, black tennis shoes, and a white shirt unbuttoned to his waist. A wrinkled red bandanna dangles from his back pocket and a black-and-silver belt wraps almost two times around his torso. He starts to speak to himself in a high nasal voice the moment his boss leaves the room. His soliloquy is a running diatribe against directors.

He pulls us over to sit in front of his dilapidated desk. His chair, on a swivel, hangs precariously to the left. It would be physically impossible to do any work in it. A huge plastic office supply container is empty except for a single heavy-duty 1950s-style pencil sharpener.

"You want information?" he squeaks. "I can give you information, and it will be much better than anything you can get from any director. All directors are *burros y payasos*."

With this he stands up and pulls out the keys to one of the two steel lockers on either side of his broken desk. He opens one and an avalanche of books and papers comes flying out. Alberto curses and mumbles while he kneels on the floor sifting through the fallen pile. He pulls out a crumpled mock-up of a brochure that looks as if it was more or less ready to go to the printer before it got smashed in the locker.

"I'm not sure I want to give this to you. If you make a copy that *burro* director might steal my information. This is ready to go to print but he has to approve it first and I don't want him to steal it. That's why I keep it locked up here. One day he'll force me to show it to him, but until then, I have the only key."

We walk out of the fort reading the bootleg brochure. Alberto's highly confidential information will be helpful to visitors if he ever lets the director approve its production. His folder explains that trade between Asia and the Americas was made feasible in 1565 when Friar Andrés de Urdaneta unraveled the mysteries of currents and prevailing winds to discover the sea lanes from east to west. Once a year a ship traveled from Manila to Acapulco loaded with furniture, silks, rugs, religious art, spices, ivory, precious stones, and fine porcelain. The trip took five or six months. A huge merchant market, the Fair of the Americas, took place in Acapulco upon the galleon's arrival. Shopkeepers and traders came from all over the New World. After two months of buying and selling, the ship would return to Manila. Any items bound for Spain were then carted across Mexico on a six-foot-wide road, the Camino Real, to the port of Veracruz.

The sea routes sailed by the galleons remained in use from 1565 to 1815, when Mexican independence released the country from its long-standing trade dependency on Spain. The fort fell into disrepair until 1986 when it was reopened as the Acapulco History Museum. We decide that Alberto should add a final line to his brochure mentioning that the fort is now used as a place of employment for eccentric Mexican slackers.

My parents' thirty-five year marriage is one to admire. Their partnership has created a home of warmth and nurturing. I enjoy going back to visit my kin and I cherish our large family dinners. Congregating in the kitchen, we sample excellent hors d'oeuvres and drinks while my mom puts the finishing touches on our meal.

For the last ten years those appetizers served in the kitchen have been presented on a colorful platter that I bought for my mother in Guadalajara. The plate was unlike anything I had seen before. Hand painted with a festive folk art scene of rural Mexican life, it was made of ceramic instead of the more commonly used baked clay. I was in graduate school, with no intention of settling down soon, and had no room or reason for a large serving plate. I left the store but kept thinking about the platter. I returned later that afternoon to buy it for my mother. Even though I had no use for it, I could at least enjoy it vicariously through her.

I should have bought two because I have wanted one of my own ever since. Over the years it has come to represent what I love about my family. When I lived in Mexico City I searched determinedly, but never found one like it. I even returned to the store in Guadalajara, but the owner said that artist no longer brought his wares around.

The artist's name and village are written on the back of the platter. I remembered that the small town was somewhere in the state of Guerrero, the same state that Acapulco is in. I phone my mother and she spells out the name of the town for me—Xalitla. Finding it on the map, I discover that Xalitla is about two hours inland from Acapulco, high in the mountains off the old highway.

I call information to get the phone number for the Xalitla mayor's office, hoping they might direct us to my talented artisan. The operator informs me that Xalitla doesn't have individual phones, just a *caseta*, a single central telephone. I dial the number and ask the woman who answers if Jesús Román, maker of ceramic platters, still lives in Xalitla. He does. The woman sends a runner to bring Jesús to the phone. I call back in thirty minutes and he's there waiting. We arrange to meet the next day.

Bryan and I are now in our second hour of weaving through the parched inland mountains. Gray rocks and a fearful wilderness of spines and cactus greet us at every turn. The landscape has gotten progressively uglier since we left Acapulco. Garbage lines the highway while sad gray houses with dried thatched roofs shelter skinny leaden people. Just when we think it can't get much worse we pass a dairy cow dead on the side of the road. It's the biggest road kill either of us has ever seen. Rigor mortis has set in and her stiff udders stand erect in the glaring noonday sun.

Fearing another Tehuacán, I have low expectations for Xalitla. We round a curve and see a little white-domed church in the distance. The dome marks a village set amid the only patch of green for miles. Can this pleasant hamlet be Xalitla? It is.

We pull up alongside two ancient women to ask where Jesús lives. A black pig scuffs his callused nose against the cobbled road. They are speaking to each other in Nahuatl, the original Aztec language. By lucky circumstance we happen to be directly in front of Jesús's house. His mother walks up, greeting the ladies in their first tongue. They tell her we are looking for Jesús and she leads us into the front gate on leathery bare feet.

Jesús approaches us with an extended hand. Fiftyish, wearing a gray T-shirt, green slacks, and work boots, he welcomes us to Xalitla. His wide face, unusually expressive, is bisected by a thick black mustache.

He leads us across a dusty yard to his workshop. Jesús learned ceramics from an old German in Taxco. Xalitla has a long history in decorative pottery, with most of the town involved in the creation of painted clay plates and bowls. This German came to Xalitla looking for artists to decorate his ceramics. Jesús was one of those chosen. He moved to Taxco and ended up working with the man for eighteen years, learning every aspect of the art of ceramic making.

"When my old boss returned to Germany I didn't have enough money or equipment to open my own ceramics studio. I could have gone back to working the traditional clay, but it's so primitive after working with ceramics. I decided to come back here to raise cattle. Two years ago one of my sons—he lives in Chicago—he offered to finance a studio for me here in Xalitla. We bought this kiln, made a few molds, and now I'm working in ceramics again. I like it better than cows."

Opening the kiln, he shows us a set of molds that has been fired for just over six hours. As soon as they finish cooling, he will extract the slate plates, platters, and cups.

From the workshop he leads us over to his pleasant, if slightly unkempt, patio. Five cages of birds—cardinals, canaries, and parakeets—fill the area with song. A slender fig tree struggles out of the concrete like the Charlie Brown Christmas tree. Two puppies wag themselves into quivering balls when they see us approach. One of them knocks over his water, which I notice is held in one of Jesús's intricately painted bowls. The birds eat off plates also painted by Jesús. Other finished works casually hold paintbrushes and enamels.

He picks up a blank platter. Instead of merely explaining how he works, Jesús sits down, grabs a paintbrush, and draws a squiggly black line across the center of the plate—the beginning of a river. He paints freehand, creating each design while he works. He's responsible for the outlines of figures and scenes, while his wife fills in the colors. When they have finished painting a piece they cover it with a glass glaze and fire it again.

"I'm the only one who works in ceramics. Everybody else here makes their pieces out of clay. You can soak mine in water for days and they will be fine. I also use lead-free paint imported from the United States and double-fire everything."

I'm happy to learn that his paint is lead-free, considering that my family has been using his platter consistently for a decade.

Standing next to him, we watch people, birds, donkeys loaded with fruit, fields of corn, and churches spring to life out of the end of his paintbrush. A line of men with rabbits' heads shuffles across one side of the platter. We ask him about the scene.

"It's the rabbit dance. It's from a festival that we have here at the beginning of December. Lots of our kids are in the United States, mostly illegally, because there are not many good paying jobs around here. But they all come back in December for the festival, and then stay through New Year's. It's a special time because of that. The rabbit dance is one of our most traditional, so it's good that the kids come back to see it."

The scenes he depicts are based on life in Xalitla. The rabbit dance, weddings, festivals, and harvests are all set against a mountainous backdrop. The river that runs through town meanders across most of his works as well, nourishing a profusion of cacti, crops, and palm trees.

Xalitla, a village of roughly six thousand, is prosperous relative to others in the area.

"Most of the people in our town make their living creating pottery *artesanía*, so there aren't many hands available to work the fields. People *mas indígena que nosotros* come down from the hills to get jobs here as laborers. They only earn about sixty cents a day, but it's more than they can get up there."

At another small table Jesús's wife is busy painting a pitcher. She smiles shyly while she works. It's eighty degrees in the shade of their patio and she's wearing a black dress with a slip that peaks out from her hem. Her luminous ebony hair is fit for a Pantene commercial. She doesn't say much, but is an active listener, constantly nodding with big black eyes.

We ask Jesús about how the pieces get from here to the stores.

"When we finish up a large batch I load them into boxes, flag down a bus on the highway, and go into Acapulco. When I first started my business two years ago I had to go from store to store to try to sell them. Now I have some clients who buy anything I bring in. When I was younger, working for the German, I sometimes took things to Guadalajara. That's how you got that platter for your mother."

I picture Jesús winding through the mountains on a crammed bus headed to Acapulco. Months of effort and income sit unprotected in old cardboard boxes in the bowels of the vehicle. A carelessly thrown suitcase or not-uncommon highway robbery would wipe him out.

"We're almost ready to take a selling trip now. We just have to finish up those unpainted pieces you saw in the kiln. We have all the finished works stored in the house. Do you want to see them?"

He leads us through their stifling living room, past an unmade bed covered with mosquito netting, into a dark room. Throwing open a shutter, he lets the sunlight tumble in. As our eyes slowly adjust to the scene before us we are confronted with the mother lode of the Román family works. Stacks of trays, platters, cups, and plates cover the entire floor. I'm paralyzed by too many choices. After searching for ten years, I now have more options than I can handle. I break out of my daze and wade through the piles. Let's just say we now have family functions covered for the next fifty years.

A voice mail message from my parents awaits us at Las Brisas. They both talk into the recorder at the same time. Recounting the highlights of their honeymoon, they are still effusive after so many years. Just before their message gets cut off they exhort us to go see the cliff divers. "President Nixon was there when we went . . ."

The cliff divers are Acapulco icons. I remember watching them on ABC's "Wide World of Sports" while growing up. At least once a year the network would feature the daring young men soaring off a jagged cliff into the waves far below.

La Quebrada, where the divers perform, is about as far as you can get from Las Brisas and still be in Acapulco. By the time we get there, hundreds of people crowd a viewing platform opposite the cliff. We decide to watch the performance from the balcony of La Perla Hotel.

Until we saw the cliff up close I hadn't comprehended all of the potential dangers. The precipice slants backward so that the performers have to jump out to clear boulders at the point where the crag meets the sea. The ocean in the constricted gash where they dive, between the cliff and the viewing platform, churns like a Maytag washer. The water rushes into the narrow opening, caroms off a rock wall in the back, and crashes back out to the sea in a swirling green foam.

It's nerve-wracking to watch, yet impossible not to. As the show begins, the divers stand at the top of the cliff to bow before an altar dedicated to the Virgin of Guadalupe. The first diver performs from forty-five feet, about halfway up the cliff. He raises his arms and the crowd becomes silent. All we can hear are the waves violently crashing against the rocks. He pushes off and the crowd sucks in a collective breath until he hits the water. His little black head surfaces amid the foam, an olive in the spin cycle, and everybody exhales together.

The next diver moves up to a jutting protrusion at seventy-five feet. The crowd, expecting another swan dive, is surprised when he somersaults through the air in one and a half flips. Again, all is silent until his little head is seen bobbing on the waves.

The last diver stands at the very top of the cliff, 105 feet. He pauses, lifts his arms, waits for the space below to fill with a large wave, and then throws himself into emptiness. Flying in full layout flips, he hits the water in perfect form.

After they surface, the divers swim to the other side of the opening, climb up to the observation platform, and make their way through the crowd, accepting tips. The entire performance is over in the time it takes to drink half a *michelada*. The divers eventually circulate on the patio where we sit. One of them arrives at our table shivering in the night breeze. Against his wet hair, dark Speedo, and skin burned black by the Acapulco sun, his white teeth and white T-shirt look radioactive. José, the man who dove from 105 feet, has been performing for nine years. We had watched him work his way through the crowd with ease, walking comfortably from table to table, pausing for photos and chatting with each group. He's twenty-six years old, strong, stocky, and about five feet tall. We ask him how much longer he thinks he'll dive.

"Well, most divers don't make it much past age thirty-five. It's funny; it's not ligament stress or anything like that that causes people to retire. No. It's their eardrums and retinas. They start to go bad after too many years of hitting the water so fast. I'll do it as long as my body holds out, I guess."

When we walk downstairs into the La Perla restaurant, an older man in a tan *guayabera* hands me a flower and makes a cheesy remark about my "beautiful blue eyes." Meet Raúl García. García is Acapulco's most famous and audacious diver. At seventy-two years old he hasn't slowed down a beat. He hands us his card as we make introductions. It reads "La Perla Hotel, Public Relations." It appears that his job only deals with 50 percent of the public—the female half. We watch him chat and flirt with every woman that walks in as he offers her a red carnation.

We sit with García in the restaurant's large foyer. A long patio in front of us dangles over the opening where the divers land. The entire wall behind us features photos of divers, mainly 8x10s and larger. Most of them are of García. He started diving here when he was eight years old, and he performed for over fifty years.

The next show starts and García provides running commentary.

"Everybody knows that the cliff is 105 feet tall, but they don't have any idea about the other difficulties of the dive. The height is the least of it. For one thing, you have to jump out twenty-one feet to clear the rocks at the base of the cliff. You can't jump too far out, because the gap where you land is only fifteen feet wide. And then, when you hit the water, you'd better curl out of your dive pretty fast because it's only 12 feet deep."

Those variables don't sound as if they are OSHA approved. I ask if anybody has ever hit the rocks.

"Nobody has ever 'splatted,' if that's what you mean. Once I grazed a rock at the base. I've got a hard head, though. I just got a bump but the rock was pulverized. No, the worst thing is the sea urchins. You hit one of those at fifty-five miles per hour—that's how fast you're going when you enter the water—you hit one of those at fifty-five miles per hour and it hurts like hell."

One of the divers over-rotates a little and penetrates the water at less than a perfect ninety degrees. García scoffs.

"I could do that dive blindfolded. I'm in the *Guinness Book of World Records*, you know, because I've done more than 35,000 dives. Look on the wall over there. I've been a Timex man twice."

We walk over to a framed magazine page, a print ad from 1990. A close-up of García's face and arm fill the picture. He wears a Timex on his wrist. The text outlines his amazing longevity as a diver and the fact that he was featured in a 1962 Timex ad as well.

We walk back over to García, who says in English, "I've got both watches at home and they're still clicking. So am I, if you know what I mean."

Clicking, ticking, whatever—I don't want to picture what he means.

García pulls a stack of photos out of his pocket and walks us through his major feats. Some of the photos, over fifty years old, show him as a barrel-chested young man, taller and stronger than the two divers we met earlier.

A shameless self-promoter, García managed to parlay his diving into a career that took him all over the world. Through contact with Hollywood big shots that vacationed in Acapulco, he managed to get stunt double parts in films for stars like Johnny "Tarzan" Weissmuller and Elvis Presley. He also traveled across the United States as a diving showman.

"Here's one of me going off the Golden Gate Bridge from 180 feet. The water in that San Francisco Bay sure is cold. I also dove off bridges into the Cumberland and Ohio Rivers."

He turns to Bryan.

"Where are you from? Seattle? I dove off the rafters in the Seattle Coliseum into a tiny pool of water. Here's a picture of that. Oh, here's one in Toronto. I dove 150 feet into 7 feet of water. That sure had 'em entertained."

García's stunts were in demand all over the world. He tells us about dives in Venezuela, Japan, Canada, and elsewhere. He also shows us pictures of himself with famous movie stars.

By this time the last show of the night has started. Every evening, for the grand finale, divers launch from the rocks holding burning torches. I want to walk to the edge of the balcony to get a closer look, but I know that García would consider it a slight. Only an unnaturally large ego would propel a man to travel the world diving into puddles from outrageous heights. A psyche like that doesn't shrink just because he's retired. I listen to the roaring applause in one ear and García's tales in the other.

We have a photo taken together at the end of the evening. García wraps his arm around me and pulls my body in so that my breasts are smashed against the side of his chest. I stick out my elbow and poke him in the ribs. He twists to the side to parry my thrust, puts his other arm across my sternum, and gives me a squeeze. He may not dive anymore, but he still manages to get his thrills.

The real Tarzan, Johnny Weissmuller, might have loved Acapulco even more than his stunt diver. Weissmuller was introduced to the city by his good friend John Wayne. Weissmuller and Wayne bought a hotel here in 1954. They closed Los Flamingos to the public and it became the retreat of the Hollywood gang. Friends that joined them included Cary Grant, Dolores del Río, Errol Flynn, and Rex Allen.

The group sold the property in 1960, but Weissmuller kept his ties with Acapulco. He lived out the last years of his life here and is buried in Acapulco's Valley of the Light Cemetery. Weissmuller's gravestone is a tall monument that towers above the other marble markers in the vicinity. It reads "Tarzan, Johnny Weissmuller, homage to a man that chose to live and lie at rest in this beautiful port of Acapulco."

Although not the dazzling hot spot that it was in Weissmuller's day, Acapulco remains a fine place to rest. *Vuelva a la vida.*

Resources

"Acapulco in the Pink." *Saturday Review*, March 8, 1958, 46.

Adano, Marcelo. *El galón del Pacífico*. Acapulco: Museo Histórico de Acapulco Fuerte de San Diego, 2000.

Alessio Robles, Vito. *Acapulco en la historia y en la leyenda*. México, DF: Ediciones Botas, 1948.

"El galón de Manila." *Acatl Carrizo*. Acapulco: Museo Histórico de Acapulco Fuerte de San Diego, abril-mayo 1997.

Fischgrund, Eugenio. *Acapulco*. México, DF: Editorial Fischgrund, 1954.

Lobato, Lillian. "The Jet-Set Glamour that Made Acapulco Famous." *Acapulco Visitors' Bureau*, March 31, 2000.

Nin, Anaïs. *Collages: A Novel.* Athens: Swallow Press/Ohio University Press, 1964.

Sutton, Horace. "Life on a Mountainside." *Saturday Review*, December 11, 1965, 52-55.

Swartz, Mimi. "The Last Resort." *Texas Monthly*, November 1997, 92-103.

PULQUE

APÁN, MEXICO CITY, AND TEPOZTLÁN

Becky and I motor along the blacktopped roads sixty miles east of Mexico City. Two days ago we drove back to the capital from Acapulco. As we crisscross the country I tell myself there is a method to our logistical madness, but at this point, I bemusedly wonder what it is.

A dozen old travelogues led us on this day trip, naming the expansive Apán Valley as the primary source of pulque, a beverage that reigned as Mexico's supreme drink for at least five centuries before the Spanish arrived in 1519 and for another four centuries after.

In his 1909 book, *Mexico*, W. E. Carson described the Apán region as

> . . . plains relieved only by the monotonous rows of maguey plants, from which the national drink, pulque, is made. Apán, in fact, is the most important district in Mexico for the cultivation of this plant, a species of agave which looks a good deal like aloe, sometimes called the "century plant," from the fiction that it blooms once in a hundred years.

We inquire in the town of Apán about the location of the nearest *tinacal*, or pulque production site. After driving about twenty minutes into the barley-stitched countryside we see a crude sign that simply states "$ PULQUE," meaning "Pulque for sale."

At the end of a dirt road, a gentle old *campesino* meanders inquisitively toward us. He is dressed in pressed threadbare jeans and weathered, carefully polished cowboy boots to which only the most tenacious dust can cling. When we explain our interest he introduces himself as Gabriel and metaphorically offers us his humble *tinacal* shack, saying, "*Es su casa.*"

Don Gabriel suggests we first inspect the agave plants that line the nearby hills. There he leads us through rows of monstrous agave plants. The pulque variety is colossal in comparison to the agave we saw in Tequila.

He shows us a cross that has been carved into the underside of an eight-foot-long agave leaf, explaining that the plant is marked for castration. "This plant is about ten years old and ready to bloom. We must take action before it sends up its flower stalk or we will be robbed of a decade invested in cultivation. Just before the flower stalk sprouts is the best time for sap production. Afterward it's too late. The sap dries up, the plant dies, and we lose everything.

Fortunately, the agave gives us signs that it is about to bloom. The new leaves on the outside turn purple and the center ones bend inward, pointing to where the single flower stalk will emerge, just as if they are trying to tell us it is time for extraction."

The agave stalk, known as a "floral peduncle," produces the world's tallest flower. It lances upward over twenty feet high like an adolescent oak, and then emits yellow pom-pom blooms around the top. We learn that a few of the cultivated plants are allowed to flower so that their thousands of offspring can be transplanted to nurseries.

Our host climbs up the thick leaves, as sturdy as tree branches and cupped like wide green drain sprouts that narrow outward to a point. When he is positioned in the center of the plant, Don Gabriel looks like some kind of agave gnome. He peaks through lazy isosceles leaves that tower and bend above him. We can see his white cowboy hat and gray furry eyebrows above his twinkling eyes, but nothing else of his body. He works with a small ladle-shaped tool with which he scrapes the walls of a cylindrical hollow within the plant's core. The agave will try to heal the fresh wound by secreting sap known as *aguamiel*, honey water, into the carved-out hollow. (The term *aguamiel*

Pulque production sites, called *tinacales*, are becoming scarce on Mexico's central plateau. Imbibed in Mexico since Aztec times, pulque reached its peak of consumption during the early 1900s, when 17,000 gallons were shipped to Mexico City each day.

was subsequently adopted by tequila and mezcal producers to describe the juice extracted from crushed agave hearts).

Don Gabriel emerges with a gourdful of *aguamiel* in hand. Like an origami master, he folds a piece of a young agave leaf into a square cup, fills it with honey water, and passes it to us. We've rarely read or heard a pleasant word about pulque's flavor, so we are surprised when the unfermented raw material tastes delicious, like a fruity sugarcane juice.

The original discovery of the sweet *aguamiel,* as well as many other facts and legends of Aztec life, were documented by a Spanish friar, Bernardino de Sahagún. He spent a decade of the sixteenth century interviewing indigenous men who had lived through the conquest, enabling him to record the life, customs, and history of pre-Hispanic Mexico in admirable detail. The invaluable published work

Don Gabriel holding a gourd filled with *aguamiel.*

is titled *Historia universal de las cosas de Nueva España,* but is more often referred to as the Florentine codex.

When asked about the origin of pulque, the indigenous men, who became known as the Informants of Sahagún, responded:

> And here is how it happened:
> the maguey was scraped out,
> the bountiful maguey was discovered
> from which aguamiel comes.
> The first to discover the art of scraping it
> was a woman, her name, Mayahuel.

Mayahuel filled an animal skin with the honey water and took it to her tribe. The three men who studied the sweet liquid found that it foamed, soured, and thickened in a day's time. Like grapes into wine, *aguamiel* ferments naturally. The honey water turned into mildly alcoholic pulque. The men drank it and grew effusive, woozy, and contented.

Mayahuel led the men to the agave plant. They extracted a copious quantity of *aguamiel*, hauled the liquid in animal skins to the top of a hill, and poured it into a large ceramic pot. While the honey water fermented into effervescent pulque, runners were sent to the surrounding villages. The lords and elders of these villages gathered on the hill, which would become known as Foam Hill due to the pulque's quality of frothing during fermentation. A feast was prepared with dishes like corn tamales stuffed with snails, sweet potatoes, white fish in tart cherry sauce, and turkey simmered in tomatoes and chiles. Each lord was served four gourds full of the fermented *aguamiel*, now in its ripe, sour state of pulque. They drank these gourdfuls and proclaimed pulque to be a libation of the gods.

One leader, Cuextecatl, demanded another round. He drank a fifth gourd of pulque. With this extra serving, he turned loud, boisterous, and, finally, outlandish. In front of his fellow chiefs and the others in attendance, he cast aside his loincloth like a barbarian. He stood there completely naked, unashamed, laughing recklessly. The other lords stepped away from the madman. Cuextecatl, realizing that he was being ostracized, led his people away. They walked until they came to the ocean, saddened that they could distance themselves no further away from the loss of dignity.

The only remedy that the Cuextecas found for their bane was to imbibe more pulque. As they did so, they enjoyed other amusements such as musicians playing flutes. The tribe performed sleight of hand tricks that made strangers look on with awe. Some reported that they could make a hut burst into fire without setting a torch to it and make water suddenly gush forth from the ground. The people went naked and drank and sang, following the ways of their chief, until the Christians arrived.

The Cuextecas were cursed with drunkenness because their chief drank five gourdfuls instead of four on Foam Hill. Like their leader, the Cuextecas drank to excess, staggering and falling as though they lived on hallucinogenic herbs.

According to the Informants of Sahagún, of anyone known to be a drunk it was said:

> He is the image of Cuextecatl
> Have you perchance drunk five pulques?
> He drank five pulques.
> He not only drank four,
> he finished off five pulques!

In addition to propagating morality legends to reduce indulgence, pre-Hispanic cultures such as the Aztecs encoded severe laws to limit the negative effects of alcohol on society. Nobles who were found drunk in private were stripped of their titles; if caught in public they were sentenced to death. For a first offense, commoners had their heads shaved and were held up to public ridicule in the square. When found guilty of a second offense, they were sentenced to death by beating or strangulation.

The threat of alcohol to public order, as perceived by the pre-Hispanic rulers, was great. According to the Informants, one emperor warned his people, "Drunkenness is a malignant storm that brings all evil with it. Before adultery, rape, debauching of girls, incest, theft, crime, cursing and bearing false witness, murmuring, calumny, riots, and brawling, there is always drunkenness."

Compare that statement to a claim by the National Council on Alcoholism five centuries later. "Alcohol is typically found in the offender or the victim, or both, in about half of all homicides and serious assaults. Thirty-seven percent of rapes and sexual assaults involve alcohol use by the offender as do 15 percent of robberies, and 25 percent of simple assaults."

Yet despite the harsh laws and the moral sway, the Aztecs partied. Access to pulque was not a barrier. The production of agave was widespread due to the number of applications the plant offered. It provided fibers for textiles and paper; needles for surgery, punishment, and ear piercings; syrup for sweetening food; and thick, sturdy leaves for roofing material. *Aguamiel* ferments naturally, even if left in the core of the plant, so no additional materials were required to make pulque. There are a sufficient number of references to pulque in the Sahagún documents to suggest that illicit consumption occurred.

There were exceptions to Aztec prohibition. The elderly were permitted to drink at their leisure throughout the year, perhaps because their contribution to society had already been collected, and thus was no longer at risk. The general public was allowed to drink on certain holidays. One such festival was held just before the "dead days" at year's end, when people stayed close to home waiting to see if the gods would bless them with a new year.

The Informants described the festival, during which a small portion of pulque was even given to children and dabbed on the lips of babies:

> There the dancing and singing continued—the songs spreading the sound, crashing like waves. And there began the giving, the giving of pulque to the people. Everyone took his pulque; it was taken in earthen jars. There was giving to each other; there was continual giving to one another; there was continual returning, there was continual reciprocating.
>
> There was no awe of pulque. It was as if it bubbled up. It was as if it gleamed. The pulque ran like water.

Tribes that came to power in central Mexico, like the Aztecs and others before them, claimed lineage to powerful ancient empires. They adopted revered legends, casting their own people into the leading roles. Such is the case of the history of *aguamiel* and pulque. In the Toltec version, the father of the Mayahuel character sends her to present pulque to the emperor to gain favor with him. The emperor falls in love with the drink and the girl, marries her, and sires a son. The son, known as the Justice Maker, assumes the throne. He attempts to prevent a civil war, but fails. It leads to the downfall of the great Toltec civilization.

Katherine Ann Porter, one of the most ardent promoters of Mexican literature during the twentieth century, wrote a short story, "Hacienda" (1932), in which she describes a *tinacal* with a mural inspired by the Mayahuel legend:

> We walked through the vat-room, picking our way through the puddles of sap sinking into the mud floor, idly stopping to watch, without comment, the flies drowning in the stinking liquor which seeped over the hairy bullhides sagging between wooden frames. The walls were covered with a faded fresco relating the legend of pulque; how a young girl discovered this divine liquor, and brought it to the emperor, who rewarded her well; and after her death she became a half goddess. An old legend, maybe the oldest: something to do with man's confused veneration for, and terror of the fertility of women and vegetation.

Mayahuel, a demigoddess, is usually depicted as having the bare upper torso of a woman and an agave plant for a lower torso. She holds a babe to her breast and a flower stalk rises from her spine. The Informants described her as the woman of four hundred breasts, attesting to her fecundity as well as the productivity of the agave plant itself.

Don Gabriel informs us that each pulque agave yields an average of three quarts of *aguamiel* per day for a period of about four months, a rough equivalent of 360 quarts per plant. To prompt this output, twice per day the aguamiel is extracted and the cavity scraped anew.

That the pulque agave acts like a living spring is an important distinction between it and those agaves used to make tequila and mezcal. The plant is not uprooted, merely carved out, so that it continues secreting *aguamiel* while living on for another four months or so. This honey water is placed in a bin to ferment, resulting in a beverage similar to wine and beer in alcohol content.

In contrast, to produce tequila and mezcal, the agave is uprooted, baked, crushed, fermented, and distilled to concentrate it into potent hard liquor. The agave varieties used to make mezcal and tequila are not used to make pulque, nor vice versa.

A century ago, the *aguamiel* was transported from the field to the *tinacal* in cowhides and pigskins, endowing it with a particularly pungent flavor from the outset. Today Don Gabriel uses plastic buckets. The *tinacal* in which Don Gabriel makes his pulque is a two-room brick shack with dirt floors. In the first room, his wife ladles the milky white pulque from a ceramic jar into mugs for a pair of farmers.

He invites us into the back room where the pulque is fermenting in a three-by-five-foot fiberglass bin. The recipe for pulque is simple. Take one part *aguamiel*, wait for it to ferment; drink. The conversion of *aguamiel* to pulque is self-induced because the sap contains both the sugar and yeast necessary for fermentation. One further step is usually taken to speed the fermentation process, which is adding some old acidic pulque in with the new pulque.

Next to the vat is a shrine to the Virgin of Guadalupe. A velvet image of her hangs between small shelves with fresh flowers, all mounted on a square background of Christmas wrapping paper. Tiny lights frame the entire composition.

Our host scoops beneath the foam in the vat to fill two glasses with the cloudy concoction. It tastes sour, like plain yogurt, but with a definite fizz to it. The color is lighter than that of nonfat milk, though more

Pulque became such a popular drink in Mexico because it was so accessible. All people had to do was scoop some *aguamiel* (sap) out of an agave and wait for it to ferment. Nothing had to be added because the sap contains both the sugar and yeast necessary for fermentation. Here pulque ferments in a fiberglass vat.

viscous in consistency. It goes down easily after the first few gulps, and because the drink is cool on a hot day, it is unexpectedly refreshing.

Don Gabriel teaches us a drinking proverb in Spanish: *Una no es ninguna, dos es la mitad, tres sí es una, y como una no es ninguna, vuelve a empezar.* ("One cup is nothing, two are about half, the third cup—you could call that one, and since one is nothing, you must start again.")

Teaching us the proverb is a genial tactic to get us to accept refilled glasses, and it works.

When we say goodbye to Don Gabriel, he insists that we come back the next day for lunch. He informs us that he will be preparing *mixiote*, meat marinated in a chili *ancho* sauce that is wrapped in an agave leaf and cooked over a fire. We would love to say yes, but decline, having already made another commitment. We request pulque to go so that we can take it back to friends in Mexico City. He fills our plastic water bottle from the batch in the fiberglass tank. He pokes a hole the cap so that the still fermenting beverage can breathe and will not explode from the bottle.

Back in Apán proper, a town of about 30,000, we decide to stop by a *pulquería*, a tavern that dispenses pulque, to check out the ambience. The *pulquería*'s compact façade is a windowless wall painted with a Victoria Beer logo. Inside, the cement blocks that compose the walls remain unadorned and gray. Bare light bulbs hang from the ceiling. The only decorations of any sort are a dog and cat asleep on the dirt floor. The place reeks of rancid pulque, inspiring in us quakes of heebie-jeebies.

The owners are an elderly couple in miniature, she with ghoulish hollows for eyes, he with a bulbous nose pocked like volcanic rock, both with obliging smiles. The gentleman serves us pulque from a five-gallon plastic bucket that sits on the crude wooden bar. Slimy and spry, the pulque hurtles from the ladle into our cups. The flavor and consistency are considerably less appealing than that which we drank at the *tinacal*. This pulque, only ten miles from the production site, is more like the infamous grog that travelers who imbibed it during its heyday vituperated. The farther away from the production bin in time and distance, the less savory pulque becomes.

Stephen Crane wrote this in an article for the *Philadelphia Press* in 1895:

> The first thing to be done by the investigating tourist of this country is to begin to drink the national beverage, pulque. The second thing to

> be done by the investigating tourist is to cease to drink pulque. Why should a man ever taste another drop having collided with it once? It resembles green milk. And it tastes like—it tastes like—some terrible concoction of bad yeast perhaps. Or maybe some calamity of eggs.

The other patrons in the bar don't seem put off by the flavor. The four men here are in various states of stupor. An old man with gray hair sprouting from beneath a John Deere cap slumps, chin against chest, snoozing for the duration of our visit. The next man, a *gordito* in his late twenties, fades in and out of consciousness. Another is awake and grinning, but not saying much. His buddy is our main channel into the mind of the pulque drinker. He has on a neat white cowboy hat, a pressed green shirt unbuttoned to his belly, gold chains garlanding a hairy chest, and a red sash around his waist as a belt. We discuss his work as a migrant farm worker in the United States. He tells us that all of the young men from Apán venture to the same town in North Dakota, which they call Apán del Norte.

What hastens our exit is the arrival of an effusive man in the image of Cuextecatl, who seizes the opportunity to settle a historical score with gringos. Our experience with these types is numerous because there seems to be one at almost every party in Mexico. The drunk usually starts off by aggressively listing grievances against the United States. Because I agree with much of what he says, I defuse the situation by diplomatically lamenting the injustices with him. I then tell the drunk what I love about Mexico. It takes a moment for him to process my input, but eventually he embraces me as an *hermano*. Once the bond is established it is difficult to be rid of him.

When we shake hands, this particular *hermano* will not let go of mine. He insists that he buy us a round of pulques. I notice that our glasses are still full, but do not want to draw attention to the fact that we barely touched the beverage. My *hermano* boasts about his wealth in English, shouting, "I am reesh, I am reesh!" He frees my hand to swing his arms in an effort indicate the extent of his riches, which sends our two glasses of pulque flying off the bar, startling the sleeping animals and patrons. Under the cover of chaos, we depart.

The rapid quality degradation of pulque, which we experienced to some degree in the *pulquerías*, limited its consumption to its immediate area of production during most of its history. In the time that it took pulque to be transported to Mexico City on horseback, it grew rather ripe. This changed dramatically in the latter half of the nineteenth century with the introduction of the railroad. The iron horse allowed for rapid movement of pulque to the capital. By luck of routing, three lines crossed the Apán plains. With the faster supply lines in place, demand increased dramatically in the capital. This in turn spurred increased cultivation. Plantations flourished, inspiring great haciendas to be built by a newly established "pulque aristocracy." The principal families in this group formed a single company, a virtual monopoly that supplied 90 percent of the pulque to Mexico City. With their newfound power they negotiated favorable rates with the railroad through which they shipped three complete trainloads per day.

William Cullen Bryant writes in his 1872 essay "A Visit to Mexico" that

> we were among the fields of maguey, the plant with stiff, thick, dark-green leaves, from which the common drink of the country, called pulque, is drawn. On each side we saw them stretching away over the Champaign country to the bare hills that enclose it. . . . at a distance the rows seemed to run together, and the earth was completely hidden, for leagues around, under what seemed to the sight a close mass of dark-green leaves. . . . it would seem as if there was nothing but the maguey cultivated, so few are the other crops at this time of the year, and such is the great breadth of the region occupied by this plant. The railways also attest to the extent of this traffic. The freight-trains drag huge cars loaded with pulque in barrels, and also in skins, the primitive method of keeping wine in Spain. At the railway stations were piles of barrels and huge heaps of skins filled with pulque waiting their turn to be transported to market. (35-6)

In 1900, during the peak of consumption, seventeen thousand gallons were being shipped to Mexico City daily. Like the Aztecs, ensuing governments initially tried to limit the consumption of pulque through prohibition and taxation. The Spanish, in an effort to protect their own wine and liquor industry, limited the number of *pulquerías* in the capital to thirty-five. After independence, the Mexican government occasionally imposed laws to maintain public order, but the tax revenue from a thirsty populace was simply too lucrative to pass up. Pulque taxation constituted nearly a tenth of government income.

A century ago, Mexico City's 600 *pulquerías* were the most ubiquitous of gathering spots. The bars were decorated with brightly colored tissue paper and flags inside and out. The exterior walls were painted in florid colors with birds, tropical flowers, warriors, chariots, martyrs, and saints. Willow branches draped over the doors. The varied green glasses ranged in size from sample shots to one-quart vases. Wry invention was key to naming the venues. Among the locales were "A Trip to the Moon," "Baco's Preoccupation," "Hangover Hospital," and the "Playground for Those Out Front," which was located across the street from the legislature building.

While some people were charmed by the folkloric aspects of the *pulquerías*, others described them in dire terms such as "reeking, foul-smelling dens with earthen floors" frequented by "ragged and filthy men, boys, and even women." Pulque was a cheap buzz, the Thunderbird Wine of its time. *Pulquerías* catered to destitute peons for the most part. Haciendas frequently paid part of their workers' salaries in pulque.

Indigenous people were particularly at risk to alcoholism and succumbed in great numbers. Physically their bodies struggled to metabolize the alcohol, and psychologically it provided an escape from oppression. Once lauded for its nutritional content of vegetable proteins, carbohydrates, and vitamins, supplements to the pre-Hispanic diet, pulque ultimately proved to be a lethal double-edged sword.

You have to search to find a *pulquería* in Mexico City today. The one that most people know of is in Plaza Garibaldi. The quality of the pulque served anywhere in Mexico City should be suspect. There are no longer three trains per day dedicated to its transport, so the city's pulque is usually slimy and vile. Of such pulque a reviewer might write, "The flavor and aroma are equally well-balanced like curdled cream with a touch of rotting plums, revealing capricious undertones of toe-jam, and endowed with a complex finish of dachshund fart." Vendors mask the poor flavor in the traditional method of "curing" it with fruit and spices.

It was this rapid deterioration and the inability to preserve it through bottling that led to pulque's demise. Similar in alcohol content and cost, beer was more shelf stable and simply tasted better. Beer wiped pulque off the map in all except a handful of countryside production areas.

The downfall of pulque is evident in Apán's landscape. The agave's dominant "mass of dark green leaves" that Bryant described has disappeared with the exception of rows grown as a fence line and the rare cultivated agave field. Barley now dominates most of the plain.

During our drive back to Mexico City we notice that the other prevalent crop is the prickly pear cactus, called *nopal* in Spanish. The cactus is a collection of green paddles tilted and turned in all directions, making it look like a Cubist rendering. The pads are stripped of their spines, cut into slices, grilled, and served in tacos and other dishes, while the prickly pear fruit (*tuna* in Spanish) is used to make juice and sauces.

The *nopal* is as old and revered as the agave in Mexican history. The Informants reported that the Aztecs left their original territory, Aztlán, located somewhere in northwest Mexico, to look for a new homeland—where they would find an eagle with a snake in its beak, perched on a *nopal* cactus. They saw the omen on a small island where Mexico City's historical center is now located, when the entire valley was a vast lake. They named their new land Tenochtitlán, which means "place of the divine prickly pear" in Nahuatl. The prickly pear was sacred because it symbolized the human heart.

To understand how the Aztecs became known as Mexicas, and subsequently, why the Spaniards called Tenochtitlán "Mexico," I consult the Sahagún documents. The Informants tell of the priest who beheld the prophecy, "According to tradition, the name of the priest who led the Aztecs, was Mexicatl. That comes from the name Mecitli: *me*, that is to say *maguey*; and *citli*, rabbit. It is said that when he was born they named him Citli. And they placed him in a maguey leaf, where he grew strong. And since he led his subjects, therefore they were given the name Mexica."

These two plants, the maguey and the *nopal*, are integral components of Mexican national identity. An eagle with a snake in its beak perched on a *nopal* graces the national flag. The image of a rabbit sheltered by a maguey is evoked when one says the country's name.

In our car, the plastic water bottle filled with pulque is fizzing and spitting through the tiny hole punched in the top. The pulque is young, still fermenting, and the gas that escapes fills up the interior with a nauseating aroma of a *pulquería*. We feel that enduring the odor is a worthy sacrifice because we are attending a birthday party this evening for our friend John. We're sure that pulque fresh from the *tinacal* will be the hit of the party.

The nopal cactus, one of the symbols on the Mexican flag, can be found growing in the fields of central Mexico. The pads of the cactus are stripped of their spines, cut into slices, grilled, and served in tacos and other dishes. The fruit, called *tuna,* is used to make juice and sauces.

We've been using John's apartment as a base during our travels in Mexico. His apartment is easy for us to find because it's my old apartment, the one I lived in during most of the five years that I spent working in Mexico. When I met John, an earnest consultant from Chicago, he was rooming with a journalist from Virginia, Hugh, one of the tallest gringos that ever ambled across the border. I convinced them to move from their dungeon into my airy three-bedroom flat that overlooked the Bohemian neighborhood of Condesa. John is now the sole resident of the apartment, so my old room is available. It feels like coming home.

The people who enlivened my neighborhood when I left Mexico five years ago are still here. The Trolls, a strange family that live under the stairs and act as superintendents, are as mystifying as ever. I buy the newspaper from the same corner newsman. I do not even have to look from the balcony to see who is offering services or goods in the street below. Their calls are familiar. The flute is played by a man who sharpens knives. He flips his bicycle over to use the pedal mechanics to power his whetting wheel. The prolonged, undulating cry of "ga-a-a-a-a-a-a-a-a-as" is yodeled by the seller of gas tanks that each apartment buys to heat the water. Loudspeakers attached to the fruit vendor's truck scratch and squeal, "*Naranjas. Naranjas. Jugosas, ricas naranjas. Diez pesos.*" This pitch for oranges is so deafening that you can't do another thing except suffer through it and hope that no one forestalls the vehicle's progress with a purchase.

John is Irish American and today, fittingly, Saint Patrick's Day, is his birthday. There are no Irish pubs in Mexico City, so he's had his annual get-together most years in a pseudo-English pub. The bar is packed to standing room only. Gradually we snag and link enough tables for most of us to sit down. Nearly everyone who sees the pulque we brought turns up a nose at it. The ultra-curious take a few polite swigs when they learn it comes directly from the *tinacal* in Apán.

Rather than push the pulque, we simply switch gears by ordering a bottle of tequila. Becky extracts a bottle of food coloring to turn the shots green. She tints everyone's beers as well. It inspires fond remembrance from the gringos and explanations to those Mexicans who are not familiar with our Irish holiday. Several people squeal when pinched.

The first time I met Becky she served me a green tequila shot. She was throwing a party at her Mexico City abode, a dual celebration for Saint Patrick's Day and John's birthday. She and John had met a few months earlier at a Thunderbird University alumni function. Becky's party fell on the first night of a four-day weekend. John and I had plans to go to the mellow beach of Zipolite the next day, so he described the undeveloped paradise to Becky. By the end of the evening she was on the phone with her twenty-four-hour travel agent changing her destination from Acapulco, where she was to spend the weekend with work associates, to the coastal airport in Oaxaca.

Our hotel room in Zipolite consisted of three cement block walls and a palm thatched roof. The fourth wall was nonexistent, open to the ocean, inviting in the salty breeze.

Zipolite is a nude optional locale favored by Europeans and anachronistic hippies. Our hotel's dining area was composed of ten tables planted on the beach and covered by a thatched roof. Each morning John and I would happily munch pancakes and ogle the voluptuous pink flesh of Scandinavian women. Becky lamented that the male exhibition consisted only of Naked Spinning Man, a long-bearded, leathery dropout who spun around in circles knee-deep in water, his appendages and privates flailing in the centrifugal force. Our dining table was only a few feet away from the beach chairs. We made it our goal to move less than ten yards per day, excepting trips to the bathroom and the ocean. Lunch was followed by afternoons of card playing that merged surreptitiously into dusk, dinner, darkness, and more cards.

At John's birthday party this year only a few of the faces are familiar, though the group reminds me of our free-flowing gang during my ex-pat time here. About two-thirds of us were foreigners, from the United States and Canada mostly, but there were also several Europeans. The other third of our social group was Mexican, bicultural folk who found satisfaction in switching from Spanish to English in mid-sentence, knowing that they could be understood. They were the reverse image of ex-pats and interlocked superbly.

The group of young ex-pats of which we were a part arrived in Mexico during a time of tremendous political and economic change. When the North American Free Trade Agreement came to a vote before the U.S. Congress, we gathered in a bar to watch on cable, cheering as if it was the Super Bowl when the tally was confirmed. Our camaraderie was an extension of college in the sense of euphoric partying, but with intensive cultural immersion and levels of responsibility in the workplace difficult to attain stateside. We ran departments, owned companies, edited newspapers, modeled for magazines, and represented federal and state government offices. Most of us were under thirty; many of us were under twenty-five. We grew older, a bit more financially stable, and became fluent in Spanish when suddenly a major currency devaluation struck, devastating the Mexican economy. We were scattered to the wind in search of livelihood beyond Mexico's borders.

Most of us left, anyway. John stuck it out. He kept his consulting business alive by expanding into other Latin American markets and now contemplates whether he'll ever go home.

Depending on the traffic out of Mexico City, it is a one- to two-hour drive south to Tepoztlán. The best route is to start on the Mexico City-Acapulco toll road, then veer off on a spur just before reaching Cuernavaca. Cuernavaca has traditionally been a sumptuous garden retreat for Mexico City residents. Over the years more and more people moved there to commute to Mexico City, so that now Cuernavaca is a major city itself, with all of the problems that go along with it. Tepoztlán, once a sleepy village, has also experienced substantial growth. Its lovely oval valley is filled with part- and full-time homes belonging primarily to artists and new-agers.

What attracts the spiritually aware are animated rock formations similar to those found in Sedona, Arizona, and Cappadoccia, Turkey. While Tepoztlán's rocks are not blessed with the engaging colors of those locales, purple jacaranda and vivid splashes of bougainvillea more than compensate. The rocks form a massive, undulating 800-foot basalt wall on one side of town, and smaller, beguiling hills the rest of the way around. Statuesque boulders, rotund towers, and teetering stalactites protrude from the imposing calico wall while lush foliage billows out of its shadowy vertical creases.

We park our car in the heart of town where a craft market dominates the street. The swirls of incense and flashes of tie-dye are wandering spirits that have taken refuge in earthly goods. My main preoccupation is finding a way to hydrate my green Saint Patrick's Day hangover, which I do with blue Gatorade. As we make our way up cobblestone roads leading to the mountain, the sun beats against our suffering heads. Our destination this morning is the Tepozteco pyramid, perched at the top of this rocky curtain. We have come to pay homage in labored steps, sweat, and gasps to the ancient agave god Tepoztecatl.

Robert Redfield's *Tepoztlán, A Mexican Village,* written in 1930, inspired our visit:

> Some one of the many gods generally shared by the highland pueblos of Mexico was regarded as the special protector of each one of the villages. That deity particularly associated with Tepoztlán was Ome Tochtli, Two Rabbit, the god generally described as that of drunkenness.
>
> The god of the temple in his capacity as patron of Tepoztlán, or perhaps another closely associated with Ome Tochtli, was known as Tepoztecatl. The ruins on the cliff above town are known as "the house of Tepozteco."

Tepoztecatl was born to a virgin mother. Afraid of losing her honor in her community, she hid the infant near an anthill. Instead of devouring the babe, the ants brought him food in a long sinuous caravan. He suckled from the leaves of a *maguey* until he was found and adopted by an elderly couple.

The couple sheltered Tepoztecatl in their home and he provided for them by becoming an expert hunter. When his frail adoptive father was to be sacrificed to the Ogre King, Tepoztecatl offered himself to the monster in his father's place. The Ogre King swallowed Tepoztecatl in one gulp. Soon after, the beast clutched his stomach and doubled over in pain. A knife blade broke through the skin of his belly from within. Tepoztecatl had secretly armed himself and cut his way out, killing the beast, and in the process became a hero to the surrounding community. No longer would the villagers be sacrificed to the Ogre King. In this way, he became the town's protector. Tepoztecatl, who is usually depicted in battle dress with a copper hatchet, frequently defended the town from marauding tribes.

Tepoztecatl's Aztec calendar name was Two Rabbit (Ome Tochtli). Like the goddess Mayahuel's four hundred breasts signifying abundant aguamiel, Aztec chronicles mention four hundred rabbits associated with drunkenness. The Informants of Sahagún recounted that when Mayahuel discovered the honey water in the maguey plant, three men took part in the creation of pulque on Foam Hill. Tepoztecatl was one of these men, supposedly the one who perfected the craft, which is how he figures as a principal god of pulque and drunkenness.

The hike to the ruins is steep, but crude stairs have been cut into the stone to make the going easier. The stairs wind around craggy walls stubbled with tenacious brush. Families, couples, and groups huff and puff their way upward. Fathers carry young ones on strong shoulders. The weary pause, drink water, and wipe the sweat from their brows. The path corners frequently, leading through rocky corridors. About 45 minutes into the hike we reach the final ascent, which is accomplished via a steel ladder welded together and cemented into the rock.

The main pyramid is built up in six rectangular levels. The top floors are partially plastered with white limestone mortar. A placard indicates that priests conducted religious ceremonies dedicated to Tepoztecatl in this temple.

Groups of teenagers dangle their legs over the sides of the upper floors. We hike up toward them, and then climb the precarious tiny steps that lead the way to the summit. From here we can see the entire valley of Tepoztlán. The main streets create a plaid pattern dotted with houses. You would expect a beatific silence in such a moment, but even from here we can hear the wail of a car alarm sounding below.

Tepoztlán was one of the first villages to be subjugated by the Aztecs after they secured power in Mexico City. The Aztec religion was open and dynamic. Tepoztecatl, like gods of other tribes that the Aztecs conquered, was adopted into the Aztec pantheon.

Likewise, the Spaniards made Tepoztlán an early acquisition. In 1521, the same year that they conquered the Aztecs, the Spaniards journeyed here. Bernal Díaz del Castillo wrote in *The Conquest of New Spain,* "In Tepoztlán we found many pretty women and much loot. Cortés summoned three or four times for the chiefs to come and make peace, and said if they did not come he would burn the town and go in search of them. They replied that they did not intend to come, therefore, so as to strike fear into other *pueblos*, Cortés ordered half of the houses to be set on fire." Tepoztlán and all of the area around Cuernavaca became part of Cortés's personal holding, giving him rights to both land and labor.

The Dominican priests were charged with converting the natives and building the cathedral, which still stands today. After the cathedral was completed in 1588, Friar Domingo de la Asunción ordered that the statue of Tepoztecatl situated on the pyramid be knocked down. When he saw that the fallen statue remained whole, he had it smashed into pieces and buried these shards at the base of a nearby church.

The people of Tepoztlán originally made offerings of papyrus, palm oil, quail, and pigeons to Tepoztecatl. As an Aztec tributary, human sacrifice had been instituted. The Spaniards tried, but could not do away with all of the pagan practices. Tepoztecatl simply would not disappear that easily.

The journalist Hart Crane reported in a letter in 1931:

> The most exciting feature of the trip and visit was the rare luck of arriving on the eve of the yearly festival of Tepoztecatl, the ancient Aztec god of pulque, whose temple, partially ruined by the Spaniards and recent revolutions, still hangs on one of the perilous cliffs confronting the town.
>
> The people, largely elderly, divided into several groups around lanterns on the roof of the cathedral and monastery (of all places!),

> which dominates the town, made a wonderful sight with their white "pyjama" suits and enormous white hats. A drummer and a flute player standing facing the dark temple on the heights, alternated their barbaric service at ten minute intervals with loud ringing of the church bells by the sextons of the church. Two voices, still in conflict here in Mexico, the idol's and the Cross. Yet there really did not seem to be a real conflict that amazing night. Nearly all of these elders go to mass!
>
> They served us delicious coffee, all the hotter with a generous infusion of pulque, straight pulque alcohol in each cup.

This festival still takes place every year on September 8, coinciding with the celebration of the birth of the Virgin Mary. A stage is set up in front of the church where a dancer dressed as Tepoztecatl does battle with representatives of the surrounding villages. In a dire moment in mid-battle, when it looks as if all will be lost to his foes, Tepoztecatl converts to Christianity, then slays his enemies to claim victory. Even the Christians could not resist adopting Tepoztecatl into their own lore.

From the swelter of the temple, we begin our hike down the mountain, our sights set on cold beverages to quench the thirst from our pilgrimage. Almost everyone stops at one of the makeshift stands at the bottom of the trail for a cold beer or *michelada*. Pulque may be nearly extinct, but Tepoztecatl, the ancient drink's crafter, god of drunkenness, protector of this village and hero in three successive religions, is still at large.

Resources

Álvarez, José Rogelio, ed. *Enciclopedia de México*. México, DF: Compañía Editora de Enciclopedias de México, 1987.

Barrios, Virginia B. de. *A Guide to Tequila, Mezcal, and Pulque*. México, DF: Editorial Minutiae Mexicana SA, 1971.

Bryant, William Cullen. "A Visit to Mexico." In *Gringos in Mexico: An Anthology*, edited by Edward Simmen. Fort Worth: Texas Christian University Press, 1988.

Carson, W. E. *Mexico*. New York: Macmillan, 1909.

Ceballos Novello, Roque J. *Culturas del Valle de México*. México, DF: El Nacional, 1941.

Chase, Stuart. *Mexico: A Study of Two Americas*. New York: Macmillan, 1938.

Crane, Hart. *Letters of Hart Crane 1916-1932*. Berkeley: University of California Press, 1965.

Crane, Stephen. *Uncollected Writings of Stephen Crane in the West and Mexico*. Stockholm: Acta Universitatis Upsaliensis, 1962.

Díaz del Castillo, Bernal (1496-1584). *The Conquest of New Spain*. Baltimore: Penguin Books, 1963.

Flandrau, Charles Macomb. *Viva Mexico!* New York: D. Appleton and Company, 1908.

Gonzales Lima, Oswaldo. *El pulque y maguey en los codices mexicanos*. México, DF: Fondo de Cultura Económica, 1978.

Humboldt, Alexander. *Political Essay on the Kingdom of New Spain*. 1811. Reprint, New York: AMS Press, 1940.

López, Virginia. "El maguey, creador de una cultura ancestral." *El Sol*, July 3, 1991.

Ober, Frederick A. *Travels in Mexico*. Boston: Estes and Lauriat, 1883.

Poblett, Martha. *En torno al pulque y al maguey*. México, DF: Grupo Editorial Siquisiri, 1995.

Porter, Katherine Anne. *Collected Essays and Occasional Writings*. New York: Delacorte Press, 1970.

Rascón, Vincent. *Myths and Gods of Ancient Mexico*. Menlo Park, CA: Education Consortium of America, 1975.

Redfield, Robert. *Tepoztlán, A Mexican Village*. Chicago: University of Chicago Press, 1930.

Sahagún, Bernardino de. *Historia general de las cosas de Nueva España* [Florentine codex]. Originally compiled 1576-1577. Reprint, Salt Lake City: University of Utah, 1975.

Corona

SAN MIGUEL DE ALLENDE

The fountain halts Bryan and me in mid-stride. Twenty feet tall and built into a wall in the street, every inch of it is overlaid with recently placed decorations. At its center a Virgin of Sorrows with a small dagger through her heart cries in her purple robe. Cadmium oranges dot the fountain's steps and ledges like brass studs. Pierced with tiny gold flags, the fruit glimmers in the gloaming. Little jars of sprouting wheat, slender emerald stalks reaching toward the burnished sky, sit tucked between each orange. Purple forget-me-nots and white calla lilies fill in leftover spaces and line the fountain's high top edge. Fresh chamomile, spread in a fragrant mat, covers the stone beneath all the adornment. It's more reminiscent of shrines in Bali than anything we've ever seen in Mexico.

A man and a woman carefully attend to the fountain's final details, straightening a plant here and placing an extra orange there. She wears a faded blue dress protected by a soft cotton apron. Her partner stands from a stooped position, hitches up a pair of khaki workpants, adjusts his crumpled straw hat, and nods in greeting.

We admire their work and question them about each of the fountain's adornments. She positions a clump of chamomile while he guides us through the decorative elements.

"Well, to start with, the oranges are bitter, not sweet. They stand for the tears and anguish of the Virgin of Sorrows—because her son is being sacrificed. The gold flags make them precious. The sprouts were planted as seeds of Christianity. Their growth means that Christ will rise again. The flowers stand for penance and royalty. You might not have noticed, but all the objects are in rows of seven. That represents the Virgin's seven sorrows."

We had heard about San Miguel de Allende's tradition of decorating the city's fountains the Friday before Good Friday, but hadn't imagined this type of extravagance. People here in the colonial heart of Mexico take their religion and its accompanying ceremonies very seriously.

Because we are at the end of the dry season, the city has been rationing water during the afternoon. Not today. Cool jets of liquid pour into every fountain in town.

Even fountains in private homes get special treatment today. We know this because we are staying in a friend's colonial-era house. It feels good to be stationary. Tired after weeks on the road, we have temporarily retired our suitcases so that we can spend some time compiling our notes and gathering steam for the final leg of our trip.

This home, our little version of paradise, features flower-filled outdoor patios, a rooftop balcony with views of the many village churches, and a tinkling fountain. Our housekeeper, Lupe, drained the fountain this morning and gave it a thorough cleaning before refilling it and putting fresh flowers around its base.

I asked Lupe about the day's events while she stood in our kitchen stirring homemade ice cream.

"All of the activities are dedicated to the *Virgen de Dolores* [Virgin of Sorrows]. There are lots of traditions associated with today. For one thing, people decorate all the public fountains in town. Then, later, at the San Francisco Cathedral, they take offerings for the church to use throughout the year.

"Many people also set up altars in their homes featuring the *Virgen de Dolores*. At night their neighbors, and even strangers, come by to honor her. I create an altar in my front room every year. When people leave my house, I give them ice cream. That's what I'm making right now. After all, you never know if one of them is Christ come back to visit his congregation."

After our fountain tour we stop by the San Francisco Cathedral. Four little girls in crooked angel costumes lead a procession to the altar. Most of the people bear traditional gifts like flowers, palms, candles, and wine. Bryan nudges me to point out that a few members of the group, more practical than their peers, lug offerings of mops and plastic buckets.

Out on the streets, hundreds of people walk from house to house visiting altars and receiving ice cream bars. Families stand in line, patiently licking their frozen treats while waiting to enter each home.

The altars, set up in front windows, entryways, and patios, range from poignantly simple to surprisingly ornate. Almost all of the designs incorporate candles, oranges, and purple flowers. Some fill entire rooms and feature intricate carpets of sand and flowers. My favorite one is a Last Supper of blond Ken dolls wearing rough cotton tunics.

Bryan and I are struck by the orderliness of the crowd. Large groups of people stand quietly, reverently, and wait for their treats. This is a night for honoring the Virgin—the goodies are secondary.

The Virgin and other symbols of the church have broad appeal in this country, where 90 percent of the population call themselves

Catholic. The history of Catholicism in Mexico goes back almost five hundred years. When the conquistadors arrived from Spain, they brought with them a special brand of Iberian Catholicism. Characterized as militant, intolerant, and uncompromising, the Spanish church, shaped by centuries of conflict with Moorish invaders, sought to convert its new subjects quickly and, if need be, ruthlessly.

The indigenous people of Mexico, when forced, were able to assimilate this new theology. In a world of human sacrifice, many of them greeted with relief the news of a god whose death sufficed for all. Already religious and practicing fasting and confession, they were accustomed to a dominant priestly class. The Spanish priests simply replaced their old shamans and holy men. They took these new Christian concepts and worked them into their own religious beliefs, creating a uniquely Mexican Catholicism. Although church and state are strictly separated today, Catholicism still plays a central role in the lives of many people, especially during Holy Week.

Although jump-started by the day dedicated to the Virgin of Sorrows, Holy Week in San Miguel de Allende officially kicks off on Palm Sunday. We walk to the town's main plaza, known as the Jardín. The square is closed to traffic today, but a blue and yellow Corona truck is parked in the middle of the street. Its pot-bellied driver flirts with a policewoman while two young men haul cases of beer into the restaurants ringing the Jardín.

Holy Week is a busy time for beer sellers. Curious about the logistics of delivering beer to even the most remote locales, we've been in contact with the Corona headquarters in Mexico City. We want to ride in one of their trucks on a San Miguel route. I wonder to myself if we'll end up spending the day with this overweight ladies' man.

We are drawn to the festivities at the San Francisco Cathedral by a frenzied pealing of bells. Two men stand in the carillon tower. One vigorously pulls a rope attached to a clapper as tall as he is, while the other wildly spins his bell around and around.

Vendors line the long pathway to the church doors. All are selling objects made of palm fronds. Woven by hand into intricate works of art, the fresh palm leaves will be used for the day and then discarded. Longer-lasting dried palms are fashioned into crosses, fans, and even candle holders. A sweet smell, like fresh hay, hangs in the air. We stop to admire a brilliant miniature crucifix. Christ, braided onto the beam, wears a straw crown dyed purple. Heads of dried wheat sprout from the top of the cross.

We're so intrigued with the palms that we don't notice the first of the day's many processions until we are almost run over by a donkey carrying Jesus. He is followed by hundreds of people who have paraded down from a chapel high above town. Jesus is wearing white robes and a sticky felt beard that must itch in this heat. A group of disciples in the same white robes and brightly-colored sashes leads a gaggle of nuns. Behind them follow the town faithful.

Every person carries a handful of the braided palm creations. Some of the designs are interwoven with purple flowers, others with small yellow buds. Many of the members of this procession are humble people from the outskirts of town. The wrinkled old women wear *rebozos*, Mexican scarves that cover their heads and drape down across their shoulders. The men, in fancy western shirts and jeans, remove their cowboy hats as they walk through the doors to reveal two-tone foreheads. Entering the church two by two, they remind me of Noah's Ark.

Inside the cavernous cathedral it's standing room only. The priest, adorned in crimson robes, stands in front of a rich purple-and-gold altar. The air is thick with incense and waving palms. Their shimmering fronds create the illusion that the church is moving, swaying to the sad rhythm of the organ. Not many people know the words to the hymn, but they make up for their lack of singing by jostling their palms vigorously. The rustling blades almost drown out the music.

As the procession enters the church it looks as if the donkey is going to head all the way to the altar. He is led off at the last second, however, and is now tied to an orange tree outside. An old ranch hand with weathered skin and a wide straw hat sits in the shade next to the tree. We ask the man, Gonzalo, about how his donkey was chosen to lead the procession.

"*Pues*, I work for a man, Señor Pérez, who is good friends with the priest. He helps the priest organize this whole procession. I live on his *rancho* outside of town. Señor Pérez told me to pick the best burro, to give it a good bath, and to prepare it to carry Jesus."

Gonzalo rubs his hand through the small donkey's white hair. The strands are fluffy and curly and smell like Pert shampoo.

"Did you know that donkeys are blessed animals? They have special protection from God because one carried Mary and Jesus from the Holy Land to Egypt. Look here at its wither. You see this cross of dark hair? All donkeys have this cross. It's a symbol of divine protection."

There is some type of religious observance or procession almost every day for the rest of the week. By Friday the city is packed to the gills. Thousands of people from all over Mexico and abroad have descended on San Miguel to witness the Easter weekend festivities. Today's procession starts at noon at the city's parochial church on the main square. Vendors make their way through the crowd selling sun umbrellas in a staggering range of colors and designs. The sea of people, spiked with hundreds of paper parasols, is like a giant party drink at a cheap Chinese restaurant. A chubby little girl in an angel costume pushes past us. Huffing and puffing, she disappears behind the church doorway. Men dressed as Roman soldiers stand guard on the roof above the entrance.

A stage has been set up on the steps of the church. A priest reads the events of Good Friday from the Bible. The actors behind him—Roman soldiers, Pontius Pilate, and Barabbas—miss all their cues. Finally, once Pilate has washed his hands of the matter, it's time for the procession.

The procession can't begin until the stage is disassembled, because the stage completely blocks the steps. Nobody in the pageant can come out of the church until the stairs are free. Rather than build a portable platform, the procession organizers created a solidly constructed stage of planks and two-by-fours held together by nails. It takes more than ten minutes to tear it apart, but the crowd doesn't seem to mind or really even notice the delay.

The first group out of the church doors is the children's choir, in purple and white robes. An out-of-tune band comes next. In between each row of musicians march little boys in white shirts. We can't figure out why the boys are there until they pass us. Clothespinned to the back of each boy's shirt is the sheet music for the band member behind him.

Litters bearing life-size statues of Jesus and various Virgins and saints follow. The heavy platforms balancing the Virgins are carried solely by women. The older ladies wear shiny black pumps with high, spiky heels—an amazing balancing act considering the cobblestones and their weighty load.

Behind them follow twenty barefoot penitents in crowns of thorns, blood trickling down their faces. They wear purple sackcloth and drag heavy wooden crosses. Many have ceramic human skulls tucked under their arms. These men, all volunteers, are atoning for their sins. They are ringed by an army of Roman soldiers playing little reed fifes. Following the soldiers are the angels, including the chubby one that stepped on my foot.

By the time Easter Sunday rolls around the town has had enough processions. Instead, we watch large *papier-mâché* figures being blown up at the Jardín. Representing Judas, these figures, about twice life size, are strung up in the street in front of the main plaza. Hung on ropes that run from roofs to the tops of trees, there are about thirty figures in all. One by one, each Judas is lowered to the ground, where a fuse is lit. Firecrackers cause the figure to spin in circles as it is being raised back into the air. The last firecracker sets off a loud M-80 that blows the Judas into a thousand bits of colorful tissue. Paper body parts fly through the air, landing in the outstretched arms of waiting kids. We watch a boy make an impressive diving catch for one Judas's head. Especially successful kids walk around with entire collections of limbs. One little girl about three feet tall clutches two legs that reach high over her head, while another has a giant arm tucked under her own puny armpit. No wonder the Easter bunny isn't very popular here. How could it compete with these explosions?

People in San Miguel are fascinated with firecrackers. They seem to go off between five and six in the morning and eleven and twelve at night on a daily basis. Once a year, however, during the independence holiday, the city's leaders create the mother of all fireworks shows. Several years ago I was here in San Miguel on September 15 for the spectacle. Packed into the Jardín with thousands of fellow spectators, I watched what seemed like hours of explosions. Set up in elaborate towers in front of the church, the fireworks mesmerized the crowd. Burning balls of fire occasionally dropped down on the throng, but miraculously nobody seemed to get hurt. Dodging these stray embers was part of the fun.

The highlight of the night was *El Grito*. Performed at 11 PM on plazas across Mexico, *El Grito* is a reenactment of the original call to independence. The mayor, waving a large Mexican flag, stood in front of the crowd and yelled, "*¡Viva México!*"

The throng, in screaming unison, replied, "*¡Viva!*"

"*¡Viva la independencia!*"

"*¡Viva!*"

"*¡Vivan los héroes!*"

"*¡Vivan!*"

The wave of voices, rising together louder and louder, brought goose bumps to my skin.

The original *Grito* was shouted by Miguel Hidalgo in 1810. Known as the father of Mexican independence, Hidalgo was a parish priest in a village nearby. Bryan and I have come to this village, known today as Dolores Hidalgo, to check out the birthplace of the independence movement.

The Independence Museum, a block off the main square, gives us some details of the uprising. By the turn of the nineteenth century the church had grown to be the most powerful fixture in New Spain. It was so wealthy that it had become the richest colonial lending institution. Many of the people who borrowed its money were *criollos*, descendents of Spanish colonists born in the New World.

The Crown resented and feared the power of the Catholic Church. In order to curb its influence, Spain decreed the immediate transfer of all church charitable funds (the assets from which the loans were made) to the royal coffers. This forced the church to call in its debts, hitting the *criollos* in the pocketbook. The *criollos*, already denied access to the highest positions in society because they weren't born in Spain, were outraged.

A group of *criollos* from the central highlands began to plot to overthrow the government. They invited Father Hidalgo to join the conspiracy. Although religion was never an issue during the revolt, Hidalgo's influence on the Indians of his parish would be vital in broadening the base of the rebellion.

The famous *Grito* took place at about 7 AM on September 16, 1810. Hidalgo issued his call from the steps of the parish church as the country folk came to mass. We now sit on the famous stairs. The exact words of the original *Grito* are lost, but they were along the lines of "Long live America! Long live religion! Death to bad government!"

We've seen these steps on television before because it's traditional for the president of the country to come to Dolores on Independence Day in the last year of his term. Church and state are now separate, so the line about religion in the original *Grito* has been changed, as has the exhortation to destroy bad government. These days that would be akin to the president calling for his own head.

Hidalgo's army of rural mestizos and Indians quickly controlled the central highlands around San Miguel and Dolores, but it would take another eleven years of fighting and other leaders to claim the capital and gain independence from Spain. Hidalgo never lived to see Mexican independence. He was captured and executed by a firing squad in 1811.

Although Hidalgo is revered throughout Mexico for his key role in the move toward Mexican independence, his impact on Dolores is much more concrete. Long an advocate for social justice, he spent most of his time in Dolores finding ways for the local population to earn economic self-sufficiency. Ignoring his priestly duties, he introduced agricultural reform, leather tanning, furniture making, and even the silkworm industry to the region. He saw these cottage industries as ways for the achingly poor indigenous population to escape their serfdom.

One of the industries he introduced, ceramic tile making, drives the economy of Dolores today. Typically white and cobalt blue with red, yellow, and green highlights, the tiles and ceramic items from Dolores are famous in Mexico and throughout the world.

Multiple stores, selling every type of ceramic item we can imagine, line the streets leading off the main plaza. We see dinnerware, coffee mugs, bowls, casserole dishes, vases, planters, pitchers, lamps, and more. Hand painted and made right on the premises, the items are astoundingly inexpensive. One too many moves has wreaked havoc on our personal Talavera supplies. We're running out of room in Gordo, but can't pass up the chance to restock.

We load our goods into Gordo and head back to San Miguel, about forty-five minutes away. On the outskirts of town we pass La Cruz del Perdón, the Cross of Forgiveness. Although people make pilgrimages to the site, the Cross is not a religious locale, but rather an outstanding restaurant. They have been selling *carnitas* here every weekend for twenty years.

There is nothing fancy about La Cruz. Located next to the highway, the chairs are plastic and the menu simple. There are only four items to choose from here—*carnitas*, beans, guacamole, and beer. We order all four.

Bryan and I wander to the back to check out the cooking area. José, the owner's fifteen-year-old son, is the chef today. Tall and skinny, with a wild crop of dark hair, he has been raised on this tender pork dish. He points to a huge copper cauldron, about four feet in diameter, set on top of a fire pit.

"*Carnitas* get their name because the pork is so tender that it breaks into small pieces. We cook the entire pig so that you can get any part you want. People come here early on Saturdays to get their favorite items—innards, skin, ears, even tails. *Los gringos* usually prefer the loin. We heat up this pot, boil the fat, stick the whole pig in there and cook it for a couple of hours. The meat gets crispy on the outside and moist and juicy inside. It's so tender people don't believe it."

The *carnitas* flake apart at the nudge of our forks. Piled into tortillas and covered with spicy salsa, these rate at the top of our list. Although the menu choices are limited, every option represents a flavor unique to Mexico. We savor our meal as we wash down each bite with an icy Corona.

Although there are other beers listed on the menu, it's hard to order any other brand because of the not-so-subliminal Corona advertising at La Cruz. All the plastic chairs sport the Corona label, as do the large refrigerators behind the cash register. A Corona logo also decorates the menu. I ask José's mother about the Corona connection.

"Well, we are *patrocinado* by Corona. They provide the furniture and the refrigerators to us for free. I guess they know that this is a popular restaurant, so they want to have their logo here everywhere they can. We sell a lot of their beer. It just goes really well with *carnitas*."

In control of almost 40 percent of the beer market, Corona obviously goes well with just about everything. We know this market share figure because we've been studying reports on Corona. Our efforts with the public relations department of the Corona headquarters have stalled in regard to our riding on a delivery route, but they've sent us a flood of corporate and marketing information.

We've learned that Corona is the number one selling beer in Mexico, the number one U.S.-imported beer, and the fifth largest selling brand of beer worldwide. (Bud, Bud Light, Brahma from Brazil, and Asahi Super Dry of Japan are the top four.)

The people at Modelo, the company that owns Corona, have been accommodating as far as information goes, but we can tell they want no part in our riding in a Corona delivery truck. As is common in Mexico, however, they find it extremely difficult to give us a direct "no." Instead, they have created barriers, hoping that we will get frustrated and leave them alone. Their current tactic is to be in a meeting every single time we call. No matter what time of day it is, as soon as the secretary hears my name she determines that her boss is busy. Occasionally I can hear him in the background instructing her to tell me he's occupied. I feel as if this is turning into a challenge, a test of wills. Well, we *will* ride in that truck.

Unlike Independence Day, Cinco de Mayo (May 5), comes and goes in Mexico without much fanfare. Commemorating a battle against French troops, the day makes the papers simply because there is a reenactment of the fight each year. It isn't a national holiday, however, so most Mexicans don't even note its passing.

That's hard for many Americans to handle. Some plan trips to Mexico to coincide with May 5, expecting huge parties, and find nothing. Bryan made the same mistake when he was living in San Diego many years ago. He and a bunch of his friends decided to spend Cinco de Mayo in Tijuana to get an authentic taste of the Mexican celebration. They crossed the border, expecting mayhem, but the city's bars were quiet. They crossed back to San Diego, however, and found raging parties in every Mexican restaurant in town. Cinco de Mayo as a festive event is a purely U.S. phenomenon, a kind of Mexican Saint Patrick's Day.

An article I found in *Brandweek*, an advertising industry magazine, explained how the day became such a big to-do north of the border. Retailers in the United States are always looking for special events to move products. Cinco de Mayo, falling in a month with not many celebrations, fits the bill perfectly. Grocery stores fill their shelves with Corona and taco shells, Mexican restaurants throw parties, and consumers buy, buy, buy. Everybody is happy, especially companies like Corona.

The success of Corona in the United States is a strange phenomenon. The brand, described by beer reviewers as "thin and almost flavorless," took America by storm in the late 1980s. Part of its popularity is due to the fact that it's very light, the way many people in the United States prefer their beer. Corona tastes similar to a U.S. beer but has the cachet of an imported product.

The rest of its acceptance can be attributed to marketing. When Corona first introduced the beer, they spent next to nothing on advertising and promotion. It was all about positioning. They took a cheap beer, put it in a retro bottle with a painted label, and priced it just below European imports. It became the hot drink for college students. The students graduated and took their hip beer with them. It was almost dumb luck for Corona.

What wasn't dumb luck, however, was their advertising once they decided to invest in the market. It was, and still is, a brilliant campaign. Their slogan, "Change Your Whole Lattitude," captures a vacation in a bottle. You take a sip of Corona and you're transported to a warm, sunny place. They never stray from their formula of Mexican beaches and a lime. That clear long-neck bottle with a wedge of lime has become an icon in America. You can't see it without picturing an exotic stretch of Mexican sand.

Corona's popularity in Mexico can also be attributed to its light flavor. The beer is quite often used as a chaser with a glass of tequila, making its watery consistency a plus. It is also downed in large quantities on hot days, a time when people prefer a lighter beer. Mexicans, however, don't add a wedge of lime to their Coronas.

Before the stonewalling began I had asked José Piso, our public relations contact at the Modelo headquarters, about the different approach.

"Bottles in Mexico are returnable, you know. We collect our empties from all over the country, wash them, and reuse them. If there is an old lime at the bottom of the bottle, we can't reuse it. In fact, we have to break any bottle with a lime in it to make sure it doesn't accidentally get put back on the line. That's a waste of resources. Here in Mexico, we avoid showing the lime in the bottle in any of our advertising material."

That was when I again broached the subject of our ride in the Corona delivery truck. José told me he was discussing the issue with his boss and that I should call back in a few days. I call and call but never manage to get him on the phone again. They probably don't understand why I can't get their not-so-subtle message.

Sometimes it's good to start at the top, but other times you have to go down a few levels to get anything done. Having given up hope of going through the corporate headquarters, our next stop is the local Corona distributor.

As we learned at the Cuauhtémoc Brewery in Monterrey, many brands of beer are strong only on a regional level in Mexico. Corona, however, was the first to make a countrywide splash. Modelo set up the initial national distribution network for beer in the 1940s. Today it's one of the most sophisticated in the country.

The Modelo distributor in San Miguel is located on a highway on the way out of town. A large Corona logo decorates the front of the wooden reception desk. Three feet behind the desk a cross about ten feet tall is the undisputed focal point of the room. A surreal crucifix, it is decorated with the hands, feet, and head of Christ, but no body. The bloody hands, impaled with iron nails, sprout out of the ends of the crossbeam. The gruesome head, stained with gore, wears a large crown of thorns. Not what you expect to find at a beer company, but we are in pious San Miguel.

Manolo Londres, general director of the San Miguel distributor, is a tall man in his late forties with a bushy skunk's tail of a mustache. He puffs with pride when he tells us about the network. "All of our agencies—distributorships really—have complex computerized systems to help us manage our inventory and coordinate deliveries. Modelo has 695 distributors and sub-distributors. Impressive, no? We—"

The ringing of his phone interrupts him. He excuses himself for a moment, explaining that the city's front-running mayoral candidate is there to visit him. We wait in his office for about ten minutes before he returns. As soon as he walks back in, his phone rings again. Somehow his boss has already gotten wind that Londres was hobnobbing with the candidate.

"*Bueno*. Oh, hello, Boss. How's the weather in Celaya today? No, no, I didn't promise him anything or make any kind of deals, I swear. I didn't even arrange the meeting. He just stopped by out of the blue."

Londres sounds about as sincere as Eddie Haskell on *Leave It to Beaver*. We can't hear his boss's response, but the tone doesn't sound positive.

"No, no, no. What's important to me is the company, not political gain. All I'm concerned about is Grupo Modelo. I just want to make sure our company is advancing. I'm not concerned about myself."

We hear more yelling coming out of the receiver. Desperate to change the subject, he looks at us and a light comes into his eyes.

"Hey, Boss, I have some writers here in my office from the United States asking some questions about our distribution system . . . Oh, yes, I was about to do that . . . Don't worry, I'll get them checked out with headquarters."

He successfully managed to divert his boss's attention, but now has to follow through with his vow to OK our meeting with the corporate office. That's bad news for us. Our contact at the headquarters will know immediately that we are trying to sneak around him to get a ride in the delivery truck. Bryan and I both start to squirm.

Londres places a call to Mexico City, but is put on hold. He can't resist talking to us while he waits.

"Our distribution system is fantastic. We can get our beer anywhere in the country in a matter of days. In this area, the longest customers go between visits is three days, no matter how remote they are. Most of our customers are attended by one of our delivery trucks every twenty-four hours, Sunday included. The trucks go on set routes and replenish customers' inventories."

His call finally goes through. "Oh, hello, señorita, I am calling from the San Miguel distributorship. I have two writers here that I need to talk about with your boss. They say they have already been in contact with him, but I need to make sure that everything is on the up and up . . . He's not there?"

Bryan and I breathe a sigh of relief and make a motion to indicate we're leaving. We want to get out of here before being confronted about our duplicitous scheme. Foiled again.

If we can't ride in a beer truck, at least we have mountain biking. San Miguel offers some wonderful off-road terrain for fat tire adventures. One of the first trips Bryan and I took after we started dating was an outing to San Miguel for a weekend of biking. Mexico's currency had recently collapsed in an unforeseen devaluation, which meant that the dollars we were earning went twice as far as they had a few months before. That, coupled with the fact that there was absolutely nothing happening in terms of business, meant that we could take off for a different Mexican destination every Friday afternoon at lunchtime. It was an adrenaline-filled courting period. We went surfing in Guerrero, rafting in Veracruz, volcano climbing in Puebla, and mountain biking in Guanajuato.

Today we have enlisted the same guide we used five years ago to steer us through the country terrain. He has suggested a route to Atotonilco, a modest community about fifteen miles from San Miguel. The church at Atotonilco played a small but key role in Mexican independence. Marching on his way from Dolores to San Miguel, Father Hidalgo stopped by there and grabbed a flag off the altar. The standard bore the image of the Virgin of Guadalupe, which became the symbol of the nascent independence movement.

The church at Atotonilco is basically all there is of the village. It's a famous place of pilgrimage. Beto tells us about the church as we rest outside. "This sanctuary was built in 1740 as a spiritual retreat. There are lots of hot springs around here. The priest that founded Atotonilco thought the area needed a religious presence to offset the depraved behavior at the springs. He couldn't stand the idea of public bathing and immodesty."

We walk inside the narrow adobe building on creaky wooden floors. Incredible murals in the style of folk art cover every inch of the walls, ceiling, and even the doors. Beto points to a scene above us. A man tears out his hair in apparent agony. "All of these pictures outline the dangers that lie in wait for the human soul."

It's a toned-down Mexican version of a scene Hieronymus Bosch would paint.

We look around for a flag bearing the image of the Virgen de Guadalupe. There isn't one to be found. I guess they haven't gotten around to replacing the original in the almost two hundred years since Hidalgo grabbed it for independence.

I buy some water from a stand outside. Along with the standard rosaries and pictures of Jesus and Virgins, I see rope whips of various sizes as well as crowns of thorns. The proprietor asks me if I'm interested in one of the *disciplinas*, small whips made from stiff cord. It's hard for me to believe that people really buy them.

"Every day. People visit Atotonilco from all over the country. They come to sleep in the small stone cells behind the church to pray and fast. Some also come here for self-flagellation. They do it in private, when nobody is around. Usually at night. They know that it's discouraged by the Vatican, but they do it anyway."

Two women walk by us, both wearing thorn crowns. Multicolored rope cords are wrapped around their bodies. They are dressed in black skirts with white aprons. I hurry to catch up with them and ask them if they are staying here at the sanctuary. The taller one answers.

"Oh, yes, we're from San Luis Potosí, but we're with a group of four hundred women that have come from as far away as Laredo. We're using a week's vacation to stay here. I'm a cook and she's a seamstress, but for this week we are pilgrims. We spend our days in mass, prayers, and meditation. There's a different priest this year, but he's pretty good."

I try to follow them into the retreat area, but am stopped at the doors by a polite but firm older gentleman. I can hear the hum of ladies' voices inside. They may be here for meditation, but four hundred Mexican women are going to be doing some talking, no matter how much prayer is going on.

These women have secluded themselves for a week, but just down the road, a group of men have chosen prayer and meditation as a way of life. Following a dirt road, which becomes an even rougher stone track, we spot a little white chapel surrounded by cactus and mesquite—La Soledad Monastery.

We knock tentatively on the door. A woman answers and we ask her if somebody can show us around. The door closes. Minutes pass. We are about to leave when we are greeted by Brother Esteban. A thin young man of twenty-three, he wears a light blue hooded tunic and little round wire glasses. More pretty than handsome, he has been at La Soledad for two years. His first six months were spent as a *principiante*, followed by another year and a half as a novice.

"Welcome to La Soledad. We are a part of the Benedictine Confederation, an international congregation with more than 65 monasteries and 1,400 monks scattered around the world."

Esteban shows us the public areas of the monastery. Light and airy, with white walls and large windows, the building is pleasant and tranquil. A garden courtyard filled with flowers is ringed by the monks' quarters and study areas. Long tables join together in a large U in the dining room. Only five places are set for lunch.

"We have six monks here on a regular basis, but our father superior is out of town right now. He's at our regional headquarters in New Mexico. Well, I say six monks, but two of us are just novices. God willing, however, we'll both be full monks soon."

I ask Esteban how he fills his days. "Basically, we pray. Some monasteries also function as schools for outsiders, so the brothers teach, but here we are dedicated to prayer. We do it all day, from 4:30 in the morning to about 6:30 at night. We also have mass once a day. It's a very fulfilling life for me."

He walks us out to the chapel. Small and simple, it is one of the prettiest we've seen in Mexico. Natural light spills in to illuminate the white crucifix against the white wall. With beautiful rustic furniture and a vaulted *bóveda* (brick ceiling), its style is a direct contrast to the heavy-handed admonitions painted on the walls of Atotonilco.

Esteban points to some simple cabins below the chapel. "We have room for up to twenty-five people to come and share the contemplative life with us for a few days at a time. They join us for mass and meals, but spend most of their time, like us, praying."

Looking over the soft green fields listening to chirping birds break the tranquil silence, I decide that I'd rather spend a day with the brothers at La Soledad, The Place of Solitude, than with the whipping crowd down the road.

Although the church has a strong hold over many Mexicans, it's obvious that not everything is as orthodox as Rome might like. Mexican Catholicism has some unique traits traceable to preexisting Indian spiritual traditions. Some aspects of the original indigenous religions are still practiced today. One of those traditions, shamanism, remains strong in the area around San Miguel.

Juventud de las Rosas, a town about an hour from San Miguel, is home to one of Mexico's highest concentrations of *curanderos*. *Curanderos* prescribe herbal mixes for medical problems and recite incantations or perform ceremonies to produce specific effects. *Webster's International Dictionary* defines a shaman as "A priest-doctor who uses magic to cure the sick, to divine the hidden, and *to control events that affect the welfare of people*." I don't think it's a stretch to call our need to ride in a Corona truck an event that will affect our welfare. With our many unanswered telephone calls and our bad luck at the distributor's office, we are in need of a Corona delivery truck incantation. We're sure that the *curanderos* of Juventud de las Rosas have heard stranger things, so we set out in search of a spell.

Our first dilemma is finding a shaman. Driving into Juventud de las Rosas, an unremarkable town with primarily cement buildings, we are surprised at its size. We were expecting a small, traditional *pueblo* and instead find a large, thriving center of local commerce. We decide to begin our search at the market. We seek out a stall selling pre-Colombian staples and locate one that fits the bill perfectly. Three old women sit gossiping in front of their piles of corn, *nopal* cactus, and chiles. They are absolutely nonplussed when we ask where to find a *curandero*. It's as if we have inquired about where to find the closest barbershop. Our question sparks a spirited debate between the three.

"How about that lady on the hill where your *hijo* went about his bicycle?"

"No, that one's too far away. What about Don Jesús, the man who buys some of his herbs here?"

"No, *no es bueno*. My sister-in-law went to him and he didn't help her at all."

"What about that lady that lives behind the church, across from where I used to live? She helped my husband once."

"Yeah, her name is María. She's a good one. And it's close. José Antonio, *mijo*, take them to her house."

The woman's son, José Antonio, is a chubby gnome with a wheeze, homemade tattoos, and a quick smile. As he leads us through the streets of town we ask if he's ever visited a *curandero* before.

"Oh, sure, lots of times. Last time was when my bicycle got stolen. I went to the *curandera* up on the hill and she told me that the person who stole it worked in a stall in the market. She also kind of described what he looked like. I knew immediately who it was. I confronted him and, wouldn't you know, I found my bike at his house."

He leads us to a well-kept house with a small tree struggling out of the sidewalk in front. It's one of the only trees we've seen in the entire town. José Antonio knocks on the door and explains that he's brought two gringos to see the shaman. We are led into what can only be described as the doctor's waiting room. Twelve plastic chairs line the peach walls of a spotless antechamber. We half expect to find year-old *Highlights* magazines sitting on the end table.

We follow our shaman across a bird-filled patio to a small room with flowered cloth hanging down in place of a door. She pulls the material back to reveal her examination room. Two chairs and a small bed fit neatly in the limited space. She motions me to the bed for my consultation. I'm fascinated with the room's décor. Hundreds of paintings of Jesus and the Virgin hang among other religious curios. Rosaries, wheat, candles, and flowers fill in every bit of blank space. A pyramid, an Aztec mask, and a stuffed owl hover behind my head. An altar behind Bryan features a mirror with three watches hung in a triangular design.

María's attitude is as professional as that of any doctor I've ever visited.

"So, what's bothering you?"

I decide to keep the story general, explaining that we have a problem at work that we can't seem to overcome, no matter what we try.

María nods her head slowly. "You both need *una limpieza*. Somebody who is jealous of your work has probably put a curse on you. How long are you going to be in town? In order for a cleansing to be effective, you need three treatments. One in the name of the Father, one in the name of the Son, and one in the name of the Holy Spirit."

Three treatments? Sounds expensive. I inquire about the cost.

"Well, for both of you it would be 300 pesos [about $30]. I charge 50 pesos a visit for a cleansing, you both need three, so that's 150 pesos per person."

Bryan is miraculously cured upon hearing the price. "Well, to tell you the truth, Becky's really the one having the problem. I think all we need is one *limpieza*. But there's another complication. We are going to be in town only today. We can't come back for any other visits."

María sadly shakes her head. "Can't be done. The cleansings have to be performed two days apart and you have to have all three of them. If I just do one, it's like giving you aspirin. It will temporarily cover the symptoms, but it won't cure the problem. No, you have to have three."

Bryan, long accustomed to Mexican negotiations, asks if there is any other way to go about this.

"Well, I guess I could give her the first *limpieza* today, and then, if she left her clothes, I could give the second and third ones to the clothes. They have the form of her body."

I mention the small detail that I can't be walking naked around the streets of Juventud de las Rosas.

"Huummmm. Do you have a photo? I could do the second two cleansings to a photo."

Bryan carries copies of our passports with us in his wallet. He pulls mine out, tears off the picture, and hands it to her.

"No, I'm sorry. This won't work. It's a copy. It has to be a real photo."

We're stymied, but Bryan comes to the rescue with a sudden brainstorm.

"Okay, how about this? You use the copy of the picture and Becky's socks. That way you have her image and her form. That will work, right?"

María ponders his suggestion and slowly starts to nod. I take off my socks, noting with chagrin that they are an expensive pair I just bought recently. María tucks my photo and our payment into the socks and tells us to leave so that she can prepare the room for the cleansing.

She calls us back about five minutes later. The chairs have been placed on the bed, leaving an empty space in the middle of the room. Trails of incense smoke curl up toward the ceiling and strains of religious music fill the air. She motions for Bryan to stand in the corner and places me in the middle of the room. I study her as she bends over a pot to collect a handful of long, fragrant brea branches. About fifty, María wears a flowered T-shirt and green pants. Short and chubby, with bulging eyes and fat sausage lips, she could be Diego Rivera's sister. We ask her about her credentials as she gathers the branches.

"I have been a *curandera* for twelve years. I was visiting a shaman once for a problem, and just felt the calling. She helped train me, but it's really God's guidance that leads me along. I refuse to perform any curses; I only liberate people. All of my work is done in the name of the Holy Trinity."

María stands, turns up the music, and begins the cleansing. Rubbing the fragrant branches over my head and face, she sings the same incantation over and over again.

"Help her, Father, cure her of the jealousies cast upon her, cure her of witchcraft, cure her of curses, cure her of envies, help her with your power. Make her free, make her clean, clean from bad things said against her, free from jealousies cast upon her, free from witchcraft, free from curses, free from envies, clean her with your power. Help her, Father, help her, Father."

She works up a sweat as she makes her way from my head down to the tips of my toes, rubbing me with the branches while repeatedly chanting the same phrases. She does not pass the shoots lightly over my body, but rather digs them into my skin and clothes, scouring the evil from my pores.

After about five minutes of brushing, she places the branches on the floor in front of me and indicates that I should rub them with the bottom of my shoes three times. As I pass the soles of my sockless Hushpuppies over the plants she raises her voice. "Father, Son, Holy Spirit. Father, Son, Holy Spirit."

She arranges the branches in a straight line and has me stand with my toes against them. Turning to her altar, she picks up a chicken egg and begins the process again. As she presses the egg into my body, rubbing everywhere, she repeats the same singsong prayer, even louder this time. She's pushing so hard I'm afraid the egg is going to break all over my belly.

After making her way down to my feet she stands and faces the altar again. On the shelf sits a bottle labeled "Legitimate Spiritual Water." She takes the egg and breaks it into a tumbler of this water.

"Look. See the red spot on the yolk? That's your curse. It was in your stomach, but the egg picked it up. You're partially liberated, but you need to be protected."

She splashes orange-scented water all over my head and begins her incantations again. Massaging the liquid into my skin and clothes, she implores the Father for my safekeeping. Every time she rubs her hands over a section of my body, she cups them and blows any residual evil off into the corner. After I've been thoroughly cleansed, she repeats the process, chanting all the while.

With her hands cupped, she directs me to extend my arms. She places what she calls protective goodness (otherwise known as air) into my hands, closes them, and folds them across my chest. One more strenuous set of prayers and massage, and the *limpieza* is over. She tells me to empty my closed hands into my pockets for continual safekeeping. I do.

She won't let me move while she cleans up the branches on the floor. Because they are imbued with the evil she has brushed from my body, she refuses to touch them with her bare skin. Placing a protective plastic bag over her hand, María stuffs them into another plastic bag and ties it off.

"There, you are clean in the name of the Father. I will perform the incantation with your socks in the name of the Son on Tuesday, and then the one in the name of the Holy Spirit on Thursday. By Thursday afternoon your work troubles will be over."

We are driving to Oaxaca on Friday morning. My work troubles will be over by Thursday afternoon whether I like it or not, because we're not going to be here after that.

Modelo owns 10,500 vehicles that it uses to cart its beer around the country. During our failed trip to the San Miguel distributorship, we learned that there are fifty delivery trucks working this area. We see these trucks everywhere during our last days in San Miguel. They mock us in their pervasiveness.

When everything else fails, there's always the final recourse—the bribe. Known in Mexico as a *mordida*, "a little bite," bribes are the grease that keeps the wheels of society spinning smoothly. Americans are quick to judge this practice, but in Mexico financial misdeeds are seen as innocuous, the equivalent of white lies.

Bryan and I decide to take advantage of this cultural loophole and approach one of the drivers directly. It's Thursday morning, our last chance. We wander the streets for less than five minutes before coming across a Corona truck. The driver and his assistant lean on the cab ogling a woman walking by with her boyfriend.

We warm them up with a few innocent questions about their job. Felipe, the driver, wears a blue-and-yellow Modelo uniform with patches representing the various beer brands. His sharp features are made even harsher by his scraggly hair and pockmarked skin. Nacho, his assistant, has a white Corona shirt and a large Marlboro belt buckle.

They make beer deliveries along the same route every day, with the exception of Thursday. Every morning they load the truck with fifty cases of Corona in twelve-ounce bottles, forty cases of Corona in one-liter bottles, and various cases of the other beer brands. Corona is by far the biggest seller.

"We visit the same shops every day, but some days we have special deliveries for private parties. Last week we delivered a bunch of beer to a party that the Highway Patrol was having. They weren't checking for drunken drivers that night, that's for sure. You can have us deliver beer to your house if it's along the route. If you tell us in advance, we can throw in plastic tables and chairs with the Corona logo for free.

We pick them up when we collect the empties. We'll even provide the ice. We're making a private party delivery today."

This is our opening.

"That sounds really neat. Would it be possible for us to ride with you while you make the delivery?"

Felipe and Nacho look at each other and answer uncomfortably. "Well, the thing is, we're not allowed to have anybody from outside the company ride in the truck with us. It's against the rules."

We act crestfallen. "Gosh, we'd really like to ride with you and see how you operate. Your job sounds so exciting. That's too bad. If only there were some way to work this out."

We then deliver the countrywide euphemism for a bribe offer. "Is there a way that we can cooperate together on this?"

Felipe and Nacho look as if they are wavering. Bryan issues the line that seals the deal. "You know, some kind of exchange."

Nervous that we'll be seen, Felipe and Nacho hide us in the back of the truck. We cram in between the plastic furniture and cases of beer. We can see through to the cab, where a crucifix and a St. Christopher medallion hang from the rearview mirror.

We make a few stops with them at the establishments on their normal route. Most of the stores are Mom and Pop businesses set up in the front rooms of people's homes. Despite their small size, many of them take a couple cases of Corona every day. One "store" consists of nothing more than a single refrigerator in somebody's entry hall.

The routine is the same at each stop. Felipe does the paperwork while Nacho picks up empty bottles and trades them out for cases of beer. Sometimes, in areas where parking is a problem, Nacho does both the paper and grunt work while Felipe stays with the truck.

Finally we get to the house for the special delivery. We stand with Felipe and Nacho while they ring the bell. The door opens to reveal an unfinished interior, a work under construction. The foreman waves us in.

"We finish roofing the house today, so we're having a party to celebrate. Just go ahead and put the tables here on the patio and the beer and ice over there."

Felipe and Nacho set to work while Bryan and I wander through the house. All of the walls are in place, but the floors are still dirt. We see a pig in what will be the living room. It's tied in place with a rope like a leash around its neck. I have a good idea about its future, but ask a man digging a hole in the floor to confirm.

"*Sí*, we're going to barbecue this pig. After I finish the pit, we'll butcher it right here and then cook it up. By the time we finish work today, it will be ready. We're going to have quite a *pachanga*."

I'll bet they are. I wonder if the people who buy this house will find it haunted by strange oinking noises. Maybe that's why Mexicans often have new constructions blessed by a priest and sprinkled with holy water.

Felipe and Nacho are running low on one-liter Coronas, so they will have to make a return trip to the warehouse. Bryan pulls a few dollars in pesos out of his pocket, we thank them, and wave them on their way. Everybody's happy.

At last we have ridden in the truck. Whether it was the work of our *curandera*, the power of the *mordida*, or a combination of both, our "prayers" were answered. No wonder this is such a pious place. We can now pack Gordo up and hit the road once again. Oaxaca awaits.

Resources

Álvarez, José Rogelio, ed. *Enciclopedia de México*. México, DF: Compañía Editora de Enciclopedias de México, 1987.

Egan Diran, Carol. "Abbot Gilbert Jones Celebrates Mass." *Atención San Miguel*, June 26, 2000, A-5.

Frees, Jeff. "Tall, Thin and Mysterious." *Esquire*, May 1988, 36.

Grupo Modelo Annual Report. Grupo Modelo, 1999.

Khermouch, Gerry. "Ron Christesson & Tom McNichols." *Brandweek*, October 20, 1997, 94-97.

Magner, James. *Men of Mexico*. Freeport, NY: Books for Libraries Press, 1968.

Pipkin, Turk. "Where the Buys Are." *Texas Monthly*, July 1996, 42-49.

Riding, Alan. *Distant Neighbors*. New York: Vintage Books, 1989.

Solange, Alberto. *El águila y la cruz*. México, DF: El Colegio de México, 1999.

Walch, Katherine. "Holy Week Events Solemnly Herald Easter." *El Independiente*, April 11-24, 2000, 1.

OAXACA

As we zoom toward Oaxaca, I can't help but think about the worm. It must be this wriggling road.

Becky drives Gordo into Oaxaca State across the Calapa Bridge, a surreally curved piece of highway that seems to float 150 feet above the Tomellín Canyon. The bridge is propped into these arid Southern Sierra Mountains by three concrete flamingo legs. The pavement is smooth licorice frosting bordered by languid white stripes and gleaming yellow guardrails. Its position high above the abyss reminds me of the plastic car track that in my childhood created a precarious link from sofa arm to coffee table.

The imposing arid walls that rise up on either side of the canyon are as dry and crumbly as day-old toast. A closer look at the occasional brush strokes of green on the hillsides reveal stands of cacti so elongated that they are laughable. The cacti are reminiscent of the classic saguaro type found in Arizona, but here the spiky green tubing of the trunk and arms is pulled straight and thin upward to stretch over twenty feet.

The new toll road that we navigate descends by twisting and winding through the rolling sierra like a tossed crepe paper streamer. Today I worship this gorgeous piece of civil engineering as it cuts open the hillsides to reveal innards of rusty clay and stratified green rock. We are more than happy to pay the exorbitant tolls rather than take the free highway to avoid bucking over speed bumps, swerving around farm animals, and passing black exhaust-spewing trucks in daredevil fashion. Normally I am not so enthusiastic about a slab of concrete, but the convenience that this one affords amid a mesmerizing expanse, combined with Lyle Lovett's waggish crooning, elevates us to a perfect state of road trip bliss.

Jagged green crowns of wild agave perforate the slope that flattens toward the valley. The agave species found in Oaxaca are quite varied, as are the region's indigenous people and languages. While the primary ethnic group is the Zapotecs, there are fifteen other indigenous languages spoken here, making it one of the most ethnically diverse states in the republic. It is also one of the least economically developed. The relationship between the native people and the agave plant is centuries old and intimate. The agave furnishes food, tools, textile fibers, building material, and beverages. An envoy reported to Carlos V of Spain in 1519, "Surely nature has never combined in one plant so many elements to satisfy man's needs."

Pulque, the fermented sap of the agave, was drunk in Mexico for centuries before the Spaniards arrived, but this beer-strength concoction was not potent enough for the marauders' hardened thirsts. The Spaniards brought with them distillation techniques, the process of concentrating alcohol through evaporation that they garnered from the invading Moors in the eighth century. Initial attempts at distilling the pulque agave, which grows in the cool central highlands, failed because its core proved to be too watery. With further experimentation the Spaniards found that the agave species that thrive in warmer conditions could be distilled. By combining an old world process with a new world raw material, mezcal (mescal in English), the first truly mestizo beverage, was created.

The difference between pulque and mezcal is similar to the difference between wine and brandy. Agave-derived pulque, like grape-derived wine, is created from a simple fermentation process that gives the beverages low alcohol content, between 6 and 12 percent. Distillation endows agave-based mezcal and grape-based brandy with higher alcohol content, usually 40 to 50 percent.

The cultivated agave in Oaxaca is primarily a sword-leafed variety called *espadín*. The plants are distinctive in that each blade is long and slender like a saber, which is exactly what *espadín* means in Spanish. There are several other types also used to make mezcal. Mezcal can happily be a mutt in this regard, a mixture of varieties. Whether the producer uses several types of agave or culls more selectively to use only one, it is still mezcal.

Tequila, on the other hand, is a mezcal that is always derived from only one type of agave—the blue agave. This is a fact that tequila producers are quick to point out, and upon which they promote tequila's superiority. There are some processing differences between mezcal and tequila as well. The main difference is that the tequila agave heart is almost always steamed, while the mezcal agave heart is baked in a fire pit, which endows it with a discernible smoky flavor.

The city of Oaxaca (like New York, Oaxaca is both a name for a city and state) spreads out on a flat valley floor like one of its vibrant artisan rugs. We find our hotel by etching a path of rectangles through the grid of cobblestone one-way streets used by its 250,000 inhabitants. As soon as we unload we walk to the tourist office to ask how best to spend our last days of research on this project, exploring Oaxaca and its mezcal production.

A budding bureaucrat named Veronica greets us. She wields an alluring combination of exotic indigenous features and bold yet professional fashion sense. Becky asks about the possibility of visiting an old-fashioned *palenque*, as the mezcal production sites are known, that we understand resemble backwoods moonshine stills. We had heard that *palenques* exist in small villages where you can still request that the owner fill up your empty bottle, paying for the mezcal by the liter.

"Oh, no. The production process here is very modern. You would never find anything like that in Oaxaca. There are several factories set up for tourist visits that you should see."

Becky's disappointment is unhidden. During our visit to Tequila, she anticipated seeing functioning *tahonas*, the broad stone wheels pulled by donkeys to crush the agave hearts, but everything had been modernized for mass production. A tractor pulled the one *tahona* we found. We thought for sure we would find more rustic methods in Oaxaca. Now she imagines more hydraulics and steel tanks, something so far from the artisanship that we hoped for, that we might as well be visiting Puebla's state-of-the-art Volkswagen plant.

"What about the worms?" I ask.

"There are many types of mezcal," Veronica replies, skirting the subject. "There is *reposado*, *pollo*, *crema*—"

"I'm interested in the *gusano* type, the one with the worm. I want to know where the worms come from and how they get into the bottle."

"I really can't tell you."

"Are there worm farms where they raise them?"

"I'm not sure."

"Do you eat them, you know, like popcorn?"

"Oh, no, that is only in Hidalgo State. We never eat them here."

"I read that the worms were eaten as snacks in Oaxaca."

"That is not true. We do not eat worms," she states indignantly.

She pushes a mezcal tourism brochure toward us and wishes us good luck in that artfully courteous Mexican way that makes you feel good even though someone is telling you that they prefer never to see you again.

That afternoon we decide to give one of the mezcal *palenques* on the tourism list a look. We drive east from the city through the parched valley, striped dark green with rows of agave blades that poke from the ground like three-dimensional asterisks. The hills are mottled with similar colors, mainly brittle brown, but bald spots reveal humps of mellow green rock. The sky is so clear and blue that the white stucco of the roadside *palenque* is delineated as sharply as a Kraft paper cutout.

A hostess greets us from behind a row of bottles on a tiled counter. She explains that each of the bottles is different flavored *crema de mezcal*, mezcal liqueur. We sample a few from tiny plastic cups. The syrupy concoctions of banana, coconut, and strawberry gag us.

We are directed toward the production area, an unimaginative concrete block bordered by a vibrant flower garden. On one side of the building is a pile of enormous agave hearts. The spiky leaves have been sheared from them, making them look like mutant pineapples. The mezcal agave hearts are about the size of a laundry basket and weigh from 125 to 175 pounds, somewhat larger than those used to make tequila. Inside the *palenque*, a yoked horse pulls a rock *tahona* wheel around a circular track measuring about five feet in diameter. At the center is a cement post from which the axle extends and which is connected to the Flintstonian wheel. A worker feeds cooked agave into the curbed ring with a pitchfork, where it is crushed into a fibrous pulp. This is done to unshield the starches and sugars vital to fermentation.

We discuss the *palenque*'s dubious authenticity. The horse is healthy and white. The worker wears a clean cotton shirt, and nary an armpit stain can be detected. The bottling operation in the next room is a haphazard collection of plastic barrels and a few filling hoses hanging from the ceiling. The whole affair reeks of a tourist trap.

Another tourist site that we can't avoid, but one that we actually seek out, is the Monte Albán archeological ruins. We are attracted to the sweeping views from the flat-topped summit.

We arrive shortly after the gates open, hoping to avoid the tour buses, but there are already several parked out front. We climb tiny, steep steps to the northern platform for the most advantageous view. Spread out below us is the vast Grand Plaza, a level field of sun-scorched crew-cut grass, ten times as large as a football field. Set up on the plain is a series of three rows of pyramids, stubby stacks of gradually narrowing square platforms notched by wide stairways. The temples are incredible, but I am still most impressed by the landscaping. The man-made mesa is so immense that it dwarfs the audacious tour groups. The groups move like amoebae, disseminating and convoluting into irregular shapes as they walk from pyramid to pyramid, then reforming into a tight blob to ingest their historical nutrients.

The Zapotec people that inhabited most of the valley first built settlements here 2,500 years ago. Halfway through their occupancy, they built the pyramids as religious temples. Food and water resources probably ran thin, so they abandoned the site.

The site was neglected until a Mexican archeologist, Alfonso Caso, began excavation in 1931. He believed that the structures in and of themselves merited exploration and preservation, but he also held out hope for discovering hidden treasure. The archeological team's initial efforts did not unearth riches. What they did uncover with their probing shovels was layer upon layer of black ceramic pots.

At the time the archeologists were digging up the ancient black pots, a young woman, Rosa Real Mateo, was busy creating new ones using the same process her ancestors had.

Burros carried the clay six miles from the mountainside to Rosa's little workshop in Coyotepec. She would shape the clay, as brown and malleable as rye dough in its raw state, on a pair of ceramic saucers until a large vaselike jug known as a *cántaro*, was formed. This foot-tall vessel was apple-shaped with a fist-sized mouth opening to a flared lip. When fired in an oxygen-starved oven, the iron-rich clay achieved the unique property of turning opaque black.

Doña Rosa was not the first to create these distinctive black pots, as the archeological team could attest, nor was she the only one who practiced the craft at the beginning of the twentieth century. Yet her skill was such that she became the most well-known artisan. She was frequently

Oaxacan clay pots were found in abundance at the ruins of Monte Albán. Coyotepec is the center of their production today. Here at the Real home, Valente Real runs the workshop created by his mother, Rosa.

referred to as "that Indian woman who makes black pots," but anyone who met her would address her with the honorific title of *doña*.

It is a ten-mile jaunt from Oaxaca City to Coyotepec. The village is one of the many simple highway-straddling populaces along the way. A blue street sign displaying a *cántaro* icon indicates that we have arrived in the correct town. Next to it, a hand-painted mini-billboard advertises "doña Rosa" with an arrow pointing down a dirt road.

The workshop's display area is inside a large cream-colored stucco square structure. A rough-beamed ceiling covers the perimeter, while the courtyard in the center is open-air. Underneath the roofed portion are freestanding shelves that display thousands of pieces of black pottery.

The wall near the entrance is a collage of newspaper clippings, awards, photos, and paintings of doña Rosa. The photos span from 1930 to the end of her life in 1982, but in every one of them she looks nearly the same age. Her face is thoroughly sun-wrinkled, gauntly handsome and intense, reminiscent of Mother Teresa in her later years, except that instead of the flowing nun's habit, doña Rosa wears a dark indigenous rebozo (scarf) of rough cotton wrapped around her head like a turban. Her bony body is folded into a loose dress from which extend two dutiful, sinuous arms, muscle strung on bone, which naturally reach out for supple earth.

"That is my mother," says a calm, proud voice behind us.

We turn to greet doña Rosa's son, Valente Nieto Real. He is dressed in a flannel shirt and blue jeans. His thick silvery black hair frames a face the same color and consistency of the unbaked clay, and his wide, prominent nose is shaped like the spout of a water jug. The hand I grasp is amazingly soft, not what you'd expect from a 70-year-old artisan.

"And that's you," I say, pointing to a framed magazine ad on the wall that shows Valente standing in front of a heap of black pots. A pair of teens in mod flower-power-inspired threads pose on either side of him. Their psychedelic fashion is perfectly contrasted by the sage potter and his venerable ceramics. The tagline translates to something like "Levi's—Ageless." The ad was published in the early 1970s, demonstrating that Valente inherited his mother's trait of appearing senior in flesh and vibrant in soul across a handful of decades.

He deflects the acknowledgement. "Come on," he says, "I'll show you how we make pots."

Valente crouches on an elfin stool in front of a thick stone tablet within reach of a few plastic-covered lumps of clay. He points to a wheelbarrow full of brown dirt clods so that we understand the origin of the soft, doughy material that he begins to knead. There is no doubt as to who is boss. He dominates that moist lump of earth, punching it, rolling it, pressuring it against the stone tablet with his palm under the full weight of his upper body.

"When the archeologists were exploring Monte Albán in the 1930s, my mother was making these pots, the opaque ones. Everyone here used them for everything." He picks up a stick, threatening various sizes and shapes of pots and bowls with it. Most of them are large, over knee-high, but some of them are dinnerware-sized.

"This one is for water. You can see how it could pour nicely with the spout." Bong! He raps it with the stick. "The clay keeps the water cool."

Bing! "This one is for corn flour."

Tink! "This one is for hot chocolate."

He breaks off a piece of the clay and forms a solid cone in his hands, then punches his fist upward into the center. Soon it takes the shape of a winter stocking cap.

In front of him are two clay saucers about the size of dinner plates, but deeper. The bottom saucer is set on the floor upside down to form a base, while the upper saucer is placed right side up, on top of the other, to improvise a crude potter's wheel. He lowers the inverted clay stocking cap onto the top saucer.

"The jug that I am working on now is the *cántaro*. It is the symbol of our village. It has always been used for water and mezcal. The villagers would buy our *cántaros,* and then take them to the *palenques* to fill them up with mezcal. That way they could carry the mezcal home for their fiestas."

As Valente spins the top saucer with one hand, his other arm is deep inside the pot, shaping it, building it up from the inside out. It gradually conceals more and more of his arm. The pot is still cylindrical until he wields a flat wedge of a dried gourd, which he calls a "half

By rubbing an unfired pot with a piece of quartz, Valente is able to create a piece that shines like ebony after being fired. This pot was rubbed in only one section, which shows the contrast between the shiny and opaque finishes.

moon." With this instrument pushing against the interior, he makes the spinning clay cylinder pregnant, then globular.

Throughout the process Valente dips a hand into a nearby clay bowl filled with water. The water jumps and dances when he flicks his fingers. A flock of fat drops leaps onto the pot, moistening it to maintain pliancy. Barely a fleck of water hits the floor.

"The mezcal producers bought a lot of the black jugs from us. We also made small ones called *tinajas* with 'Souvenir of Oaxaca' painted on them. They filled our jugs with mezcal and shipped them all over the country. Later, though, factories started making plastic bottles, so people didn't want our *cántaros* for mezcal any more."

"About that time my mother and I discovered how to make the pots shine. That innovation is what made us different. People sought us out."

You can see by looking around the gallery that the opaque pots are not nearly as attractive as the shiny vessels. Valente picks up a brown pot that has dried but has not yet been fired. He rubs the pot with a piece of quartz. A bright spot appears. It shimmers brown now and will shine black once it is fired in the kiln. The downside of the luster is that the glossy black beauty is porous. If filled with water, it will bleed, gradually weaken, and disintegrate. Yet modern buyers prefer form over function.

"The foreigners really liked these shiny ones. They came here, took an interest, and wrote about us in magazines and newspapers."

After admiring Valente as he engages in this craft that has been around since the time of Monte Albán, we can't help but take several pieces home. There is a lot to choose from, and not just tastefully configured pots. There are also macabre skulls, grinning suns, and tiny pawing kittens. We opt for a pair of brilliant ebony candlesticks, a basket of shiny balls that look as if they could be fired from a cannon, and an opaque *cántaro* for mezcal.

There are four well-known brands of mezcal, all owned by big companies that can afford to acquire name recognition through advertising. These are Chagoya, Gusano Rojo, Benevá, and Monte Albán.

The Monte Albán factory is located in the small industrial town of San Agustín not too far from the outskirts of Oaxaca City. Huge gray doors open for us. Past the wall, the plant looks abandoned. There are rusting tanks and steel supports under an open-walled warehouse roof. There is not an agave heart to be seen, not even a whiff of fermentation. We notice that the office is in an even worse state of dilapidation. A huge picture window is broken so that a thick sheered piece of glass hangs down like a guillotine blade.

The manager greets us with droopy eyelids and a fuzzy-wuzzy head that makes him seem newly awoken at midday. Ashes from chain-lit cigarettes topple onto his rumpled shirt. His personal upkeep is equal to that of the factory.

The few basic questions that we ask him go vaguely answered between phone calls from creditors. We can't believe he invited us into this catastrophe area. Much of the damage was inflicted by an earthquake two years ago, but never repaired. When we ask to see the production area, he explains that they now buy from several small producers in the countryside. The mezcal is shipped to a plant in Mexico City where it is mixed, homogenized, and bottled. This plant is no longer really in the production loop. The manager hangs on to his job by shooing away creditors and squatters, while the brand hangs on to its market with a famous name.

From our hotel it is a short amble down cobblestone streets to the Regional Museum. The houses we pass are squat, thick-walled, and run together in uninterrupted rows. Often the only way you can tell where one house starts and the next begins is by an abrupt change in sublimely garish colors. One house is cobalt blue with lemon-yellow trim, the next is bright pink with lime green, and the following mustard yellow with maroon. The trim is so wide—broad bands highlight doors, windows, and rooflines—that it rivals the base color in volume. Wrought iron bars stripe and checker the bottom-floor windows for thief deterrence while the upper windows are shadowed in florid iron designs. It's like cursive lettering scrolled above block print.

The museum is located in a four-hundred-year-old Dominican convent, a tasteful, keenly retooled labyrinth of galleries, arches, and courtyards. The fact that this superb museum is in one of the poorest states of a developing country makes it all the more impressive.

We visually nibble at the Monte Albán display, admiring closely a few exquisite pieces of jewelry crafted from gold, turquoise, and seashell.

Wandering down the hall, we see a room with a sign that says "*Producción de Bebidas,*" beverage production. In it is an old distillery vat with serpentine copper coiling. There are samples of the black pottery. A computer encased in a polished wooden pedestal offers background on mezcal.

The screen glows with images of the different types of mezcal, which are broken down into classifications of species, flavor, process, and region.

Almost all of the mezcal in Oaxaca is made from *espadín*. The mezcal most noted for using a different species is *tobalá,* made from a wild agave of the same name.

The two most common flavors of mezcal are the strangest. That which contains the worm in the bottle is called *de gusano,* or *gusanito*. The other is mezcal *de pechuga*, chicken breast. Raw chicken breast is added to the tank during the distillation process, during which time it is cooked and the flavor steeps into the alcohol.

Mezcals are also distinguished by process. The first is plain mezcal, which is the end product of the double distillation. Like tequila, if plain mezcal is aged in an oak barrel for two months, it is classified as *reposado*. If it is aged in an oak barrel for a year or more, then it is *añejo*. The oakiness acquired with aging smooths out the flavor and in doing so makes it taste more like smoky, aged tequila.

Finally a few regional designations are used for products from the small villages around Oaxaca. The two most well known are *Minero* from Minas, and *Matlateco* from Matatlán.

The last thing we learn is that the traditional snacks that accompany mezcal are Oaxaca cheese and *chapulines*, fried grasshoppers. You really have to search for delicacies like grasshoppers because they are not that commonly eaten anymore.

Grasshoppers aside, recognition is merited in regard to Mexico's grand tradition of *botanas*. This is a country of world-class snackers. They squeeze lime and sprinkle chile on anything and call it a snack—pork rinds, potato chips, vegetable sticks, fruit wedges, miniature tacos, baked squash seeds—the list goes on and on. When a snack appears, *chile y limón* can't be far behind.

Oaxaca isn't just the land of mezcal, it is also black bean and *mole* country!

In the afternoon we drive east toward the rug-weaving town of Teotitlán del Valle, though we're not here to buy rugs. We've been told that Demetrio, the owner of the La Cupola restaurant, offers tasty Oaxacan fare and knows a fair bit about mezcal.

We observe that a loom and stacks of rugs occupy half the restaurant's floor space. These have been woven in the traditional manner with yarn colored with natural dyes. When we ask where the bathrooms are, Demetrio spouts the usual *al fondo a la derecha* directions and adds, "but to get there you have to look at the rugs." It's a great strategy because even though we don't have the slightest interest in buying a rug, all it takes is one glance for us to be snared by the intricate designs.

The last time I came on a rug-buying adventure to Teotitlán I was not interested in buying rugs, either. I should have been; they were much cheaper then. It was about eight months after the December '94 devaluation rendered the Mexican currency worthless and the economy dead.

That was the year Becky and I met in Mexico City, where we both lived. We traveled together every weekend to take advantage of the slack work situation caused by the devaluation. Hauling mountain bikes or surfboards with us wherever we went, each found in the other the perfect traveling companion. Our nirvana was abruptly halted when Becky's company transferred her to Cincinnati on short notice. We engaged in the wearisome gyrations of phone calls and e-mail and air travel to try to keep the relationship going, all the while wondering how long it could continue.

So instead of being with my preferred travel mate on my first trip to Oaxaca, I came with a crew of ex-pat friends, a consolation because they were all stimulating and fun people, but they could not distract my thoughts for long from the one person who dominated them. As the sun set on Teotitlán and my friends sparred with rug vendors, I contemplated my options in a dusty café. At that moment, I became determined to travel with Becky again.

This time she is here with me. She orders a *tlayuda*, a giant dried tortilla gooey with Oaxaca cheese and seasoned with pork and spices. Oaxaca cheese is a lot like mozzarella. It comes in different shapes but is usually sold in lumpy balls like wadded string cheese. I ask for the *sopa de guías*, a soup made from the wandering vines of a squash plant found only in Oaxaca. I also chow down on the *encina*, a thin cut of beef, slicing it into hot corn tortillas. Everything in Oaxaca is served with black refried beans, rather than with the pinto beans common in central Mexico. I stuff the black legumes into the tortilla for good measure.

Oaxaca is known as the land of seven *moles*, the complex sauces that are the cornerstone of the local cuisine. Some of the sauces are reputed to contain over 100 ingredients, but they usually have about twenty. Typical ingredients include dried chiles such as *anchos* and *guajillos*, an array of spices such as cinnamon and marjoram, and fruit. Ground almonds or pumpkin seeds are used to thicken the delicacy.

Ask someone to name Oaxaca's seven *moles* and you're likely to get only a partial answer. We finally tracked down the complete list in Zarela Martínez's superb book *The Food and Life of Oaxaca*. The *moles* are *amarillo* (yellow), *coloradito* (reddish), *negro* (black), *rojo* (red), *verde* (green), *chichilo* (very dark, but not *negro*), and *manchamantel* (fruit based).

I pursue these exotic sauces aggressively. Last night I had chicken with the light red *mole* called *coloradito*. Thick and robust, it was chock full of ground pecans, garlic, three types of chiles, tomatoes, an array of spices, and chocolate. I plan to knock out the yellow *mole* tonight and green *mole* tomorrow.

After our meal, Demetrio brings several unlabeled bottles of mezcal to our table. He sets down mezcal glasses, which are about half the size and twice as wide as the slender shot glasses used for tequila. A small saucer holds *sal con chile*, a mixture of chile powder and salt. You pinch and dab it on your tongue between sips of mezcal. Sometimes dried *gusano* worms are added to the mix and in such a case it is called *sal de gusano*. Unlike with tequila, lime wedges are not traditionally served with mezcal.

Demetrio pours us a sample of *tobalá* mezcal, which is made from a wild agave of the same name. It is a rare species becoming more so because it grows only in the damp upper regions of the forest, it is not commercially cultivated, and it makes an extraordinarily smooth, naturally flavorful mezcal. Demetrio, whose family speaks Zapotec at home, explains that the name for *tobalá* is from the Zapotec *doblía*. *Do* means "maguey" and *blía* means "shade." The Zapotec used the leaves of these hardy magueys to build hut roofs to block out the harsh Oaxacan sun.

When Demetrio finishes telling us about *tobalá*, he broaches the subject of the rugs he saw us coveting. Our resolve is weakening, but our budget resists. We ask him where we might find an authentic, rustic *palenque*. He mentions two places, one somewhat near, Albarradas, and another farther away, Santa Catarina de las Minas. He draws a map to Albarradas and points us in the direction of some shadowy mountains blurred purple like copies from an old mimeograph machine.

On the way to the hills we notice a sign that states, "Welcome to Santiago Matatlán, Oaxaca—Mezcal Capital of the World." We can't ignore the advertisement, even though it detours us from seeing our first true *palenque*.

The mezcal capital has been proclaimed as such by Benevá, a leading mezcal manufacturer that is located here. Rodrigo, a technician, informs us that most of the plant's product comes from the *palenques* in town and the surrounding countryside, then is refined at this plant. It is now clear that the industry relies on a network of rustic stills for its production. This realization only makes us more eager to get to one.

However, on a shelf in Rodrigo's office I spy a gallon-size jar with thousands of worms soaking in mezcal. Noticing my stare, Rodrigo scoops a handful onto a plate for us to inspect. While mezcal has been around for nearly five hundred years, he informs us that the worms have been added to bottles of commercial mezcal for only about fifty. It's a marketing tool and it works.

Most of the worms are about an inch or two long, with a dozen segments like little cream-colored inner tubes linked together. A few of them have a two-tone coloring of crimson and cream. We each pick one up.

Becky and I look at each other and at the tidbits pinched by our fingers. The worm's vile black head unsettles me. Becky and I know that if one of us munches the vermin, the other is obligated, as a point of pride, to do the same.

Rodrigo explains that the worm lives in and nourishes itself from the roots of the agave. It is most commonly called *gusano de maguey* in

Spanish, but is also known as *chinicuil*. During a life cycle of one year it proceeds from egg to larva to worm to caterpillar to butterfly. The butterfly deposits eggs on the agave leaves. The worms are collected during the rainy season, usually in September, when they seek moisture and nourishment in the wet earth. Like all edible insects, worms have high protein content. Pre-Hispanic Mexico did not have many domesticated animals, mainly only turkeys, so insects like maguey worms, grasshoppers, and ant eggs complemented the Oaxacan diet. The worms can be prepared in salsa, fried for tacos, or dried as a snack. Sometimes the dried *gusanos* are ground and added to the traditional salt and chile powder mixture consumed with mezcal.

The chubby little guys we hold in our fingers are definitely not dry. They are gorged with mezcal, which is now starting to run down our wrists. Becky tosses the worm into her mouth, as do I. The tubular segments burst as we bite down, igniting a chain reaction of mezcal splashes along the sides of our mouths. Pop! Pop! Pop! It's like biting down on tiny mezcal-filled balloons. I think the worst is over, but Rodrigo informs us that those we sampled were small worms. Soon we are chewing grubs so formidable that I swear each contains an entire straight shot.

Climbing into the hills toward Albarradas, the road grows increasingly twisting and worn. Asphalt flapjacks patch the entire surface.

The tallest plants on the scrubby mountainside are the robust floral stalks emanating from agaves. These shoot up like adolescent oaks and burst bright yellow like sunflowers at the top. The appearance of this twenty-foot-high stem known as a *quiote* signals the plant's demise. When the plant is about ten years old, the lanky *quiote* sprouts and blossoms with a dozen levels of vibrant flowers. The agave blades brown and eventually die around the stalk. Cultivators usually let a few selected plants reach this stage, then remove the flowers, which serve as cuttings. These plantings, up to 2,500 on a single stalk, are raised in a greenhouse for three years until they are transplanted to the field. In the case of the wild stalks, the flowers simply drop to the soil and the seedlings take root.

We finally find the dirt road that leads to Albarradas by asking a pair of goat herders. Hearing our approach, a group of soiled machete-wielding young men returning from a day's work reluctantly moves to the side of the road. As we pass they shout for us to give them a ride, but it goes against our survival instincts to share close quarters with all of those machetes. We try to compensate the men with friendly waves, but they do not seem appeased.

As the village comes into view, we can see that it is shaded by the summit of the mountain to which it clings. In the distance, a gorgeous tide of rusty peaks lights up in a golden glow. The distinction between light and shade highlights the fact that the town is situated on a ledge, high above a canyon.

Gordo consumes much of the dirt road that leads into town, so mules, scroungy dogs, women in shawls, and men with tools on their backs and cowboy hats on their heads must step to the side so we can proceed. A dozen school children outfitted in navy blue-and-white school uniforms carry enormous grapefruits that glow as big and yellow as suns in their tiny hands. Pockets bulge and sweaters sag from the weight. The greediest of them struggle with book bags made cumbersome with the hefty orbs.

Most of the fences are sadly tilted rows of bamboo. While some of the houses are built of red bricks or cement blocks, few of them are painted, and most are built of adobe cubes of mud, straw, and stones.

At the end of town, on a curve threatening to drop houses into the canyon, we arrive at our rustic *palenque*. We introduce ourselves to Sergio, the proprietor, who leads a mule as it pulls a *tahona*. Becky eagerly pats the shaggy mule on the head. She is so happy to see an authentic mule-powered *tahona* in action that I think she might kiss the beast.

Sergio is pot-bellied with an amiable, chubby face that squeezes his eyes into tiny slits whenever he smiles. He wears a droopy camouflage hunter's hat and an oversized T-shirt stitched with the words "Planet Reebok" that cascades over his ample paunch, reaching nearly to his knees.

Nearby is a smoking earthen mound. Sergio explains that this is where the agave hearts are baked. A wide, round pit about four feet deep has been dug out. Firewood is stacked in the pit and burned until there are sufficient coals to bake the agave. Next, the coals are covered with rocks about the size of softballs to insulate the agave. The quartered agave hearts are placed on the hot stones and then capped with

Fire pit in which agave hearts are baked.

agave leaves and earth to seal in the heat. Three days' cooking unlocks and concentrates the agave's fermentable sugars.

We break off a piece of baked agave protruding from the fermentation bin. It is the color of brown sugar and tastes like a fibrous, charbroiled sweet potato. While tequila is steam-cooked, mezcal's fire roasting endows it with its most prominent characteristic—a uniquely smoky flavor.

We enter a shack comprised of one sturdy adobe wall and a roof supported by knobby tree trunks. Sergio pours his moonshine in a cup that is actually half of a dried gourd called *jícara*. As he hands me the gourd, he offers a toast that is an oft-repeated saying in Mexico, "*Para todo mal, mezcal. Para todo bien, también.*" Suddenly I recall a newspaper article I read while vacationing on a Oaxacan beach several years ago. The article described several people dying and others going blind from drinking liquor from an unauthorized *palenque*, not that a *palenque* anywhere is actually authorized by anyone.

Sergio eyes me. I smile weakly, and then put the gourd to my lips, wetting them, but not actually drinking from the cup. I need some kind of reassurance. A quick inquiry reveals that the *palenque* has been in business for forty years and that all of the product is double-distilled. I notice that equipment in the shack, various plastic containers, tools, buckets, and jugs, are well organized.

I finally take a real gulp. The concoction sears down my gullet like liquid coals, but it is quite palatable. Becky swigs from the gourd and agrees that it is a tasty blaze.

Soon another man arrives, more of a friend than a paying client, it seems. Ricardo is a slender fellow who resembles the great Mexican comedian Cantinflas in his facial characteristics—dark black hair and a feeble moustache. He dresses in typical cowboy duds complete with hat, boots, jeans, and big buckled belt, with one odd exception—his light yellow shirt is tied off in the front with two knots like a woman's halter top to expose his midsection.

Ricardo counsels us, "To stimulate my appetite I drink four cups of mezcal at breakfast, four before lunch, and four before dinner, but not more than this. If you drink five at once, you will become a drunk." Sergio's eyes crease as he nods in agreement.

We chat with Ricardo and Sergio about the distillation for quite some time as clients come and go. One indigenous woman in a bright dress has her green Sprite bottle filled up for about ten cents. A preteen girl with a motor oil cap on and her younger sister buy a juice bottle's worth for their father.

A two-foot-high copper tank built into a brick fireplace is filled with fermenting pulp and juice. As fire heats the watery pulp, vapor flows through a tube to a cooling tank filled with water. Here the tube narrows into a copper coil, where the condensation collects, finally draining from a copper spout into a blue plastic jug at a rate of ten liters per day.

I ask about putting worms in the mezcal. The derision that the question receives makes me suspect that worms might be a gringo fixation and not an appropriate request in Oaxaca's finer *palenques*.

Just as the laughter dies down, two new customers arrive. We greet them amiably. Dusk has set in, so it is not until we see their machetes that we recognize them as two of the young men from the hitchhiking group we passed. One gives us a smile that seems genuine, but the other stares sullenly at Gordo. We linger nervously a few minutes. Boisterous backslapping and handshaking seem like a more appropriate farewell than inching away, so we say our goodbyes with enthusiasm. We are happy to depart before the mezcal complies with its notorious task of loosening tensions, emotions, and machetes.

Mezcal distillation takes place in rustic stills like the one shown here. Customers stop by with whatever vessel will hold the amount of mezcal they want—anything from a used soft drink or juice bottle to a large plastic bucket.

On our last day in Oaxaca, we look forward to visiting the most remote *palenque*, that of the famed mezcal Minero. A market takes place today in a village near there, Ocotlán, which we plan to see as well.

We dodge and bump our way through the crowded Ocotlán market seeking *gusanos de maguey*. Even though the town is only about an hour from Oaxaca City, the people here are more traditionally dressed. Most of them trek from the surrounding mountains to sell their wares and do their weekly shopping. Almost all of the women wear the scarf-shawl-baby sling-in-one *rebozo*. Some of the older women wind bright fabric into their long, distinguished braids. Straw cowboy hats are abundant, both on display and on the heads of men.

We ask in various stalls about the worms, weaving through the bread section where vendors shoo away flies with tiny plastic pom-poms to the fruit area, then back to the bread section until we find a woman who says yes, she sells worms. She extracts an enamel bowl of dry, salty, deflated worms. We buy one-half dollar's worth, a dozen worms at the going rate.

The drive to Santa Catarina Minas is one that eliminates any environmental guilt we feel for owning a sport utility vehicle. Without high clearance and four-wheel drive we would not get far on the dirt road rutted and gullied by thundershowers. Dump trucks, acting as market day taxis, force us off the road; tightly packed villagers overflow from the deep, square beds and sit on the roofs of the cabs.

The *minas* in Santa Catarina Minas translates to "mines." It was so christened for the silver that was extracted from the surrounding hills. The mezcal that comes from the town is known as *Minero* or Miner's Mezcal. Though the name has been used to describe the local mezcal for decades, a U.S. enterprise, the Del Maguey Company, is now promoting it as a brand.

Ron Cooper, an artist from Taos, New Mexico, came to Oaxaca in 1990 for creative inspiration. While in Oaxaca, the artist's fondness for mezcal grew. He crafted 500 hand-blown bottles in the shape of the pre-Hispanic god of drunkenness, Ometochtli, which he filled with the area's best spirits. When U.S. customs would not allow him personally to cart the product across the border, he decided to import it commercially.

He came up with the plan to market "single village mescals," thus distinguishing his product from that of larger producers who mix and blend mezcal from many locales to achieve volume. Cooper used his artistic skills to design sleek bottles representing four villages—San Luis del Río, Chichicapa, Albarradas, and Santa Catarina Minas. We learn that Cooper's supplier in Santa Catarina Minas was a gentleman named Florencio Sarmiento.

A burly woman in her fifties sweeps near a large metallic gate described to us as Florencio Sarmiento's *palenque*. Her baked apple face is connected to a body strengthened by years of country labor. When we inquire if don Florencio Sarmiento is in, she gruffly demands, "Who wants to know?"

I explain our research in what I believe to be a cordial and respectful manner.

She replies, "Go away."

We've never encountered such a forceful denial in Mexico, which is famous for sugarcoating rejections. She slams the gate shut. Her manner is so brazen in the context of Mexican politeness that it slaps us into a fit of giggles.

Curiosity overpowers her will of rejection. She cracks open the gate.

"What do you want?" she demands again.

We offer a slew of pandering words to explain why it was important to meet Sr. Sarmiento, *el estimable . . . respetado . . . maestro del famoso mezcal Minero . . .*

Without a word she shuts the gate again. We have no idea if she plans on coming back, but decide to wait it out. We stare at the ten-foot adobe wall that surrounds the house as Gordo's air-conditioning struggles against the triple-digit heat.

At last the gate belches forth the orneriest of codgers that you can imagine. It is our respected and estimable master of Minero mezcal, don Florencio. An intent squint from below a rumpled cowboy hat fixes on us, analyzing our motives and net worth.

"How did you get my name?" he demands.

I advise him that Demetrio the rug maker and restaurateur sent us. This is a mistake because he doesn't know Demetrio and spends the next ten minutes telling us so.

Becky hopefully jumps in, name-dropping Ron Cooper, whom we know only from hearsay at this point.

"Coooop-air?" Don Florencio utters the name reverently when he says it. He ponders and then catches himself. "You come back with Coooop-air then. He'll be here next month."

He doesn't walk away, however.

The señora pipes up, "What benefit is there for us?"

We dimly take this to mean that they would like to know what kind of positive public relations is in it for them. We spin our wheels hatching benefits over the next ten minutes.

They are unimpressed. The gate shows signs of closing again.

Finally, I say, "You know, we were up in Albarradas yesterday. We had some of their mezcal. Have you ever tasted it?"

The squint intensifies.

"Now that's good mezcal."

It is a direct hit. The defense system is wavering.

I continue, "We've never tasted mezcal Minero, but we really have to tell everyone about how good that Albarradas mezcal is. It's the best we've ever tasted."

Soon we find ourselves balancing on short, wobbly stools by a mountain of drying corncobs in the corner of don Florencio's patio. A calico cat nestles into a wooden box filled with coffee beans. We are seated near several casks of mezcal, stored in unusual twenty-five-gallon pear-shaped ceramic vessels covered with nylon net. In the adjacent room are twenty large black ceramic *cántaros*, kept upright by cylindrical baskets that wrap around the bases. Don Florencio limps toward the jugs in battered leather sandals. He adroitly funnels a healthy portion of the moonshine into a dry gourd cup.

He hands the cup to me with tough, stubby fingers. I look at the quantity knowing that to be polite, almost all of it will have to be drunk by someone who doesn't have the car keys, which are in my pocket. I sample the smooth, smoky liquid that is quite chilled from the ceramic pot, and then pass it to Becky, who sips with trepidation. The mezcal is silken and cool, so she indulges in another long, approving draw.

Don Florencio's gray whiskered face softens now that we are guests instead of intruders. We discuss the rising price of agave. He pries open his squint to reveal astute reddened eyes, then conjures up fleet-footed logic to blame the increasing price of the agave on "outsiders." He takes a precautionary glance, and then discloses that it is the president of the republic who is to blame. We momentarily buy into the conspiracy until we remember the blue agave shortage in Jalisco. Further inquiry reveals that traders from outside of Oaxaca have recently arrived, bidding up the price of the agave, which has always gone into local mezcal production.

There is a pause in the conversation as Becky and I absorb the implications of tequila producers substituting Oaxaca's agave *espadín* for the only legally sanctioned raw material to make tequila, the now scarce blue agave.

Don Florencio interrupts our contemplation. "I told Coooop-air I want to go to the United States, but he hasn't taken me yet. I'm getting old, you know; maybe he'll get around to taking me when I'm dead." His face brightens. "You should take me with you to the United States. I'd like to see it. You live there. We'll go together." He is relentless on the subject. No matter what topic we bring up, it returns to our future travels together that he now recognizes as a done deal.

We ask to see his *palenque*, and of course, given his habitual obstinacy, he refuses.

"What benefit is there for me if you see my *palenque*?" he demands, pushing his hat to a slant over one eye, withdrawing into his former hedgehog stance.

The señora, who has been busying herself with chopping up tree limbs into firewood with a machete, perks up at this inquiry. She has been constantly doing chores since our arrival, sometimes chafing blanched squash seeds, other times throwing stones at the obstinate pigs that wander into the yard. Now she is still with anticipation.

The implied meaning of the word *beneficio* finally hits on us. We've heard "cooperation" and a dozen other terms used to suggest payment, but for some reason the significance of "benefit" didn't dawn on us until now. We agree to buy two liters of his mezcal at about four times the going rate. You can probably buy Del Maguey "Minero" mezcal cheaper off the retail shelf in the United States even after duties, taxes, and transportation have been added. He also extorts us for a couple of bucks to buy *refrescos,* sodas, for his workers.

The first time I heard this payoff term, "*refresco,*" was during my rookie month living in Mexico City when attempting to park on a busy commercial street. Everyone was double parking, so I felt fairly confident my illegally, yet single-parked car would not be the first to be towed. A brown-uniformed city cop suggested that I give him some money for a *refresco* as I ran toward the bank. I ignored him and came out of the bank to see my car levitating with the assistance of a tow truck. After a lengthy negotiation to return the car to earth, I believe I ended up buying sodas for the entire police department.

We have paid don Florencio for the mezcal, but a snafu arises. There is no container in which to put the liquor. I suggest we just give him the money and forget about the mezcal, but Becky has really taken to the concoction, which is now completely drained from the big gourd. She jumps up and runs out the gate, returning triumphantly with the black *cántaro* we purchased in Coyotepec—problem solved, in the most customary of manners.

Don Florencio's *palenque* is a wondrous thing to see in terms of pure, unadulterated tradition. Instead of copper kettles and vats, don Florencio employs ceramic pots. Instead of copper pipes, the mezcal drains through hollowed bamboo. He doesn't even use a stone wheel driven by a donkey. Instead, "the boys," as he calls them, utilize an even more primitive method, pounding the agave to a pulp with a giant mortar and pestle.

Don Florencio takes his seat on a stone throne to admire his boys' work. The two "boys" in truth are rugged geriatrics perhaps even older than the boss.

As we say goodbye, don Florencio, in a voice loud enough for his boys to hear, reprimands us for not leaving any soda money, even though he already stashed the money we outlaid for them at home. Speaking equally loudly, I recount the exact amount we gave him for the boys and add that I hope their sodas will be of the tastiest, bubbliest sort.

Now having met the source, we feel that any profit that Coooop-air makes as a middleman while dealing with a scheming (yet admittedly lovable) old *cabrón* like don Florencio, he most definitely earns.

We are eating worms again, this time the dried, salted ones we purchased in the market. They accompany stubby shots of mezcal *añejo* and a balcony view of Oaxaca City's lively plaza. The one worm I eat reminds me of a shred of fried fish skin. Becky happily munches one after another, which I believe is an effort to taunt me, a successful tactic.

A cargo truck traversing the city blasts its horn below our balcony. Our attention is drawn to its hefty load—dozens of agave hearts. We can only speculate about the truck's ultimate destination, but since it is headed away from the *palenques*, we guess that it is furtively hustling toward Jalisco to supplement the blue agave shortage.

We toast with the last of our mezcal—*salud*! Usually an empty glass signifies deficiency, but in our case the thick blue-rimmed glasses overflow with experience and knowledge. We sought to investigate Mexico's traditional drinks, but serendipitously ventured into the country's culture of celebration. When we embarked on this trip, many of our friends imagined us on an extended drinking binge. Instead—or simultaneously—we have reveled in the country's music, art, architecture, history, industry, archeology, athletics, and crafts. We will return home with our thirst for Mexican culture momentarily quenched.

The hardest part about finishing our journey is leaving Oaxaca. It is a strange, enchanting place, still greatly removed from an ever-homogenizing world. On the way out of town we stop by the Basilica de la Soledad. Thousands of pilgrims visit the basilica hoping to glimpse its revered wooden Virgin, found centuries ago on this spot in a box strapped to an unattended mule.

Outside the church silver buckets of sugary cream are spun by hand within chipped wooden kegs of salt to make ice cream the artisanal way. Flavors to be contemplated include common ones like strawberry, indigenous fruits like *mamey* and *zapote*, and familiar but unimagined flavors like corn. It is easy for me to choose. I savor the rich, smoky mezcal ice cream, all the while hoping that I will not find a frozen worm at the bottom of the cone.

Resources

Álvarez, José Rogelio, ed. *Enciclopedia de México*. México, DF: Compañía Editora de Enciclopedias de México, 1987.

Barrios, Virginia B. de. *A Guide to Tequila, Mezcal, and Pulque*. México, DF: Editorial Minutiae Mexicana SA de CV, 1971.

Cowley, Geoffrey. "Highbrow Hooch Goes North." *Newsweek*, November 13, 1995, 77.

Martínez, Zarela. *The Food and Life of Oaxaca*. Hoboken, NJ: John Wiley & Sons, 1997.

Valle Septien, Carmen, ed. *Mezcal, elixir de larga vida*. Oaxaca: CVS Publishing, 1997.

EPILOGUE

JACK'S WEDDING

Bryan's great-aunt Madge, age eighty-three, leans toward me with a conspiratorial grin. We've been treading the sizzling streets for more than an hour shopping for gifts for her grandchildren.

"It sure is hot, don't you think?"

I reply in the affirmative as I wipe the sweat off the back of my neck.

"It sure would be nice to have a cold drink right now."

I look around for a small store where we can buy some water or a Coke.

"Oh, I wasn't thinking of water." She tilts closer and her smile gets bigger. "Let's go have a margarita!"

Tempting idea. I hesitate. It's 4:30 in the afternoon and I'm supposed to meet Bryan at the gym in an hour and a half. Madge, always on the ball, has the perfect response.

"Those are stationary bikes . . . You won't fall off even if you have a couple margaritas. Come on. I'll buy. It'll be fun."

How can you turn down the corrupting forces of an octogenarian?

The next thing I know we're in a leafy patio bar enjoying the perfect happy hour margaritas—100 percent agave tequila, Cointreau, and freshly squeezed key limes. We talk about the upcoming wedding over our drinks. Madge knows all the details.

Bryan's cousin Jack met his fiancée, Claudia, in San Miguel de Allende two years ago. Jack was visiting from Seattle, here to attend a wedding. He was walking across the plaza when he saw a beautiful Mexican woman. She gave him a big smile. He smiled back, but didn't stop because he was walking with his dad and his sister. When they got to the front door of their hotel he turned to his father and said, "I just have to go back to the plaza to talk to that cute girl who smiled at me." Jack and Claudia have been an item ever since.

They chose to celebrate their wedding in San Miguel because their relationship began here. For Claudia's family, it's an easy drive from Mexico City. For many of Jack's friends and relatives, it's an excuse for a Mexican vacation. For Bryan and me, it's the perfect bookend to this south-of-the-border excursion. What better way to end our trip than with a Mexican celebration on our way out of the country?

The invitation says 7:30, but we get to the church at 8 PM because we know that Mexican weddings never start on time. As we walk up to the chapel, colorful paper flags cut into intricate patterns dangle from rooftop to rooftop along the entire length of the street. Flickering luminarias, paper bags lit from within by candles, line the stairs leading to the church. People stand in shifting groups, chatting and waiting for the church doors to be unlocked.

About half an hour later the doors creak open and we're let into the chapel. The elegant sanctuary, festooned with huge flower arrangements, seats about fifty. The couple and their families finally arrive at 9 PM. As we had expected, Claudia didn't even get into the shower until 7:30, the hour the invitation indicated the wedding would start. She's stunning in a delicate white lace gown made from her great-grandmother's wedding dress. Her bronze skin glows against the pale fabric, matched by the radiance of her smile. Jack, handsome in his tux, towers above his bride.

The Catholic ceremony is performed in both English and Spanish. The priest reads a passage about Jesus's first miracle at the wedding in Cana.

> When they had not enough wine, the mother of Jesus said to him, They have no wine.
>
> Jesus said to her, Woman, this is not your business; my time is still to come.
>
> His mother said to the servants, Whatever he says to you, do it.
>
> Now six pots of stone, every one taking two or three firkins of water, were placed there for the purpose of washing, as is the way of the Jews.
>
> Jesus said to the servants, Make the pots full of water. And they made them full to the top.
>
> Then he said to them, Now take some, and give it to the master of the feast. So they took it to him.
>
> After tasting the water which had now become wine, the master of the feast (having no idea where it came from, though it was clear to the servants who took the water out) sent for the newly-married man,
>
> And said to him, Every man first puts out his best wine and when all have had enough he puts out what is not so good; but you have kept the good wine till now.
>
> (John 2:3-10, BBE)

The priest looks up at the audience. "Now, I'm sure that almost all of you have heard that passage before, particularly at weddings. I want to expand on it and clarify something, though. Not many people even think about this, but a 'firkin' is equal to roughly 10 gallons. That means that each of the stone water jars held 20 to 30 gallons. Let's say they averaged 25 gallons apiece. Jesus transformed the water in six of them. That's 150 gallons of wine.

"One hundred fifty gallons of wine is not just a token transformation. If Jesus's sole purpose was to show that he could perform miracles, he could have stopped with just one jar. But he didn't. He converted water into the equivalent of 757 bottles of wine. That's an abundance, an absolute overflowing!"

His arms spread and he comes to his tiptoes to pantomime the copiousness. In his white robe he looks like a dove about to take flight. Coming back to roost, he continues. "This miracle demonstrated the abundance of Jesus's love. There's something else about it that's important, however. It also led to a heck of a party."

The congregation laughs. "I'm serious. It's significant to understand that Jesus loved celebration. He wanted people to have a good time, to come together in jubilation. That's why we're here. It's a momentous and thoughtful occasion, but also a joyful one. We too will celebrate."

What a great image. Jesus must have been part Mexican.

Fireworks explode outside as we file from the church. Bryan and I, with plenty of experience around Mexican pyrotechnics, hang back under the eaves. Sure enough, a few pieces of burning embers whiz into the crowd.

Jack and Claudia step into a flower-strewn horse-drawn carriage, which we follow on foot through San Miguel's colonial streets. The reception is held in a beautiful home featuring extensive gardens and museum-quality Mexican folk art. The dining tables are set up under the stars in a large courtyard. The wedding that Jack had attended two years previously took place in this home. It's decorated in much the same manner that it was that night, with candles lining the outdoor walkways and gardenias and floating candles covering the pool. The flickering lights reflecting off the water envelop the scene in romance.

Most of Bryan's immediate family has come down for the event. We're seated together at what turns out to be "the rowdy table." We laugh and tell stories all through the excellent four-course dinner. The wine flows in abundance, as it did after Jesus's first miracle.

Because dinner is not served until 11 PM, we lose all sense of time. We are living in the moment. The dancing starts after midnight and goes on and on. We salsa, swing, merengue, twist, and even dance the dreaded macarena. Two cultures, two families merging together in a night of merrymaking. Tonight there are no language barriers that can't be crossed with a hug and a smile.

At about three in the morning the U.S. contingent starts to fade. Many have to make the long trek back to Seattle in a matter of hours. Bryan and I are determined to stay for the chilaquiles, a Mexican treat made from tortillas, chile sauce, cheese, and sour cream. Traditionally offered at weddings after a few hours of dancing, chilaquiles sustain guests and fortify them to keep the celebration going. We know that the chilaquiles served at this house are excellent because we too were at the wedding that Jack attended here two years ago.

Around 4:30 AM the mariachis arrive. The guests stand in a large circle around the ten-piece band, requesting song after song. We sing, clap, and "ayyy, yaiii, yaiii" at the top of our lungs.

Bryan spots a tray of chilaquiles coming out of the kitchen. He intercepts the waiter and relieves him of two plates—one with red sauce, one with green. The white sour cream completes the trio of colors of Mexico's flag. Icy beers in hand, we move over by the pool to enjoy our snack. The essence of Mexico takes over our senses. We hear the mariachis play on the patio above us, filling the predawn hours with their song. On our tongues, the hot chile sauce is doused with sips of cold lager. The perfumed scent of fresh flowers lingers in the air. We love this country and its traditions, many of which we have adopted as our own.

We put down our plates as the sun starts to rise. It's been a great night, special for us in many ways. Mexico is always special because this is where our relationship began. After Jergens moved me back to the United States, Bryan and I endured the long-distance shuffle for almost eight months before convincing our companies that we should both be transferred to Santiago, Chile. We lived there for a number of years until we quit our jobs to write and travel, but Mexico was always first in our hearts. Tonight has brought that fact home. Not only have we relished in the ceremonies of this extraordinary country with our family, but we've also celebrated an anniversary.

It wasn't just any wedding that Jack was down here attending two years ago. It was the wedding of a couple who adored Mexico. The wedding of a couple who couldn't think of a better place to start a lifelong union. The wedding of a couple who wanted to introduce the flavors of Mexico to friends and family. It was our wedding.

abrazo: A traditional greeting between male friends and family consisting of a handshake, hug, and pats on the back.

agave: *Maguey* in Spanish. Also called the "century plant" in English. A plant primarily known for its use in the production of alcoholic beverages—tequila, mezcal, and pulque—but which was also utilized for centuries by the pre-Hispanic cultures for textiles, needles, building materials, and medicine.

aguamiel: The sweet sap of the pulque agave plant before fermentation. Also, the juice of a crushed mezcal/tequila agave before distillation.

añejo: A class of tequila that has been aged in oak barrels for at least one year.

birria: Beef rib cooked in a broth of *guajillo* chiles, onion, garlic, cumin, and bay leaves, usually served in tacos.

blanco: A class of tequila that has been aged for less than two months before being bottled.

burros y payasos: Asses and clowns.

caballito: The tall, slender shot glass in which *blanco* and *reposado* tequilas are traditionally served.

cántaro: A ceramic vaselike jug.

carnitas: Tender little morsels of pork.

century plant: See agave.

chela: The slang word that residents of Mexico City use for "beer."

chilango: A slang term for any resident of Mexico City.

chilaquiles: Tortillas and chicken baked in red or green hot sauce, topped with sour cream.

churro: A dessert made by frying sweet dough in hot oil, served as cakelike sticks.

coa: The tool that agave harvesters use to uproot the agave and trim its leaves so that they are left with the heart of the plant, the *piña.* The *coa* looks something like a shovel with a sharp, rounded blade.

comadre: *Comadre* and *compadre* literally translate as "co-parent" and apply to the relationship between godparents and parents. The term is often used with close friends, regardless of any godparent connection. It implies a relationship that is not of blood but that has the same strong ties.

crema: Literally "cream," but also flavored liqueurs such as *crema de mezcal.*

cuarto: A quarter of a liter.

curandero: A type of healer or shaman.

danzón: A formal social dance that originated in Cuba and is a descendant of *contradanza.*

distillation: The process of concentrating alcohol through evaporation to create "hard liquors."

falta de moral: Immoral.

gringo: A term used for foreigners, especially people from the United States and Great Britain. It can have many connotations depending on the circumstances and tone of voice. It can be pejorative, belittling, friendly, playful, or simply innocuous. Live in Mexico for any length of time and you will be called "gringo" so much that you'll begin to use the term as well.

(El) Grito: Literally, "the yell." El Grito is the call for Mexican independence from Spain shouted by Father Miguel Hidalgo from the steps of his parish church. With this yell, the fight for Mexican independence began.

guitarrón: An oversized guitar originally crafted for and played by mariachi musicians.

gusano: A worm, such as that found in mezcal (not tequila!).

helado/a: Icy cold.

-ito/-ita: The diminutive suffix added to words in Spanish to literally transform them to "small" or convey endearment or belittlement, depending on the syntax.

jimador: An agave harvester.

limpieza: A ceremonial cleaning performed by *curanderos*.

maguey: See agave.

mezcal: Alcohol distilled from an agave plant, including tequila, which uses a specific type of agave. All tequila is mezcal, but not all mezcal is tequila. Most mezcal is produced in the state of Oaxaca.

mosto: Must; the unfermented or fermenting juice used to produce wine, tequila, and other alcoholic beverages.

nopal: A type of cactus. The pads are stripped of their spines, cut into slices, grilled, and served in tacos and other dishes, while the prickly pear fruit (*tuna* in Mexican Spanish) is used to make juice and sauces.

pachanga: A party (slang).

palenque: Though *palenque* usually refers to a cockfight yard, in Oaxaca the term is commonly used for mezcal production sites.

paso doble: Literally, "two step"; dramatic dance step from Spain symbolizing a bullfight in which the man represents a matador and the woman a cape.

patrocinado: Sponsored.

piña: The heart of a harvested and trimmed agave plant.

pipián: A sauce often made of ground pumpkin seeds and served over chicken or other meats.

pulque: Precursor to mezcal and tequila, pulque is a pre-Hispanic alcoholic drink made from the fermented juice of a distinct type of agave. Unlike tequila and mezcal, the plant is not uprooted but rather "milked" by cutting a bowl into the plant's core. Another important distinction is that the juice is fermented like beer, not distilled, so it has a lower alcohol content than mezcal and tequila.

pulquería: A simple tavern that dispenses pulque.

raicilla: A regional variety of mezcal produced in the area of Puerto Vallarta, Jalisco.

reposado: A class of tequila that has been aged in oak barrels no less than two months and no more than one year.

sangría: A Spanish wine-based drink made with wine, fruit juices, soda water, and fresh fruit.

sangrita: Literally translates to "little blood"; a nonalcoholic side drink sipped with tequila. Sangrita usually consists of tomato juice, orange juice, lime juice, hot sauce, and onion.

sotol: A regional variety of mezcal produced in the state of Chihuahua.

tahona: A stone wheel traditionally used to crush agave hearts during the tequila and mezcal-making processes.

tehuacanazo: A method of torture used by Mexican police in which a bottle of carbonated mineral water is shaken vigorously and then sprayed up a person's nose. Often chile powder is included in the water. It is extremely painful but leaves no bruising or other marks.

Tepoztecatl: A highland deity who was thought to be a protector of villages and a god of drunkenness.

tequila: A type of mezcal made from a specific type of agave. Industry norms define tequila as a double-distilled spirit made from at least 51 percent Blue Weber agave. The blue agave must originate in one of five Mexican states: Jalisco, Nayarit, Michoacán, Guanajuato, or Tamaulipas.

tinacal: A pulque production site, often a shacklike structure with a simple fermentation bin.

tomatillo: Green tomato often used for making salsa.

vihuela: A small guitar played by a mariachi musician.

Viuda de Sánchez, La: A commercial brand of *sangrita,* which translates to "Sánchez's Widow."